Lecture Notes in Computer Science

Edited by G. Goos and J. Hartmanis

T0222966

79

Language Design and Programming Methodology

Proceedings of a Symposium
Held in Sydney, Australia,
10–11 September, 1979

Edited by Jeffrey M. Tobias

Springer-Verlag
Berlin Heidelberg New York 1980

Lecture Notes in Computer Science

Lecture Notes in Computer Science

Edited by G. Goos and J. Hartmanis

79

Language Design and Programming Methodology

Proceedings of a Symposium
Held in Sydney, Australia,
10–11 September, 1979

Edited by Jeffrey M. Tobias

Springer-Verlag
Berlin Heidelberg New York 1980

Editor

Jeffrey M. Tobias
Computer Science Group
Applied Mathematics and Computing Division
Australian Atomic Energy Commission
New Illawarra Road
Lucas Heights, Sydney 2232
N.S.W.
Australia

AMS Subject Classifications (1979): 68-02, 68 A 05
CR Subject Classifications (1974): 4.2, 4.6

ISBN 3-540-09745-7 Springer-Verlag Berlin Heidelberg New York
ISBN 0-387-09745-7 Springer-Verlag New York Heidelberg Berlin

Library of Congress Cataloging in Publication Data Symposium on Language
Design and Programming Methodology, Sydney, 1979. Language design and
programming methodology. (Lecture notes in computer science; 79) Sponsored
by the Australian Atomic Energy Commission and the University of New South
Wales. Bibliography: p. Includes index. 1. Programming languages (Electronic
computers) --Congresses. 2. Electronic digital computers-- Programming--Con-
gresses. I. Tobias, Jeffrey M., 1953- II. Australia. Atomic Energy Commission.
III. New South Wales. University, Kensington. IV. Title. V. Series.
QA76.7.S94 1979 001.64'24 80-10637
ISBN 0-387-09745-7

Printing and binding: Beltz Offsetdruck, Hemsbach/Bergstr.
2145/3140-543210

PROGRAM COMMITTEE

Mr. I. Hayes, University of New South Wales
Dr. J. Hext, University of Sydney
Professor P. Poole, University of Melbourne
Professor J. Reinfelds, University of Wollongong
Professor J. Rohl, University of Western Australia
Professor A. Sale, University of Tasmania
Dr. J. Sanderson, University of Adelaide
Mr. J. M. Tobias, Australian Atomic Energy Commission (Chairman)
Dr. J. Welsh, University of Queensland

SPONSORS

AUSTRALIAN ATOMIC ENERGY COMMISSION   UNIVERSITY OF NEW SOUTH WALES

CONTENTS

PROCEEDINGS OF THE SYMPOSIUM ON
LANGUAGE DESIGN AND PROGRAMMING METHODOLOGY
SYDNEY, 10-11 SEPTEMBER, 1979

"When you're lying awake with a dismal headache,
and repose is taboo'd by anxiety,
I conceive you may use any language you choose
to indulge in, without impropriety."

Iolanthe
Sir William Gilbert

PREFACE

If the seventies are to go down in the annals of computer science history as a decade of technological achievement in the manufacture of semiconductor devices, then one might predict that the eighties would see a commensurate expansion in the development of programming tools and methods. It would be unfortunate if the comparatively primitive tools of today, which are being so widely distributed as a result of a burgeoning computer industry, bind us to an obsolete methodology.

With the challenge of the next decade in mind, over two hundred members of the scientific community interested in the future of programming and its methodology met at a Symposium in Sydney in September, 1979, to discuss language design and programming techniques. Professor Niklaus Wirth of ETH Zurich, renowned for his development of a number of superbly engineered programming languages, was invited to address the Symposium, together with Dr Dennis Ritchie, of Bell Laboratories USA, the originator of the programming language C and co-author of the UNIX time-sharing system.

Twenty-five extended summaries were submitted for review by the program committee. Only fourteen papers were finally accepted following a second review, and I would like to thank the members of the Program Committee for serving as referees. The papers in this Proceedings were printed from camera-ready copies supplied by the authors, and special thanks must go to Mr Ken Tate of the AAEC and his editorial group for so carefully proofreading the papers and assisting in the preparation of this volume.

The planning of this Symposium was largely undertaken by the Chairman with the sponsorship of the Australian Atomic Energy Commission and the University of New South Wales. It is impossible to list in a brief preface all those to whom thanks are due, but I am certainly very grateful to Dr Donald Richardson of the AAEC and Professor Murray Allen of the UNSW for their continued encouragement and guidance. Thanks also go to the management of the AAEC, in particular Professor Don George, Mr Keith Alder and Dr Grant Miles, for their enthusiasm in supporting the Symposium. Special thanks are due to Mrs Melania Moore for her invaluable assistance in all aspects of organisation, to Mr Gordon Evans for the first-class printing of the Proceedings, to Mrs Margaret Bray for the typing of correspondence, and to all those who helped during the Symposium itself.

Jeffrey M. Tobias
Symposium Chairman

PROCEEDINGS OF THE SYMPOSIUM ON
LANGUAGE DESIGN AND PROGRAMMING METHODOLOGY
SYDNEY, 10-11 SEPTEMBER, 1979

THE MODULE : A SYSTEM STRUCTURING FACILITY IN HIGH-LEVEL PROGRAMMING LANGUAGES

Niklaus Wirth

Institut für Informatik
ETH Zürich

ABSTRACT

The key to successful programming is finding the "right" structure of data and program. A programming language concept called module is presented here as a means to partition systems effectively. The module allows to encapsulate local details and to specify explicitly those elements that are part of the interface between modules.

Modules as presented here are part of the language Modula-2. Problems of separate compilation and of splitting a module into definition (interface) and implementation parts are discussed.

*   Institut für Informatik
    ETH-Zentrum
    CH-8092 Zürich

Introduction

The predominant factor influencing the field of computing today is the advent of the microprocessor and of LSI semiconductor technology in general. Depending on one's point of view, it is assessed as positive or negative; in any case it is exciting. I have recently heard the remark that it has set back the practice of programming by some 20 years. Considering the resurgence of the use of rather primitive techniques of assembly and even numeric coding one tends to agree.

Yet I prefer to see recent trends in an opposite perspective. The microprocessor spreads the availability of computing in an unforeseen degree. Hence, it also spreads the need for programming know-how and tools. In fact, it makes adequate programming techniques not only an advantageous convenience but an indispensable asset. Economically it becomes the longer the more penny-wise and pound-foolish to use antiquated programming techniques in order to save a few cheap chips. However, we must not make the mistake of adopting this doctrine to a degree that we ignore possibilities to use modern programming methods and save chips at the same time. This, I think, is the true challenge of computer engineering today.

Programming appears as an activity in many contexts. When I subsequently use the word "programming", I refer to the construction of relatively complex systems for long-time use, rather than the formulation of a small program which is discarded and forgotten after the intended result has been computed. As such, programming is computer engineering.

Computers, i.e. the hardware, are unique among the products of modern technology in many respects, but perhaps their most unique characteristic is their incompleteness. A so-called complete hardware system is an utterly useless gadget without software, i.e. programs. Each program extends the hardware creating that machine which is capable of computing or behaving in the desired manner. Hence programming is constructing that machine, starting from the basis of some given multi-

purpose elements. These elements may indeed be specific hardware components of a given kind. But the modern view is that they are the constructs
which are offered by a programming language. Hence we tend to abstract
from a given concrete machine and to work with idealized building blocks.
We have recognized that abstraction allows us to suppress (to hide)
details that are irrelevant to our ultimate goal, a process that is indispensable in the construction of complex machinery. The division of a
computing system into hardware and software was and is the most clear-
cut borderline that hides details (of the hardware from the software
and vice versa). It appears that we need a large number of such border-
lines, and that the one usually given between hard- and software is by
no means a good one.

As a side remark, let me point out that the mentioned incompleteness
of computers is also the key to their flexibility and universality. As it
is, against widespread beliefs, much more costly to realize a given
system entirely in hardware than partly with software, the tendency is to
implement as hardware only those parts that are very universally applicable. Therefore it is possible to produce components in very large
quantities necessary to become cost-effective. As a consequence, the trend
is to increase the percentage of a system implemented by software. And
this is the reason for steadily increasing software cost and decreasing
hardware cost.

I have tried to motivate my view of (system) programming languages
as abstract tool sets for the construction of computing machinery. This
is in strong contrast to the view of a language as a medium of communication between man and machine. Admittedly this latter view is not only
more common but has also coined the term "programming language", which
in my opinion is ill-chosen and misleading. "Program notation" would
be eminently more appropriate.

Historical development

Let us now consider in which ways programming languages aid the system designer in his task to develop complex machinery, and in particular to hide details of some part from other parts.

The first step with this goal in mind has been the introduction of subroutines in Fortran. Their purpose had always been proclaimed as avoidance of code replication (and saving the programmer from having to write so much!). But equally important is the fact that a subroutine can be accompanied with objects (variables) that are unknown to other subroutines.

This aspect was clearly recognized by the designers of Algol 60. It resulted in the concepts of locality and block structure. It is noteworthy that a necessary ingredient was the insistence on explicit declaration of objects, a rule that has been heavily criticized by Fortran programmers, but nevertheless has proved to be extremely helpful in discovering mistakes at an early stage by the compiler. Blocks in Algol 60 are properly nested, i.e. each block is fully contained in another one (except of course the outermost block).

```
                                          a   b   e
BEGIN INTEGER a, b ;
     S1 ;
     BEGIN REAL c ;                   c
          S2
     END ;
     S3 ;
     BEGIN BOOLEAN d, b ;            d,b
          OWN INTEGER e ;
          S4
     END ;
     S5
END
```

In Algol 60, visibility and existence are intimately connected: Whenever an object is visible, it exists (i.e. is allocated) and vice-versa. There are, however, two exceptions to this intentional rule, one being accidental, the other planned but unsatisfactory. The accidental exception is shown in Fig. 1 by the integer variable b: in statement S4 it is invisible, although it exists, because the identifier b is there taken to denote a local Boolean variable. The intended exception is the concept of own variables. As it proved to be an unsatisfactory solution, we shall not pursue it any further here.

Block structure proved to be an extremely important concept and was adopted by virtually all subsequently designed programming languages, notably PL/I and Pascal.

Yet it became apparent that Algol 60's intriguingly simple rule of "whenever an object exists, it is also visible" was inappropriate in certain situations. Simula was the language that presented a construct which departed from this rule, although the language, based on Algol 60, retained most of its ancestor's characteristics [2] . I refer to the concept of the class. A class is defined similar to a procedure; it specifies a set of local objects, a set of parameters and a statement body. In contrast to the procedure, however, the statement body represents a coroutine, i.e. a process that is executed concurrently with other processes in the realm of abstraction, but in time-interleaved fashion in reality. Hence, a coroutine can be suspended and later resumed. During the period of suspension, its local objects exist, but are invisible. This rule follows very naturally from the premise that one process' local data should not be manipulated by other processes (even when suspended). The intended exception from the rule is provided by the external accessibility of a class' parameters.

The class structure of Simula was inspired by particular requirements of discrete event simulation. From the point of view of programming language theory it represents a feature which combines several distinct concepts, and this conglomeration makes it rather difficult to understand. With respect to Algol, the novel concepts introduced

by the Simula class feature are
- concurrency (or quasi-concurrency) of execution
- definition of a class, i.e. of a template of data objects associated
  with executable statements vs. creation of instances of this class
- distinction between visibility and existence of objects
- access of class instances via pointers, and explicit facilities
  to manipulate pointers (instead of referenced objects).

   The process of disentangling these concepts took considerable time
in the history of language development, as it was only slowly recognized
that such a separation of issues would add useful flexibility to languages.

   Algol W introduced the class idea into a purely sequential language
and disconnected the data template from its association with a body of
executable statements. This resulted in the so-called record class
[4, 8] . The Algol W class declaration defines a template of data
(records) without associated statements. However, it retains the rule
that instances of this record class are accessed exclusively via explicit
pointers, whereas all other data are accessed directly.

   The following are examples of Algol W record class declarations:
   RECORD Node (REFERENCE (Node) left, right)
   RECORD Person (STRING name;
                  INTEGER age;
                  LOGICAL male;
                  REFERENCE (Person) father, mother)
An instance of the class is generated by use of the class name and
argument of the generated element's pointer to a reference variable:
   REFERENCE (Node) root
   REFERENCE (Person) p
   root := Node (NIL, NIL)
   p := Person ("Albert", 0, TRUE, p1, p2)

Pascal went a step further, disentangling also the concepts of access, structure, and instantiation of data: all variables can be either accessed directly or via pointers, be unstructured or structured (i.e. be arrays, records, or sets), be defined as a single instance or by a template of which many instances can be created. The record class, in fact, led to the generalization of the template declaration, called type definition in Pascal [9].

The gradual process of disentangling these distinct concepts led to one definitely remarkable discovery. C.A.R. Hoare and P. Brinch Hansen recognised that the association of data and procedure declaration as embodied in the class concept would be an ideal frame for promoting the idea of program design with various levels of abstraction. If the class body is regarded as an initialization statement of local data instead of as a coroutine, and if the procedures are made globally accessible instead of local to the coroutine body, and if the associated variables are local, i.e. hidden from the environment of the class declaration, then such a structure would be an ideal tool for representing abstract objects in terms of more concrete details. This was the origin of the idea of the abstract data type.

In fact the class concept with hidden variables and visible (public) procedures was inspired by considerations of multiprogramming needs. The grouping of those variables that are accessed by several concurrent processes together with the procedures that embody these accesses created the concept of a so-called monitor [1, 5].   It enables a compiler to automatically insert interlocks (among the processes) at the appropriate places in the program, namely at all entries and exits of a monitor's procedures (instead of upon each individual reference to a shared variable). Such interlocks are a sufficient means to guarantee the absence of unintended process interference (mutual exclusion), which in turn is a sufficient condition to assert the integrity of the shared data.

```
TYPE Stack =
    CLASS  i : INTEGER ;
           el : ARRAY [1..N] OF INTEGER ;
           PROCEDURE push (x : INTEGER) ;
               BEGIN i := i + 1 ; el[i] := x END ;
           PROCEDURE pop : INTEGER ;
               BEGIN pop := el[i] ; i := i - 1 END ;
           PROCEDURE  nonempty : BOOLEAN ;
               BEGIN nonempty := i > 0 END ;
    BEGIN (* initialize *) i := 0
    END
```

Once postulated, the concept of the abstract data type led to a considerable amount of research activities. Only a few matured into implemented systems [6, 7]. It was soon recognized that a truly useful facility would have to offer parameters to type definitions, whose actual values could vary from one instantiation to another. This generalization,however, has considerable implications on the complexity of implementation. At this time, the question about the practical usefulness of the abstract data type to the programmer is still not settled, and factual experience with this concept is largely missing.

```
TYPE Stack (n : INTEGER ; T : TYPE) =
    CLASS i : INTEGER ;
          el : ARRAY [1..n] OF T ;
          PROCEDURE push (x : T) ;
              BEGIN (* assume i < n *)
                  i := i + 1 ; el[i] := x
              END ;
    ...
    END
```

A careful observer will notice that in spite of the enthusiasm with which the abstract data type was received, there are relatively few successful applications. They are therefore widely used as typical examples (e.g. the stack and the queue). This is in strong contrast to

the general data and statement structures earlier introduced by high-
level languages. The reason for this lack of proven applications may
lie in the current lack of good implementations of data type facilities;
perhaps it also points out that it is inherently difficult to discover
suitable abstract data types for a given problem.

Modules

In Modula [10], we proposed another, similar construct for information hiding, namely the so-called module. The guiding idea was once again
the separation of issues. Whereas the class of Concurrent Pascal (and
Portal) combines both a facility for information hiding (i.e. a class
declaration establishes a scope of identifiers) and for defining a
template of data (i.e. a type) for possible instantiation, the module
represents a facility serving the first purpose only. The module concept is oriented towards the need of separating large programs into
partitions with relatively "thin" connections, and to make the elements
establishing this connection more evident in the program text.

The module is effectively a bracket around a group of (type,
variable, procedure, etc.) declarations establishing a scope of identifiers. In the first instance, we may regard this bracket as an impenetrable
wall, objects declared outside of the module are invisible inside it, and those
declared inside are invisible outside. This wall is punctured selectively by
two lists of identifiers: the import list contains those identifiers defined outside which are to be visible inside too, and the export list
contains the identifiers defined inside that are to be visible outside.
This scheme is of a very attractive conceptual simplicity. As a consequence, it is relatively easy to find appropriate applications and to
develop a methodology (a style?) for its usage. Implementation is quite
manageable, although not trivial.

As the module allows grouping of data and procedure declarations and
making only selected elements of this group externally visible, it
may also serve to define "abstract data types" that can be instantiated
in arbitrary numbers.

As an example, the following Concurrent Pascal class declaration

```
TYPE C  = CLASS
                VAR x, y : T ;
                PROCEDURE p ;
                    BEGIN ... x ... y ... END p ;
                PROCEDURE q ;
                    BEGIN ... x ... y ... END q
            END
```

can be expressed by a module as

```
MODULE M ;
    IMPORT T ;
    EXPORT p, q, C ;
    TYPE C = RECORD x, y : T END ;
    PROCEDURE p (c : C) ;
        BEGIN ... c.x ... c.y ... END p ;
    PROCEDURE q (c : C) ;
        BEGIN ... c.x ... c.y ... END q
END M
```

For creating two instances of the class (type) C we declare "VAR a, b : C" in Concurrent Pascal as well as in Modula. In order to invoke a procedure applied to a class object, we write p(a), q(b) in a conventional manner, instead of a.p, b.q as in Concurrent Pascal.

This analogy between module and class hides one important ingredient of the abstract data type concept that must be mentioned for the sake of fairness and clarity. A crucial idea of the abstract data type is that each instance is governed by some condition (called the type's invariant) which holds for the hidden data at all times (more specifically: whenever control is outside the procedures defined within the class). This invariant is established as soon as an instance is created by some initialization body of the class declaration (not shown above). In the solution using a module, this initialization would have to be performed by an additional, explicit procedure declared within M. Its call might be forgotten by a programmer - missing initialization is indeed a common error - whereas for the class instance it is automatically implied by its declaration.

The sacrifice of this benefit perhaps shows that in choosing the module in place of the class, formal verification techniques have not been foremost on our mind. Instead, our motivation was to provide a facility whose purpose is unique and easy to understand. Experience with programming in Modula - designing compilers and other large programs - has justified the presence of the module facility in a very convincing manner. Most of us would never wish to design another large program without an encapsulation feature such as the module. A revealing fact was also that in the average only a few percent of the modules occurring in a program serve in the sense of an abstract data type as template with several instances. More important is the possibility to nest modules. The distinct asset, however, is the simple but general rule about import and export, the freedom to select objects for import and export, and to have the same rule govern procedures as well as variables, types, and other objects.

In spite of these virtues, the module as described so far has its shortcomings. We have tried to overcome some of them in Modula-2 [11] and during these efforts came to the conclusion that the belief in the existence of an ideal solution satisfying all needs is not only too optimistic but mistaken.

Let me nevertheless present a few points of controversy and point out our choices for Modula-2, a language oriented towards system programming.

Primarily if programs are to be composed from collections of existing modules, i.e. if the writer of a module may not know the environment in which his modules will be embedded, the described solution is unsatisfactory. For, if two inner modules export, by coincidence, the same identifiers, a conflict arises:

```
MODULE M ;
    MODULE MO ;
        EXPORT x ;
        VAR x : CARDINAL ;

            ...
    END MO ;
    MODULE M1 ;
        EXPORT x ;
        VAR x : BOOLEAN ;
    END M1 ;
    (* at this point x denotes two different variables *)
END M.
```

In order to disambiguate the above situation, a qualification of x is introduced. In the above example, x must be exported in so-called qualified mode. In this case (see below), no naming conflict arises, because the Cardinal variable x is to be referred to as MO.x, and the Boolean as M1.x.

Qualified export has its drawbacks too, however, and in our experience it is used almost exclusively in the case of utility modules only. Typically, modules are named by relatively long identifiers. They have to be used whenever an object exported in qualified mode is referenced. This results in a "heavy" and cumbersome notation.

In Modula-2, we have eased this situation by providing a facility with an effect similar to that of a WITH statement for records.

Consider the following example:

```
MODULE M ;
    MODULE MO ;
        EXPORT QUALIFIED x, y ; ...
    END MO ;
    MODULE M1 ;
        EXPORT QUALIFIED x, y ; ...
    END M1 ;
    MODULE M2 ;
        FROM MO IMPORT x ;
        FROM M1 IMPORT y ;
        ... x ... y ...
    END M2 ;
    ... MO.x ... M1.y ...
END M.
```

An import list of the form

FROM M IMPORT x

will allow reference by unqualified x, although x has been exported from M in qualified mode.

The simple export rules indicated above have consequences that are undesirable in some situations. If a module is employed to implement an abstract data type as indicated above, then external visibility of the record field identifiers x and y is definitely undesirable. A strict interpretation of the given rules, however, exports x and y automatically together with C. Here we are confronted with the dilemma of transparent vs. obscure export of types. In Modula, we had decided for obscure export - to cater for the view of abstract data types - in Modula-2 we opted for transparent export, which not only allows for a simple export rule, but is highly desirable in many practical cases.

```
MODULE M ;
    MODULE M1 ;
        EXPORT A, R, P ;
        TYPE A = ARRAY 0..9 OF CHAR ;
        TYPE R = RECORD x, y : CARDINAL END ;
        PROCEDURE P (a : A ; r : R) ;

            ...
        END P ;

        ...
    END M1 ;
    VAR a0, a1 : A ; r0, r1 : R ;
BEGIN ...
    (* assume obscure type export *)
    a0[i] := a1[j] ;
    (* illegal because it is unknown here that a0, a1 are arrays *)
    r0.x := r1.y ;
    (* illegal because it is unknown here that r0, r1 are records;
    x, y are  here unknown identifiers *)
    P(a0, r1) (* legal call *)
END M.
```

Our experience has been that transparent export is rather the normal
case, and obscure export is desired, if the module is designed in the
sense of an abstract data type. Modula-2 offers transparent type export
as default, and obscure export in special cases (see below).

Separate modules

Large systems are built in layers with a hierarchical structure.
The very large number of elementary components asks for a fair number of
logical layers, each being described by a set of abstractions and by
conditions governing them. It would indeed be surprising, if the same
constructs would be optimally suited for the decomposition on all levels
of the hierarchy. But of course, a careful designer has a natural tendency
not to introduce different concepts and mechanisms for each level; in fact,

one should _like_ to use the same concept for all layers.

We feel that a certain compromise may yield the best results, and recognize a primary distinction of requirements between the level on which components are designed and implemented by different people, and the levels below it. If different people are involved, the incentive to specify thin interfaces, and to nail them by binding agreements, is very much more pronounced, than if the parts are designed, combined, and tested by one person. In the former case, it appears desirable to separate the specifications of a program from the specification of the interface, i.e. of those items that are exported and imported. Such a separation has the decisive advantage that the interface specification can be widely distributed, whereas the actual program is kept private to its implementor. Such a scheme is used in MESA [3].

This scheme is particularly useful if a compiler is designed to check for the consistency of the individual program parts. It must verify that a program is consistent with its specified interface, and that users of a module M are consistent with M's interface. Only in this way can it be determined whether or not changes in a program P can be implemented without changes in any of the users of P; the condition is that P's _interface_ remains unchanged.

At this point, we have quiescently abandoned the view of a system defined by a program written on one piece of paper. Instead, it is specified by many such pieces (we call them modules) designed and developed by different people. For several reasons, it is desirable to be able to compile these modules separately. This facility, belonging entirely to the realm of technical realization should, however, not influence the conceptual design of the language. A program, being a piece of text, must be understood without resort to explanations of its execution and preparation. If it consists of several pieces, it must be regarded as a concatenation of these pieces, and the language rule must cover this case.

In Modula-2 we regard the concatenated modules as able to export
into and to import from a vacuous environment. Typically, such a concatenation consists of one module representing the so-called main program and a set of modules with data and procedures used by the primary
module. The primary module imports only, the others export and may
import. From the foregoing it follows that only the secondary modules
have reason to be specified in two parts, namely as an interface specification and a program implementation. We have decided that they must
be specified in two parts, and therefore obtain three different species
of modules:

- The "normal" module. It can be nested. If it occurs as a separate
  piece of text, it cannot export and is regarded as a main program.

- The definition module. It specifies the interface of a module, in
  particular all objects that are exported. (Modula-2 allows qualified
  export only in this case.)

- The implementation module. It belongs to the definition module
  carrying the same name. It contains the bodies of the procedures
  whose headings are listed in the definition module, and possibly
  declarations of further objects that are local, i.e. not exported.

Definition and implementation modules occur as pairs and as separate pieces of text, i.e. they cannot be nested in some other module.
The implementation module is assumed to import all objects defined in its
associated definition module.

```
DEFINITION MODULE IO ;
     EXPORT put, get ;
     PROCEDURE put (ch : CHAR) ;
     PROCEDURE get ( ) : CHAR ;
END IO.

IMPLEMENTATION MODULE IO ;
     VAR inbuf, outbuf : ARRAY 0..15 OF CHAR ;
     PROCEDURE put (ch : CHAR) ;
          BEGIN (* body of put *)  END put ;
     PROCEDURE get ( ) : CHAR ;
           BEGIN (* body of get *)  END get ;
  BEGIN       (* initialization of data *)
  END IO.
```

```
MODULE Main ;
      FROM IO IMPORT put, get ;
      VAR ch : CHAR ;
BEGIN
      ... put (ch) ... ch := get ( ) ...
END Main.
```

The separation into definition and implementation modules yields an unexpected benefit. It solves the problem of transparent vs. obscure export of types in a most natural manner: If a type is fully specified in the definition module, this signals transparent export. Obscure export is achieved by listing merely the identifier in the definition module and by "hiding" the full declaration within the implementation module.

```
DEFINITION MODULE M ;
      EXPORT T0, T1, ... ;
      TYPE T0 ;  (* obscure type export *)
      TYPE T1 = ARRAY 0..15 OF CHAR ;  (* transparent export *)
END M.

IMPLEMENTATION MODULE M;
      TYPE T0 = POINTER TO
                          RECORD x, y : CARDINAL ;
                                   ...
                          END ;
      ...
END M.
```

The use of the module facility

It is a well-known truth that any new facility requires not only an appropriate formulation and specification, but also a "theory and practice" of its use. Although well-motivated examples for the principle of information hiding have been circulating for some time, and although they appeared to demonstrate convincingly where classeś and modules would be useful, we have experienced that it is by no means an easy task to determine the best modularization of a program in development. This is particularly the case for the larger partitions, except perhaps when a hierarchical structure of procedure layers is fairly evident, such as e.g. in the case of input/output utilities, file handlers, and drivers.

In general, a module is established whenever a collection of procedures share a set of variables that is accessed exclusively by these procedures. (These variables are typically *own* in the sense of Algol 60). We have gradually shifted, however, from the view of a module being a collection of procedures sharing common variables towards the view of a data structure whose access is restricted by having to occur via a small set of operators. Hence, the data rather than the procedures move into the foreground of attention. A module is typically characterized by the *data* it contains (and perhaps hides) rather than by its set of exported procedures.

Often - in the case of larger partitions - these data are structured in quite complex manners. In particular, structures with several different kinds of elements occur. It therefore is inappropriate to characterize a module as a type. Instead, the exported procedures often access and alter data elements of several types. This fact may explain partly the earlier mentioned lack of practical success of the class structure which effectively exports a single type only. The module does not suffer from this restrictiveness; it allows arbitrary definition of many data types and structures, and export of all of them if desired.

In essence, then, the recognition of a useful modularization of the involved data structure is the key to finding the appropriate decomposition of a program into modules. As any experienced programmer knows, this is the hardest task; often one discovers the right data structures only while developing the entire program. Without experience and foresight, one is condemned to restructure a program's module decomposition from time to time. The obvious alternative is, of course, not to bother to improve the program.

But I must draw attention to the fact that - owing to the explicit modules - the inappropriateness of a program's structure is much more obvious than it is (or was) when written in a language without modules. Programming with a module facility is indeed more difficult, as it forces the programmer to reason from the start more carefully about a program's structure. However, the benefit is that such programs are - once designed - easier to reason about, to change, to document, and to understand. For system programs, which in general are expected to have a long life span, the gain in "maintainability" is well worth a heavier investment in the effort of their design. In many cases, finding the right structure initially is not merely a benefit, but simply a matter of success or failure.

The module also appeared as an aid towards a solution of another longstanding problem typical of systems programming languages. I refer to the use of low-level, perhaps machine-dependent facilities in a high-level language with program-defined data types. Whereas machine-dependent facilities such as special operators and data types like WORD or BYTE are virtually indispensable in, for example, a disk driver, we strongly wish to hide them from most program parts. The module provides exactly this hiding capability, and therefore emerges as the means to make all levels of a system expressible in one and the same language, without being restrictive in low-level modules, nor being too "permissive" in high-level modules.

In Modula-2, we have postulated a (machine-dependent) pseudo-module, called SYSTEM, that is typically imported in low-level modules only. It contains data types such as ADDRESS, WORD, and procedures corresponding to specialized machine instructions. Moreover, it also contains the primitives used for coroutine handling, from which typically a process scheduler could be programmed. We call this a pseudo module, because its components must be known to the compiler, which acts according to special rules (e.g. generates the specialized instructions instead of regular procedure calls).

Of importance besides the availability of the system module are
the additional compatibility rules of these system types with other
types. For example, the type ADDRESS is said to be compatible with all
pointer types. This holds for both assignment and actual-formal parameter substitution. Compatibility also exists between the types WORD
and INTEGER (or CARDINAL). Thus it becomes possible to perform arithmetic operation on pointers, but only in the low-level module, where
the pointers are typed as addresses (such as e.g. in a storage manager,
see below).

```
MODULE Storage ;
    FROM SYSTEM IMPORT ADDRESS ;
    EXPORT new ;
    VAR LastAdr : ADDRESS ;
    PROCEDURE new (VAR a : ADDRESS ; size : CARDINAL) ;
        BEGIN a := LastAdr ;
            LastAdr := LastAdr + size
        END new ;
BEGIN LastAdr := 0
END Storage.

MODULE Main ;
    IMPORT Storage ;
    TYPE T = ... ;
    VAR p : POINTER TO T ;
BEGIN ...
    Storage.new (p, SIZE(T)) ...
END Main.
```

(Note: The decomposition of the module Storage into definition and
implementation parts is not shown here).

Exception handling

When a programmer is experienced in the use of a structured
language with sufficiently flexible control statements (such as IF,
WHILE, etc.), the GO TO statement will appear as quite dispensable to

him. The introduction of modules, however, in particular of separate modules,
reintroduces the need for a jump. The major need arises from the handling
of exceptional cases, i.e. of exit jumps from procedures. Although this
case might be handled by the passing of additional output parameters,
the exceptional exit jump is desirable, because parameters would cause
additional, unacceptable overhead upon each call. A regular GO TO
statement is inadequate, however, if the point of resumption is unknown
in the module where the exceptional condition arises.

For this purpose, Modula-2 provides a feature called _exception_.
It is worth emphasizing that the need for it is mainly a consequence
of the module facility. We distinguish between three constructs, called
exception declaration, exception call, and exception handler.
The following example illustrates their use:

```
MODULE M ;
      EXCEPTION ex ;      (* declaration *)
      PROCEDURE p ;
            BEGIN ...
                  ex  (* transfer to S1, which is invisible here *)
            END p ;
      PROCEDURE q ;
            BEGIN ... p ; ...
            WHEN ex DO S1  (* exception handler *)
            END q ;
   BEGIN ... q ; ...
      ex ; (* exception call, handled by S2 *)
            ...
   WHEN ex DO S2
   END M.
```

When an exception is called, control exits the called procedures
up to the first one which provides a corresponding handler. This
handler is executed, whereupon the procedure is terminated and
execution resumes at the point of its call. The handlers (WHEN ...)
occur at the end of procedure bodies. They can be regarded like
procedures; however, when called, the search follows the dynamic history

of procedure activations instead of the static, nested scopes of
identifier visibility.

Implementation

A pleasant property of the module concept as described here is
that it does not present any major problems to implementors. In essence,
its influence is restricted primarily to the mechanisms for symbol table
access in the compiler. In effect, the module structure is invisible
in the code ultimately generated, as it only concerns the scopes
(visibility ranges) of objects, but not the semantics of a program.

Large modules specified as separate entities should be separately
compilable. This requirement complicates matters to a considerable extent; it does not merely require the generation of relocatable instead
of absolute code. The emphasis is on separate compilation in contrast
to independent compilation. Thereby we understand that upon compilation,
syntax and type consistency checks are performed regardless of whether
or not a program is presented in its entirety or in separate pieces.
As a consequence, a compiler processing a module M must have access to
information about all modules imported by M. Acutally, this information can be restricted to the items exported and, in order to expedite
matters, can be stored in a compiled form. A compiler now does not only
generate an object (code) file and a listing, but additionally (in the
case of a definition module) a symbol table file describing all exported objects. It not only reads from a source file, but also inputs
compiled symbol table files of all modules it imports.

This implies that a module M0 being used by M1 must be compiled
prior to compilation of M1. Circular references are thereby prohibited.
Fortunately, the split into definition and implementation parts solves
this problem, if perhaps not fully, then at least for the practically
relevant cases. A definition module is compiled - resulting in a
symbol table file - before its corresponding implementation module is
compiled. If two modules both contain references to the other, then
these imports belong to the implementation parts. Hence, both definition

parts can be compiled separately (in any sequence), whereupon both implementation parts are processed, yielding the actual code files.

An important consideration is that a compiler should have to consult only the symbol table files of directly imported modules. For example, if M2 imports M1 which in turn imports M0, then the table of M1 should contain processed information on those selected objects of M0 that are referenced in M1. If this were not the case, M2 would have to consult the tables of both M1 and M0. In practical cases, this might quickly lead to an unacceptably large volume of tables to be loaded for modules on higher levels.

Although the complications induced on a compiler by a scheme of separate compilation is by no means minor, a separate compilation facility for modules is virtually indispensable for the construction of large systems. The simple solution of replacing separate by independent compilation is unacceptable, as it would eliminate type consistency checking across module boundaries, thereby giving away one of the most effective assets of a structured language.

References

[1]   P. Brinch Hansen. The programming language Concurrent Pascal.
      IEEE Trans. Software Eng., 1, 2, 199-207 (1975)

[2]   O.J. Dahl, K. Nygaard. Simula - An Algol-based simulation language.
      Comm. ACM 9, 9, 671-678 (Sept. 1966)

[3]   Ch. M. Geschke, J.H. Morris, E.H. Satterthwaite. Early experience
      with Mesa. Comm. ACM, 20, 8, 540-553 (Aug. 1977)

[4]   C.A. R. Hoare. Record handling; in Programming Languages, F. Genuys,
      Ed., London and New York, 1968. (pp. 291-347)

[5]   C.A. R. Hoare. Monitors: An operating system structuring concept.
      Comm. ACM, 17, 10, 549-557 (1974)

[6]   H. Lienhard. The real-time programming language PORTAL. R. Schild.
      Parallel processes in PORTAL, exemplified in a group project.
      Landis & Gyr Review 25, 2, 2-16 (1978)

[7]   B. Liskov et al. CLU Reference Manual. Computation Structures Group
      Memo 161. MIT Lab. for Comp. Sci. July 1978

[8]   N. Wirth and C.A. R. Hoare. A contribution to the development of
      Algol. Comm. ACM, 9, 6, 413-432 (June 1966)

[9]   N. Wirth. The programming language Pascal. Acta Informatica 1,
      35-63 (1971).

[10] N. Wirth. Modula: A language for modular multiprogramming.
      Software - Practice and Experience, 7, 3-35 (1977)

[11] N. Wirth. Modula-2. Tech. Report 27, Institut für Informatik ETH.
      Zürich, Dec. 1978.

THE EVOLUTION OF THE UNIX TIME-SHARING SYSTEM

Dennis M. Ritchie

Bell Laboratories

U.S.A.

ABSTRACT

This paper presents a brief history of the early development of the Unix operating system. It concentrates on the evolution of the file system, the process-control mechanism, and the idea of pipelined commands. Some attention is paid to social conditions during the development of the system.

Introduction

During the past few years, the Unix operating system has come into wide use, so wide that its very name has become a trademark of Bell Laboratories. Its important characteristics have become known to many people. It has suffered much rewriting and tinkering since the first publication describing it in 1974,[1] but few fundamental changes. However, Unix was born in 1969 not 1974, and the account of its development makes a little-known and perhaps instructive story. This paper presents a technical and social history of the evolution of the system.

Origins

For computer science at Bell Laboratories, the period 1968-1969 was somewhat unsettled. The main reason for this was the slow, though clearly inevitable, withdrawal of the Labs from the Multics project. To the Labs computing community as a whole, the problem was the increasing obviousness of the failure of Multics to deliver promptly any sort of usable system, let alone the panacea envisioned earlier. For much of this time, the Murray Hill Computer Center was also running a costly GE 645 machine that inadequately simulated the GE 635. Another shake-up that occurred during this period was the organizational separation of computing services and computing research.

From the point of view of the group that was to be most involved in the beginnings of Unix (K. Thompson, Ritchie, M. D. McIlroy, J. F. Ossanna), the decline and fall of Multics had a directly felt effect. We were among the last Bell Laboratories holdouts actually working on Multics, so we still felt some sort of stake in its success. More important, the convenient interactive computing service that Multics had promised to the entire community was in fact available to our limited group, at first under the CTSS system used to develop Multics, and later under Multics itself. Even though Multics could not then support many users, it could support us, albeit at exorbitant cost. We didn't want to lose the pleasant niche we occupied, because no similar ones were available; even the time-sharing service that would later be offered under GE's operating system did not exist. What we wanted to preserve was not just a good environment in which to do programming, but a system around which a fellowship could form. We knew from experience that the essence of communal computing, as supplied by remote-access, time-shared machines, is not just to type programs into a terminal instead of a keypunch, but to encourage close communication.

Thus, during 1969, we began trying to find an alternative to Multics. The search took several forms. Throughout 1969 we (mainly Ossanna, Thompson, Ritchie) lobbied intensively for the purchase of a medium-scale machine for which we promised to write an operating system; the machines we suggested were the DEC PDP-10 and the SDS (later Xerox) Sigma 7. The effort was frustrating, because our proposals were never clearly and finally turned down, but yet were certainly never accepted. Several times it seemed we were very near success. The final blow to this effort came when we presented an exquisitely complicated proposal, designed to minimize financial outlay, that involved some outright purchase, some third-party lease, and a plan to turn in a DEC KA-10 processor on the soon-to-be-announced and more capable KI-10. The proposal was rejected, and rumor soon had it that W. O. Baker (then vice-president of Research) had reacted to it with the comment 'Bell Laboratories just doesn't do business this way!'

Actually, it is perfectly obvious in retrospect (and should have been at the time) that we were asking the Labs to spend too much money on too few people with too vague a plan. Moreover, I am quite sure that at that time operating systems were not, for our management, an attractive area in which to support work. They were in the process of extricating themselves not only from an operating system development effort that had failed, but from running the local Computation Center. Thus it may have seemed that buying a machine such as we suggested might lead on the one hand to yet another Multics, or on the other, if we produced something useful, to yet another Comp Center for them to be responsible for.

Besides the financial agitations that took place in 1969, there was technical work also. Thompson, R. H. Canaday, and Ritchie developed, on blackboards and scribbled notes, the basic design of a file system that was later to become the heart of Unix. Most of the design was Thompson's, as was the impulse to think about file systems at all, but I believe I contributed the idea of device files. Thompson's itch for creation of an operating system took several forms during this period; he also wrote (on Multics) a fairly detailed simulation of the performance of the proposed file system design and of paging behavior of programs. In addition, he started work on a new operating system for the GE-645, going as far as writing an assembler for the machine and a rudimentary operating system kernel whose greatest achievement, so far as I remember, was to type a greeting message. The complexity of the machine was such that a mere message was already a fairly notable accomplishment, but when it became clear that the lifetime of the 645 at the Labs was measured in months, the work was dropped.

Also during 1969, Thompson developed the game of 'Space Travel.' First written on Multics, then transliterated into Fortran for GECOS (the operating system for the GE, later Honeywell, 635), it was nothing less than a simulation of the movement of the major bodies of the Solar System, with the player guiding a ship here and there, observing the scenery, and attempting to land on the various planets and moons. The GECOS version was unsatisfactory in two important respects: first, the display of the state of the game was jerky and hard to control because one had to type commands at it, and second, a game cost about $75 for CPU time on the big computer. It did not take long, therefore, for Thompson to find a little-used PDP-7 computer with an excellent display processor; the whole system was used as a Graphic-II terminal. He and I rewrote Space Travel to run on this machine. The undertaking was more ambitious than it might seem; because we disdained all existing software, we had to write a floating-point arithmetic package, the pointwise specification of the graphic characters for the display, and a debugging subsystem that continuously displayed the contents of typed-in locations in a corner of the screen. All this was written in assembly language for a cross-assembler that ran under GECOS and produced paper tapes to be carried to the PDP-7.

Space Travel, though it made a very attractive game, served mainly as an introduction to the clumsy technology of preparing programs for the PDP-7. Soon Thompson began implementing the paper file system (perhaps 'chalk file system' would be more accurate) that had been designed earlier. A file system without a way to exercise it is a sterile proposition, so he proceeded to flesh it out with the other requirements for a working operating system, in particular the notion of processes. Then came a small set of user-level utilities: the means to copy, print, delete, and edit files, and of course a simple command interpreter (shell). Up to this time all the programs were written using GECOS and files were transferred to the PDP-7 on paper tape; but once an assembler was completed the system was able to support itself. Although it was not until well into 1970 that Brian Kernighan suggested the name 'Unix,' in a somewhat treacherous pun on 'Multics,' the operating system we know today was born.

The PDP-7 Unix file system

Structurally, the file system of PDP-7 Unix was nearly identical to today's. It had

1) An i-list: a linear array of *i-nodes* each describing a file. An i-node contained less than it does now, but the essential information was the same: the protection mode of the file, its type and size, and the list of physical blocks holding the contents.

2) Directories: a special kind of file containing a sequence of names and the associated i-number.

3) Special files describing devices. The device specification was not contained explicitly in the i-node, but was instead encoded in the number: specific i-numbers corresponded to specific files.

The important file system calls were also present from the start. Read, write, open, creat (sic), close: with one very important exception, discussed below, they were similar to what one finds now. A minor difference was that the unit of I/O was the word, not the byte, because the PDP-7 was a word-addressed machine. In practice this meant merely that all programs dealing with character streams ignored null characters, because null was used to pad a file to an even number of characters. Another minor, occasionally annoying difference was the lack of erase and kill processing for terminals. Terminals, in effect, were always in raw mode. Only a few programs (notably the shell and the editor) bothered to implement erase-kill processing.

In spite of its considerable similarity to the current file system, the PDP-7 file system was in one way remarkably different:

there were no path names, and each file-name argument to the system was a simple name (without '/') taken relative to the current directory. Links, in the usual Unix sense, did exist. Together with an elaborate set of conventions, they were the principal means by which the lack of path names became acceptable.

The *link* call took the form

link(dir, file, newname)

where *dir* was a directory file in the current directory, *file* an existing entry in that directory, and *newname* the name of the link, which was added to the current directory. Because *dir* needed to be in the current directory, it is evident that today's prohibition against links to directories was not enforced; the PDP-7 Unix file system had the shape of a general directed graph.

So that every user did not need to maintain a link to all directories of interest, there existed a directory called *dd* that contained entries for the directory of each user. Thus, to make a link to file *x* in directory *ken*, I might do

```
ln dd ken ken
ln ken x x
rm ken
```

This scheme rendered subdirectories sufficiently hard to use as to make them unused in practice. Another important barrier was that there was no way to create a directory while the system was running; all were made during recreation of the file system from paper tape, so that directories were in effect a nonrenewable resource.

The *dd* convention made the *chdir* command relatively convenient. It took multiple arguments, and switched the current directory to each named directory in turn. Thus

chdir dd ken

would move to directory *ken*. (Incidentally, *chdir* was spelled *ch*; why this was expanded when we went to the PDP-11 I don't remember.)

The most serious inconvenience of the implementation of the file system, aside from the lack of path names, was the difficulty of changing its configuration; as mentioned, directories and special files were both made only when the disk was recreated. Installation of a new device was very painful, because the code for devices was spread widely throughout the system; for example there were several loops that visited each device in turn. Not surprisingly, there was no notion of mounting a removable disk pack, because the machine had only a single fixed-head disk.

The operating system code that implemented this file system was a drastically simplified version of the present scheme. One important simplification followed from the fact that the system was not multiprogrammed; only one program was in memory at a time, and control was passed between processes only when an explicit swap took place. So, for example, there was an *iget* routine that made a named i-node available, but it left the i-node in a constant, static location rather than returning a pointer into a large table of active i-nodes. A precursor of the current buffering mechanism was present (with about 4 buffers) but there was essentially no overlap of disk I/O with computation. This was avoided not merely for simplicity. The disk attached to the PDP-7 was fast for its time; it transferred one 18-bit word every 2 microseconds. On the other hand, the PDP-7 itself had a memory cycle time of 1 microsecond, and most instructions took 2 cycles (one for the instruction itself, one for the operand). However, indirectly addressed instructions required 3 cycles, and indirection was quite common, because the machine had no index registers. Finally, the DMA controller was unable to access memory during an instruction. The upshot was that the disk would incur overrun errors if any indirectly-addressed instructions were executed while it was transferring. Thus control could not be returned to the user, nor in fact could general system code be executed, with the disk running. The interrupt routines for the clock and terminals, which needed to be runnable at all times, had to be coded in very strange fashion to avoid indirection.

Process control

By 'process control,' I mean the mechanisms by which processes are created and used; today the system calls *fork*, *exec*, *wait*, and *exit* implement these mechanisms. Unlike the file system, which existed in nearly its present form from the earliest days, the process control scheme underwent considerable mutation after PDP-7 Unix was already in use. (The introduction of path names in the PDP-11 system was certainly a considerable notational advance, but not a change in fundamental structure.)

Today, the way in which commands are executed by the shell can be summarized as follows:

1) The shell reads a command line from the terminal.

2) It creates a child process by *fork*.

3) The child process uses *exec* to call in the command from a file.

4) Meanwhile, the parent shell uses *wait* to wait for the child (command) process to terminate by calling *exit*.

5) The parent shell goes back to step 1).

Processes (independently executing entities) existed very early in PDP-7 Unix. There were in fact precisely two of them, one for each of the two terminals attached to the machine. There was no *fork*, *wait*, or *exec*. There was an *exit*, but its meaning was rather different, as will be seen. The main loop of the shell went as follows.

1) The shell closed all its open files, then opened the terminal special file for standard input and output (file descriptors 0 and 1).

2) It read a command line from the terminal.

3) It linked to the file specifying the command, opened the file, and removed the link. Then it copied a small bootstrap program to the top of memory and jumped to it; this bootstrap program read in the file over the shell code, then jumped to the first location of the command (in effect an *exec*).

4) The command did its work, then terminated by calling *exit*. The *exit* call caused the system to read in a fresh copy of the shell over the terminated command, then to jump to its start (and thus in effect to go to step 1).

The most interesting thing about this primitive implementation is the degree to which it anticipated themes developed more fully later. True, it could support neither background processes nor shell command files (let alone pipes and filters); but IO redirection (via '<' and '>') was soon there; it is discussed below. The implementation of redirection was quite straightforward; in step 3) above the shell just replaced its standard input or output with the appropriate file. Crucial to subsequent development was the implementation of the shell as a user-level program stored in a file, rather than a part of the operating system.

The structure of this process control scheme, with one process per terminal, is similar to that of many interactive systems, for example CTSS, Multics, Honeywell TSS, and IBM TSS and TSO. In general such systems require special mechanisms to implement useful facilities such as detached computations and command files; Unix at that stage didn't bother to supply the special mechanisms. It also exhibited some irritating, idiosyncratic problems. For example, a newly recreated shell had to close all its open files both to get rid of any open files left by the command just executed and to rescind previous IO redirection. Then it had to reopen the special file corresponding to its terminal, in order to read a new command line. There was no /dev directory (because no path names); moreover, the shell could retain no memory across commands, because it was reexecuted afresh after each command. Thus a further file system convention was required: each directory had to contain an entry *tty* for a special file that referred to the terminal of the process that opened it. If by accident one changed into some directory that lacked this entry, the shell would loop hopelessly; about the only remedy was to reboot. (Sometimes the missing link could be made from the other terminal.)

Process control in its modern form was designed and implemented within a couple of days. It is astonishing how easily it fitted into the existing system; at the same time it is easy to see how some of the slightly unusual features of the design are present precisely because they represented small, easily-coded changes to what existed. A good example is the separation of the *fork* and *exec* functions. The most common model for the creation of new processes involves specifying a program for the process to execute; in Unix, a forked process continues to run the same program as its parent until it performs an explicit *exec*. The separation of the functions is certainly not unique to Unix, and in fact it was present in the Berkeley time-sharing system,[2] which was well-known to Thompson. Still, it seems reasonable to suppose that it exists in Unix mainly because of the ease with which *fork* could be implemented without changing much else. The system already handled multiple (i.e. two) processes; there was a process table, and the processes were swapped between main memory and the disk. The initial implementation of *fork* required only

1) Expansion of the process table

2) Addition of a fork call that copied the current process to the disk swap area, using the already existing swap IO primitives, and made some adjustments to the process table.

In fact, the PDP-7's *fork* call required precisely 27 lines of assembly code. Of course, other changes in the operating system and user programs were required, and some of them were rather interesting and unexpected. But a combined *fork-exec* would have been considerably more complicated, if only because *exec* as such did not exist; its function was already performed, using explicit IO, by the shell.

The *exit* system call, which previously read in a new copy of the shell (actually a sort of automatic *exec* but without arguments), simplified considerably; in the new version a process only had to clean out its process table entry, and give up control.

Curiously, the primitives that became *wait* were considerably more general than the present scheme. A pair of primitives sent one-word messages between named processes:

smes(pid, message)
(pid, message) = rmes()

The target process of *smes* did not need to have any ancestral relationship with the receiver, although the system provided no explicit mechanism for communicating process IDs except that *fork* returned to each of the parent and child the ID of its relative. Messages were not queued; a sender delayed until the receiver read the message.

The message facility was used as follows: the parent shell, after creating a process to execute a command, sent a message to the new process by *smes*; when the command terminated (assuming it did not try to read any messages) the shell's blocked *smes* call returned an error indication that the target process did not exist. Thus the shell's *smes* became, in effect, the equivalent of *wait*.

A different protocol, which took advantage of more of the generality offered by messages, was used between the initialization program and the shells for each terminal. The initialization process, whose ID was understood to be 1, created a shell for each of the terminals, and then issued *rmes*; each shell, when it read the end of its input file, used *smes* to send a conventional 'I am terminating' message to the initialization process, which recreated a new shell process for that terminal.

I can recall no other use of messages. This explains why the facility was replaced by the *wait* call of the present system, which is less general, but more directly applicable to the desired purpose. Possibly relevant also is the evident bug in the mechanism: if a command process attempted to use messages to communicate with other processes, it would disrupt the shell's synchronization. The shell depended on sending a message that was never received; if a command executed *rmes*, it would receive the shell's phony message, and cause the shell to read another input line just as if the command had terminated. If a need for general messages had manifested itself, the bug would have been repaired.

At any rate, the new process control scheme instantly rendered some very valuable features trivial to implement; for example detached processes (with '&') and recursive use of the shell as a command. Most systems have to supply some sort of special 'batch job submission' facility and a special command interpreter for files distinct from the one used interactively.

Although the multiple-process idea slipped in very easily indeed, there were some aftereffects that weren't anticipated. The most memorable of these became evident soon after the new system came up and apparently worked. In the midst of our jubilation, it was discovered that the *chdir* (change current directory) command had stopped working. There was much reading of code and anxious introspection about how the addition of *fork* could have broken the *chdir* call. Finally the truth dawned: in the old system *chdir* was an ordinary command; it adjusted the current directory of the (unique) process attached to the terminal. Under the new system, the *chdir* command correctly changed the current directory of the process created to execute it, but this process promptly terminated and had no effect whatsoever on its parent shell! It was necessary to make *chdir* a special command, executed internally within the shell. It turns out that several command-like functions have the same property, for example *login*.

Another mismatch between the system as it had been and the new process control scheme took longer to become evident. Originally, the read/write pointer associated with each open file was stored within the process that opened the file. (This pointer indicates where in the file the next read or write will take place.) The problem with this organization became evident only when we tried to use command files. Suppose a simple command file contains

    ls
    who

and it is executed as follows:

    sh comfile >output

The sequence of events was

1) The main shell creates a new process, which opens *outfile* to receive the standard output and executes the shell recursively.

2) The new shell creates another process to execute *ls*, which correctly writes on file *output* and then terminates.

3) Another process is created to execute the next command. However, the IO pointer for the output is copied from that of the shell, and it is still 0, because the shell has never written on its output, and IO pointers are associated with processes. The effect is that the output of *who* overwrites and destroys the output of the preceding *ls* command.

Solution of this problem required creation of a new system table to contain the IO pointers of open files independently of the process in which they were opened.

IO Redirection

The very convenient notation for IO redirection, using the '>' and '<' characters, was not present from the very beginning of the PDP-7 Unix system, but it did appear quite early. Like much else in Unix, it was inspired by an idea from Multics. Multics has a rather general IO redirection mechanism[3] embodying named IO streams that can be dynamically redirected to various devices, files, and even through special stream-processing modules. Even in the version of Multics we were familiar with a decade ago, there existed a command that switched subsequent output normally destined for the terminal to a file, and another command to reattach output to the terminal. Where under Unix one might say

   ls >xx

to get a listing of the names of one's files in *xx*, on Multics the notation was

   iocall attach user_output file xx
   list
   iocall attach user_output syn user_i/o

Even though this very clumsy sequence was used often during the Multics days, and would have been utterly straightforward to integrate into the Multics shell, the idea did not occur to us or anyone else at the time. I speculate that the reason it did not was the sheer size of the Multics project: the implementors of the IO system were at Bell Labs in Murray Hill, while the shell was done at MIT. We didn't consider making changes to the shell (it was *their* program); correspondingly, the keepers of the shell may not even have known of the usefulness, albeit clumsiness, of *iocall*. (The 1969 Multics manual[4] lists *iocall* as an 'author-maintained,' that is non-standard, command.) Because both the Unix IO system and its shell were under the exclusive control of Thompson, when the right idea finally surfaced, it was a matter of an hour or so to implement it.

The advent of the PDP-11

By the beginning of 1970, PDP-7 Unix was a going concern. Primitive by today's standards, it was still capable of providing a more congenial programming environment than its alternatives. Nevertheless, it was clear that the PDP-7, a machine we didn't even own, was already obsolete, and its successors in the same line offered little of interest. In early 1970 we proposed acquisition of a PDP-11, which had just been introduced by Digital. In some sense, this proposal was merely the latest in the series of attempts that had been made throughout the preceding year. It differed in two important ways. First, the amount of money (about $65,000) was an order of magnitude less than what we had previously asked; second, the charter sought was not merely to write some (unspecified) operating system, but instead to create a system specifically designed for editing and formatting text, what might today be called a 'word-processing system.' The impetus for the proposal came mainly from J. F. Ossanna, who was then and until the end of his life interested in text processing. If our early proposals were too vague, this one was perhaps too specific; at first it too met with disfavor. Before long, however, funds were obtained through the efforts of L. E. McMahon and an order for a PDP-11 was placed in May.

The processor arrived at the end of the summer, but the PDP-11 was so new a product that no disk was available until December. In the meantime, a rudimentary, core-only version of Unix was written using a cross-assembler on the PDP-7. Most of the time, the machine sat in a corner, enumerating all the closed Knight's tours on a 6×8 chess board—a three-month job.

The first PDP-11 system

Once the disk arrived, the system was quickly completed. In internal structure, the first version of Unix for the PDP-11 represented a relatively minor advance over the PDP-7 system; writing it was largely a matter of transliteration. For example, there was no multi-programming; only one user program was present in core at any moment. On the other hand, there were important changes in the interface to the user: the present directory structure, with full path names, was in place, along with the modern form of *exec* and *wait*, and conveniences like character-erase and line-kill processing for terminals. Perhaps the most interesting thing about the enterprise was its small size: there were 24K bytes of core memory (16K for the system, 8K for user programs), and a disk with 1K blocks (512K bytes). Files were limited to 64K bytes.

At the time of the placement of the order for the PDP-11, it had seemed natural, or perhaps expedient, to promise a system dedicated to word processing. During the protracted arrival of the hardware, the increasing usefulness of PDP-7 Unix made it appropriate to justify creating PDP-11 Unix as a development tool, to be used in writing the more special-purpose system. By the spring of 1971, it was generally agreed that no one had the slightest interest in scrapping Unix. Therefore, we transliterated the *roff* text formatter into PDP-11 assembler language, starting from the PDP-7 version that had been transliterated from McIlroy's BCPL version on Multics, which had in turn been inspired by J. Saltzer's *runoff* program on CTSS. In early summer, editor and formatter in hand, we felt prepared to fulfill our charter by offering to supply a text-processing service to the Patent department for preparing patent applications. At the time, they were evaluating a commercial system for this purpose; the main advantages we offered (besides the dubious one of taking part in an in-house experiment) were two in number: first, we supported Teletype's model 37 terminals, which, with an extended type-box, could print most of the math symbols they required; second, we quickly endowed *roff* with the ability to produce line-numbered pages, which the Patent Office required and which the other system could not handle.

During the last half of 1971, we supported three typists from the Patent department, who spent the day busily typing, editing, and formatting patent applications, and meanwhile tried to carry on our own work. Unix has a reputation for supplying interesting services on modest hardware, and this period may mark a high point in the benefit/equipment ratio; on a machine with no memory protection and a single .5 MB disk, every test of a new program required care and boldness, because it could easily crash the system, and every few hours' work by the typists meant pushing out more information onto DECtape, because of the very small disk.

The experiment was trying but successful. Not only did the Patent department adopt Unix, and thus become the first of many groups at the Laboratories to ratify our work, but we achieved sufficient credibility to convince our own management to acquire one of the first PDP 11/45 systems made. We have accumulated much hardware since then, and labored continuously on the software, but because most of the interesting work has already been published, (e.g. on the system itself[1, 5, 6] and the text processing applications[7, 8, 9]) it seems unnecessary to repeat it here.

Pipes

One of the most widely admired contributions of Unix to the culture of operating systems and command languages is the *pipe*, as used in a pipeline of commands. Of course, the fundamental idea was by no means new; the pipeline is merely a specific form of coroutine. Even the implementation was not unprecedented, although we didn't know it at the time; the 'communication files' of the Dartmouth Time-Sharing System[10] did very nearly what Unix pipes do, though they seem not to have been exploited so fully.

Pipes appeared in Unix in 1972, well after the PDP-11 version of the system was in operation, at the suggestion (or perhaps insistence) of M. D. McIlroy, a long-time advocate of the non-hierarchical control flow that characterizes coroutines. Some years before pipes were implemented, he suggested that commands should be thought of as binary operators, whose left and right operand specified the input and output files. Thus a 'copy' utility would be commanded by

inputfile copy outputfile

To make a pipeline, command operators could be stacked up. Thus, to sort *input,* paginate it neatly, and print the result offline, one would write

input sort paginate offprint

In today's system, this would correspond to

sort input | pr | opr

The idea, explained one afternoon on a blackboard, intrigued us but failed to ignite any immediate action. There were several objections to the idea as put: the infix notation seemed too radical (we were too accustomed to typing 'cp x y' to copy *x* to *y*); and we were unable to see how to distinguish command parameters from the input or output files. Also, the one-input one-output model of command execution seemed too confining. What a failure of imagination!

Some time later, thanks to McIlroy's persistence, pipes were finally installed in the operating system (a relatively simple job), and a new notation was introduced. It used the same characters as for I/O redirection. For example, the pipeline above might have been written

sort input >pr>opr>

The idea is that following a '>' may be either a file, to specify redirection of output to that file, or a command into which the output of the preceding command is directed as input. The trailing '>' was needed in the example to specify that the (nonexistent) output of *opr* should be directed to the console; otherwise the command *opr* would not have been executed at all; instead a file *opr* would have been created.

The new facility was enthusiastically received, and the term 'filter' was soon coined. Many commands were changed to make them usable in pipelines. For example, no one had imagined that anyone would want the *sort* or *pr* utility to sort or print its standard input if given no explicit arguments.

Soon some problems with the notation became evident. Most annoying was a silly lexical problem: the string after '>' was delimited by blanks, so, to give a parameter to *pr* in the example, one had to quote:

sort input >"pr −2">opr>

Second, in attempt to give generality, the pipe notation accepted '<' as an input redirection in a way corresponding to '>'; this meant that the notation was not unique. One could also write, for example,

opr <pr<"sort input"<

or even

pr <"sort input"< >opr>

The pipe notation using '<' and '>' survived only a couple of months; it was replaced by the present one that uses a unique operator to separate components of a pipeline. Although the old notation had a certain charm and inner consistency, the new one is certainly superior. Of course, it too has limitations. It is unabashedly linear, though there are situations in which multiple redirected inputs and outputs are called for. For example, what is the best way to compare the outputs of two programs? What is the appropriate notation for invoking a program with two parallel output streams?

I mentioned above in the section on IO redirection that Multics provided a mechanism by which IO streams could be directed through processing modules on the way to (or from) the device or file serving as source or sink. Thus it might seem that stream-splicing in Multics was the direct precursor of Unix pipes, as Multics IO redirection certainly was for its Unix version. In fact I do not think this is true, or is true only in a weak sense. Not only were coroutines well-known already, but their embodiment as Multics spliceable IO modules required that the modules be specially coded in such a way that they could be used for no other purpose. The genius of the Unix pipeline is precisely that it is constructed from the very same commands used constantly in simplex fashion. The mental leap needed to see this possibility and to invent the notation is large indeed.

High-level languages

Every program for the original PDP-7 Unix system was written in assembly language, and bare assembly language it was—for example, there were no macros. Moreover, there was no loader or link-editor, so every program had to be complete in itself. The first interesting language to appear was a version of McClure's TMG[11] that was implemented by McIlroy. Soon after TMG became available, Thompson decided that we could not pretend to offer a real computing service without Fortran, so he sat down to write a Fortran in TMG. As I recall, the intent to handle Fortran lasted about a week. What he produced instead was a definition of and a compiler for the new language B.[12] B was much influenced by the BCPL language;[13] other influences were Thompson's taste for spartan syntax, and the very small space into which the compiler had to fit. The compiler produced simple interpretive code; although it and the programs it produced were rather slow, it made life much more pleasant. Once interfaces to the regular system calls were made available, we began once again to enjoy the benefits of using a reasonable language to write what are usually called 'systems programs:' compilers, assemblers, and the like. (Although some might consider the PL/I we used under Multics unreasonable, it was much better than assembly language.) Among other programs, the PDP-7 B cross-compiler for the PDP-11 was written in B, and in the course of time, the B compiler for the PDP-7 itself was transliterated from TMG into B.

When the PDP-11 arrived, B was moved to it almost immediately. In fact, a version of the multi-precision 'desk calculator' program *dc* was one of the earliest programs to run on the PDP-11, well before the disk arrived. However, B did not take over instantly. Only passing thought was given to rewriting the operating system in B rather than assembler, and the same was true of most of the utilities. Even the assembler was rewritten in assembler. This approach was taken mainly because of the slowness of the interpretive code. Of smaller but still real importance was the mismatch of the word-oriented B language with the byte-addressed PDP-11.

Thus, in 1971, work began on what was to become the C language.[14] The story of the language developments from BCPL through B to C is told elsewhere,[15] and need not be repeated here. Perhaps the most important watershed occurred during 1973, when the operating system kernel was rewritten in C. It was at this point that the system assumed its modern form; the most far-reaching change was the introduction of multi-programming. There were few externally-visible changes, but the internal structure of the system became much more rational and general. The success of this effort convinced us that C was useful as a nearly universal tool for systems programming, instead of just a toy for simple applications.

Today, the only important Unix program still written in assembler is the assembler itself; virtually all the utility programs are in C, and so are most of the applications programs, although there are sites with many in Fortran, Pascal, and Algol 68 as well. It seems certain that much of the success of Unix follows from the readability, modifiability, and portability of its software that in turn follows from its expression in high-level languages.

Conclusion

One of the comforting things about old memories is their tendency to take on a rosy glow. The programming environment provided by the early versions of Unix seems, when described here, to be extremely harsh and primitive. I am sure that if forced back to the PDP-7 I would find it intolerably limiting and lacking in conveniences. Nevertheless, it did not seem so at the time; the memory fixes on what was good and what lasted, and on the joy of helping to create the improvements that made life better. In ten years, I hope we can look back with the same mixed impression of progress combined with continuity.

Acknowledgements

I am grateful to S. P. Morgan, K. Thompson, and M. D. McIlroy for providing early documents and digging up recollections.

Because I am most interested in describing the evolution of ideas, this paper attributes ideas and work to individuals only where it seems most important. The reader will not, on the average, go far wrong if he reads each occurrence of 'we' with unclear antecedent as 'Thompson, with some assistance from me.'

References

1. D. M. Ritchie and K. Thompson, "The UNIX Time-Sharing System," *Comm. Assoc. Comp. Mach.* **17**(7), pp. 365-375 (July 1974).

2. L. P. Deutsch and B. W. Lampson, "SDS 930 time-sharing system preliminary reference manual," Doc. 30.10.10, Project GENIE, Univ. Cal. at Berkeley (April 1965).

3. R. J. Feiertag and E. I. Organick, "The Multics input-output system," *Proc. Third Symposium on Operating Systems Principles*, pp. 35-41 (October 18-20, 1971).

4. *The Multiplexed Information and Computing Service: Programmers' Manual,* Massachusetts Institute of Technology Project MAC, Cambridge, Massachusetts (1969).

5. K. Thompson, "UNIX Time-Sharing System: UNIX Implementation," *Bell Sys. Tech. J.* **57**(6), pp. 1931-1946 (1978).

6. S. C. Johnson and D. M. Ritchie, "UNIX Time-Sharing System: Portability of C Programs and the UNIX System," *Bell Sys. Tech. J.* **57**(6), pp. 2021-2048 (1978).

7. B. W. Kernighan, M. E. Lesk, and J. F. Ossanna, "UNIX Time-Sharing System: Document Preparation," *Bell Sys. Tech. J.* **57**(6), pp. 2115-2135 (1978).

8. B. W. Kernighan and L. L. Cherry, "A System for Typesetting Mathematics," *Comm. Assoc. Comp. Mach.* **18**, pp. 151-157 (March 1975).

9. M. E. Lesk and B. W. Kernighan, "Computer Typesetting of Technical Journals on UNIX," *Proc. AFIPS NCC* **46**, pp. 879-888 (1977).

10. *Systems Programmers Manual for the Dartmouth Time Sharing System for the GE 635 Computer,* Dartmouth College, Hanover, New Hampshire (1971).

11. R. M. McClure, "TMG—a Syntax Directed Compiler," *Proc. 20th ACM National Conf.*, pp. 262-274 (1965).

12. S. C. Johnson and B. W. Kernighan, "The Programming Language B," Comp. Sci. Tech. Rep. No. 8, Bell Laboratories, Murray Hill, New Jersey (January 1973).

13. M. Richards, "BCPL: A Tool for Compiler Writing and Systems Programming," *Proc. AFIPS SJCC* **34**, pp. 557-566 (1969).

14. B. W. Kernighan and D. M. Ritchie, *The C Programming Language,* Prentice-Hall, Englewood Cliffs, New Jersey (1978).

15. D. M. Ritchie, S. C. Johnson, M. E. Lesk, and B. W. Kernighan, "UNIX Time-Sharing System: The C Programming Language," *Bell Sys. Tech. J.* **57**(6), pp. 1991-2019 (1978).

PROCEEDINGS OF THE SYMPOSIUM ON
LANGUAGE DESIGN AND PROGRAMMING METHODOLOGY
SYDNEY, 10-11 SEPTEMBER, 1979

PASCAL VERSUS C : A SUBJECTIVE COMPARISON

Prabhaker Mateti

Department of Computer Science
University of Melbourne

ABSTRACT

The two programming languages Pascal and C are subjectively
compared. While the two languages have comparable data and
control structures, the program structure of C appears
superior. However, C has many potentially dangerous
features, and requires great caution from its programmers.
Other psychological effects that the various structures in
these languages have on the process of programming are also
conjectured.

"At first sight, the idea of any rules or
principles being superimposed on the creative
mind seems more likely to hinder than to
help, but this is really quite untrue in
practice. Disciplined thinking focusses
inspiration rather than blinkers it."

– G. L. Glegg,
The Design of Design.

---

1 Introduction

Pascal has become one of the most widely accepted languages
for the teaching of programming. It is also one of the most
thoroughly studied languages. Several large programs have been
written in Pascal and its derivatives. The programming language
C has gained much prominence in recent years. The successful
Unix operating system and most of its associated software are
written in C.

This paper confines itself to a subjective comparison of the
two languages, and conjectures about the effect various
structures of the languages have on the way one programs. While
we do occasionally refer to the various extensions and compilers
of the languages, the comparison is between the languages as they
are now, and in the context of general programming. The official

documents for this purpose are Jensen and Wirth(1974) and the C-book [Kernighan and Ritchie 1978]. The reader who expects to find verdicts as to which language should be used in what kind of project will be disappointed and will instead find many statements supported only by personal experience and bias; when I felt it necessary to emphasise this, the first person singular is used.

1.1 'Methodology' of Comparison

We do not believe that objective (all-aspect) comparisons of programming languages are possible. Even a basis for such comparison is, often, not clear. (However, see Shaw et al. 1978 .) We can attempt to use such factors as power, efficiency, elegance, clarity, safety, notation, and verbosity of the languages. But elevating these factors from the intuitive to the scientific level by tight definitions renders them useless for the purpose of comparison. For example, all real-life programming languages are as powerful as Turing machines, and hence equally powerful. It is difficult to discuss efficiency of a language without dragging in a compiler and a machine. Furthermore, many of the other notions listed above are based heavily on human psychology, as are the useful insights gained under the banners of structured programming, programming methodology and software engineering. Thus, universal agreement as to the level these notions are supported in a given language will be difficult to reach.

One of the most important factors in choosing a language for a project should be the estimated debugging and maintenance costs. A language can, by being very cautious and redundant, eliminate a lot of trivial errors that occur during the development phase. But because it is cautious, it may increase marginally the cost of producing the first (possibly bugged) version. It is well-known that a programming language affects programming only if the problem is non-trivial and is of substantial size. Also, it seems a language has little effect on the logical errors that remain in a software system after the so-called debugging stage. This is clearly highly correlated with the competence of the programmer(s) involved.

This suggests a method of comparison based on estimating the total cost to design, develop, test, debug and prove a given program in the languages being compared. However, controlling the experiment, and adjusting the results to take care of the well-known effect that the second time it is easier to write (a better version of) the same program (in the same or different language) than to write it from scratch, may prove to be infeasible. Also, very large-scale experiments with a large

piece of software are likely to be so expensive and the results
so inconclusive that it is unlikely to be worthwhile. In any
case, I do not have the resources to undertake such an
experiment.

This comparison is, therefore, necessarily subjective. And
this, as can be expected, depends to a large extent on one's own
biases, and faith in the recent programming methodology. When
the growing evidence supporting this methodology is sufficiently
convincing, we can replace the word "faith" by "xxxx".

In the following, we shall

1. compare how "convenient" the languages are to code our
   favourite solution to a programming problem,

2. play the devil's advocate, and try to list all possible things
   that can go wrong in a program expressed in a language.

Some of us, including myself, have reservations about the
validity of the second technique for comparison, the most
persuasive argument being that even though some of the features
are potentially dangerous, people rarely use them in those
contexts. There is certainly some truth in this, but until we
have experimentally collected data convincingly demonstrating
this, it is wiser to disbelieve it. Take note of the observed
fact of increased difficulty in formally proving the properties
of programs that use these potentially hazardous features in a
safe way. This is one of the reasons behind the increased
redundancy (and restrictions) of the newer languages like
Alphard [Wulf et al. 1976], CLU [Liskov et al. 1977], Euclid
[Lampson et al. 1977], Mesa [Geschke et al. 1977], and others.

1.2 Hypotheses

It should be clear that neither language is perfect, nor
should there be any doubt about the truth of the following:

Axiom [Flon 1975]

There does not now, nor will there ever, exist a programming
language in which it is the least bit hard to write bad
programs.

Since this is a subjective comparison, it is necessary to

identify as many of the underlying assumptions as possible.

1. We believe: (i) That programs should be designed (i.e. conceiving the abstract data structures, and the operations on them, detailing, but not overspecifying, the algorithms for these operations, and grouping all these) in a suitably abstract language, which may not be a formal language. (ii) That the coding (i.e. the translation into a formal programming language) of the abstract program is strongly influenced by the programming language. This paper offers several conjectures about these influences; the word "programming" is used instead of coding, in several places, to emphasise the unfortunate fact that many of us design our programs straight into the programming language.

2. We make a lot of trivial mistakes. Examples : uninitialised or wrongly initialised variables, overlooked typing errors, array indices out of range, variable parameter instead of value, or vice versa, ...

3. The effort spent in physically writing and typing during the development of a large program is negligible compared to the rest of effort.

4. Simple things that could be done mechanically, without spending much thought, should be done by a program.

5. Permissive type checking should be outlawed.

6. It is dangerous to use our knowledge of the internal representation, as chosen by a compiler, of a data type [Geschke et al. 1977].

7. The overall efficiency of a large program depends on small portions of the program [Knuth 1971, Wichmann 1978].

1.3 General Comments

One may wonder: Why compare two languages whose projected images are so different? For example, Sammet's Roster of Programming Languages (1978) lists the application area of Pascal as multi-purpose and that of C as systems implementation.

That Pascal was designed only with two objectives -- viz., a language for teaching programming as a systematic discipline and as a language which can be implemented efficiently -- is quoted often, ignoring four other aims that Wirth(1971) lists. The hidden implication of this attitude is that since Pascal is suitable for beginners learning to program, it is ipso facto unsuited for adult programming. In fact, an increasing number of complex programs of wide variety from an operating system for the Cray-1 to interpreters on the Intel 8080 are (being) written in Pascal and its dialects.

C is being promoted as a convenient general purpose language. In reviewing the C-book, Plauger(1979) pays his tributes to its authors and claims "C is one of the important contributions of the decade to the practice of computer programming..."

Neither language includes any constructs for concurrent programming. The flexibility of C makes it possible to access nearly all aspects of the machine architecture; low-level programs such as device drivers can thus be written in C. One contention of this paper is that it achieves this flexibility at a great sacrifice of security. Such compromises can be added to Pascal by any implementor, but most have left it relatively pure and unchanged from that described in the revised report [Jensen and Wirth 1974]. Extensions of Pascal to include concurrent programming constructs have resulted in new languages in their own right (Concurrent Pascal [Brinch Hansen 1977], Modula [Wirth 1977a], and Pascal Plus [Welsh and Bustard 1979]).

Thus I believe the domain of application of both languages to be nearly the same.

A great deal of criticism of Pascal has appeared in the open literature ([Conradi 1976], [Habermann 1973], [Lecarme and Desjardins 1975], [Tanenbaum 1978], [Welsh et. al. 1977], [Wirth 1974, 1975, 1977b] and in nearly every news letter of the Pascal User Group [Pascal News]). The little published criticism of C that exists is by people associated with its design and implementation and hence is benevolent. Thus, this paper devotes a greater portion to criticism of C, and repeats some of the criticism of Pascal only when necessary in the comparison.

2. Data Types

One of the greatest assets of both languages is the ability to define new data types. The languages provide a certain number of standard (i.e. predefined) simple types from which other types are constructed. The well-known arrays are composite types whose components are homogeneous. Records of Pascal, structs of C are composite types that (usually) contain heterogeneous components. Other composite types of Pascal that contain homogeneous elements are sets and files. Types are not allowed to be defined recursively, except when they involve a pointer

type. Note that both languages consider a type to be a set of
values [Morris 1973].

2.1 Simple Types

Integers, reals, characters, and Booleans are standard types
in Pascal. All other types are user defined.

<u>type</u>
```
        zeroto15    = 0..15;
        minus7to7   = -7..7;
        aritherror  = (overflow, underflow, divideby0);
        kindofchar  = (letters, digits, specials);
```

Whereas C has integers, reals, and characters, it does not have
Booleans (which is sad), nor does it have a mechanism for
defining enumerated types (like the above kindofchar),   or
subranges (zeroto15). Instead, in some implementations of C, by
declaring a variable as short, or char, one obtains smaller sized
variables; note the following statement from the C Reference
Manual (p182):

  Other quantities may be stored into character variables, but
  the implementation is machine dependent.

In contrast, the Pascal declarations do not guarantee that
smaller units of storage will be used; they simply inform the
compiler that it may choose to do so.   More importantly, they
provide useful documentation; compiling with range checks on, one
can have any violations of these caught at run time. In C, this
is not possible. The conscious programmer may document the range
of some integer variable in a comment, but the compiler cannot
help enforce it.

The useful abstraction that Pascal offers in its enumerated
types is of considerable value.   That this is no more than a
mapping of these identifiers into 0..? does not decrease its
value. What we, the humans, have to do in other languages, is
now done by the compiler, and much more reliably.   (It is now
rumoured that C will have enumerated types in a future version.)

2.2 Arrays

In Pascal, the index type of arrays is any subrange of
scalars (which include enumerated types), whereas in C, arrays
always have indices ranging from 0 to the specified positive
integer. For example, int a[10] declares an array of ten
integers with indices from 0 to 9. Sometimes this leads to

rather unnatural constructs. Consider the following example.

```
line[-1] = '*';        /* any char other than blank,\t, \n */
while  (( n = getline(line, MAXLINE)) > 0) {
    while (line[n] == ' ' || line[n] =='\t' || line[n] =='\n')
        n--;
    line[n+1] = '\0';
    printf("%s\n", &line[0]);
}
```

(In C, = denotes the assignment, == the equality test, and || the
McCarthy's OR.)

I find this program clearer, more elegant, and more efficient
than the one on p61 of the C-book. However, since arrays cannot
have negative indices (as in line[-1]), we are forced to write
differently and use a <u>break</u> to exit from the inner loop.

    Many people do not appreciate the use of sentinels.   Often
the argument against them is that you don't have the freedom to
so design your data structure. I have not found this to be true
in real life situations. This does happen in cooked up classroom
situations. It rarely, if ever, is the case that you cannot
modify the data structure slightly. The reason for this appears
to be a misunderstanding of a fundamental principle of algorithm
design :

    Strive to reduce the number of distinct cases whose
    differences are minor.

The use of sentinels is one such technique. In the above example
it guarantees that a non-blank, non-tab, non-new-line character
does appear in the array.

    The usefulness of negative indices, in these and other
situations, should be obvious even to the Pascal-illiterates.

    One aspect of Pascal arrays that has come under strong
attack is the fact that the array bounds must always be
determinable at compile time. This rules out writing generic
library routines.   There are several suggested extensions to
overcome this problem; the signs are that one of these will be
incorporated into the language soon.

2.3   Records / Structures

The records and variant records of Pascal are similar to structs and unions of C. However, one important difference must not be forgotten. Pascal does not guarantee any relationships among the addresses of fields. C explicitly guarantees that "within a structure, the objects declared have addresses which increase as their declarations are read left-to-right" (see p196, C-book); otherwise some pointer arithmetic would not be meaningful. Some of the efficiency of pointer arithmetic is provided, in Pascal, by a much safer with statement.

2.4   Pointers

Pointers in Pascal can only point to objects in the heap (i.e., those created dynamically by the standard procedure new), whereas C pointers can point to static objects as well. It is well-known that the latter scheme has the problem of "dangling pointers", and several authors (notably Hoare(1975)) have argued for the abolition of pointers to static objects. The only argument supporting their existence appears to be that they provide an efficient access. It is not known how much this gain in efficiency is in real programs.

On the other hand, unless great caution is exercised, program clarity and correctness are often sacrificed in the process. "A very essential feature of high-level languages is that they permit a conceptual dissection of the store into disjoint parts by declaring distinct variables. The programmer may then rely on the assertion that every assignment affects only that variable which explicitly appears to the left of the assignment operator in his program. He may then focus his attention to the change of that single variable, whereas in machine coding he always has, in principle, to consider the entire store as the state of the computation. The necessary prerequisite for being able to think in terms of safely independent variables is of course the condition that no part of the store may assume more than a single name" [Wirth 1974].

Pascal pointers satisfy the following :

1.   Every pointer variable is allowed to point to objects of only one type, or is nil. That is, a pointer is bound to that type; the compiler can still do full type checking.

2.   Pointers may only refer to variables that have no explicit

name declared in the program, that is, they point
exclusively to anonymous variables allocated by the new
procedure when needed during execution.

C pointers, on the other hand, can point to virtually any
object -- local, global, dynamically acquired variables, even
functions -- and one can do arithmetic on these pointers. The
pointers are loosely bound to the type of object they are
expected to point; in the pointer arithmetic, each 1 stands for
the size of this type. Most C compilers do not check to see that
the pointers do indeed point to the right things. Furthermore,
the C language definition is such that genuine type confusion
occurs. The C-book claims that "its integration of pointers,
arrays and address arithmetic is one of the major strengths of
the language"; I tend to agree, as their current unsafe setting
can be made very secure [Mateti 1979a].

2.5 Type Checking

It is true that one of the basic aims behind the development
of strongly typed languages such as Pascal, Euclid, Mesa,
Alphard, CLU, etc. is to make it difficult to write bad programs.
In realising this goal, all programs become slightly more
difficult to write. But this increase in difficulty is of a
mechanical kind, as we now expect the programmer to provide a lot
of redundant information.

Type checking is strongly enforced in Pascal, and this is as
it should be. Errors caused by incompatible types are often
difficult to pinpoint [Geschke et al. 1977]. Strong type
checking does increase the time to produce the first version of a
syntactically correct program, but this is worthwhile. It is
true that Pascal has not satisfactorily defined when two types
(with different names) are equivalent [Welsh et al. 1977] but
the problems are easily avoided by appropriate declarations. Any
required type conversion occurs only through predefined functions
for the purpose, or through user-defined variant records. (The
latter are unsafe; see Section 8.)

In sharp contrast, all kinds of type conversions are either
blessed in C, or ignored by its compilers. For example, our
Interdata 8/32 C compiler detected only one error in the program
of Figure 1. In fact, it is rare that you see a C program that
does not convert the types of its variables, the most common
conversion being that between characters and integers. More
recently, however, C designers have provided a special program
called lint that does type checking. A few points should be

```
main()
{
                /* See Section 2.5                         */
    int         /* integer                                 */
        i,
        xx,
        a[10],
        f(),        /* f is a function returning integer   */
        (*pf)();    /* pointer to a function returning int */

    printf(" exponent part of 123.456e7 is %d \n",
           expo(123.456e7));

    i = a;          /* i now points to a[0]                */
    a[1] = f;       /* a[1] points to the function         */
    2[a] = f();     /* 2[a] is equivalent to a[2]          */
    a[3] = f(0);    /* f called with 1 argument            */

    pf = &xx;       /* pf now points to xx                 */
    i = (*pf)();    /* now call the "function" pointed to by pf
                                                           */

    a = i;          /* This is the only illegal statement  */
                    /* in this program caught by C compiler */
                    /* because a is not a left-value.      */

}

f(a,b)              /* f in fact has 2 formal parameters    */
char    a, b;
{
    if (a)  return (b);
}

expo(r)                     /* see Section 9.2              */
float   r;
{
        static struct s {
                char c[4];      /* uses 4 bytes             */
                float f;
        } c4f;
        static char *p = &(c4f.c[3])+1;
                /* points to first byte of f                */

        c4f.f = r;
        return(*p);
}
```

Figure 1

remembered in this context:

1. Type compatibility is not described in the C Reference Manual. Presumably this is similar to that of Pascal, and Algol 68. It is not clear exactly what it is that lint is checking.

2. The need for type checking is much greater during program development than afterwards. In fact, a good argument can be made that the primary goal of a compiler is this kind of error checking and code generation its secondary goal; the function of type checking should be an integral part of a compiler. To separate it from the compiler into a special program whose use is optional is a mistake, unless it is a temporary step.

3. Type checking is not something that you can add on as an afterthought. It must be an integral part of the design of the language.

It is fair to say that type conversion is difficult in Pascal but frequent need for this is a sign of bad program design. The occasional real need is then performed by explicit conversions.

2.6 Control of Storage Allocation

It is possible to specify in Pascal that certain variables be packed thereby saving storage. The semantics of such variables is the same as if they were regular variables. There are standard procedures to unpack. It should be noted that specifying packing simply gives permission to the compiler to pack; however, the compiler may decide otherwise.

C does not have a corresponding facility. But C structures can have "fields" consisting of a specified number of bits. These fields are packed into machine words automatically. It is also possible to suggest that a variable be allocated a register.

3. Statements and Expressions

C is an expression language, a la Algol 68, in a limited way; only assignments, function calls, special conditional expressions have values. Thus , for example, a function that does return a value can be called like an ordinary procedure in C, which would be illegal in Pascal, as Pascal is strictly a statement language. Below, we take a more detailed look at these aspects.

3.1 Boolean Expressions

C does not have genuine Boolean expressions. Where one
normally expects to find these (e.g., in if and while
statements), an ordinary expression is used instead, and a non-
zero value is considered "true", a zero being "false". Relations
yield 1 if true, 0 if false. The operators & and ¦ are bitwise
AND and OR operators, && and ¦¦ are similar to McCarthy's
"logical" AND and OR operators : x && y is equivalent to the
conditional expression if x ≠ 0 then y ≠ 0 else 0 fi and x
¦¦ y is equivalent to if x = 0 then y ≠ 0 else 1 fi. For
example,

4 & 6	is	4	4 && 6	is	1	
4 & 8	is	0	4 && 8	is	1	
4 ¦ 6	is	6	4 ¦¦ x	is	1	
4 ¦ 8	is	12	0 ¦¦ x	is	(x ≠ 0)	
			0 && x	is	0	

where x is any expression, including the undefined one. The
operators &, ¦ are commutative, but &&, ¦¦ are not. The left-
to-right evaluation of the "logical" operators && and ¦¦ of C
does save, occasionally, a few micro-seconds. The traditional AND
and OR operators have a nice property that they are commutative,
in conformity with their use in mathematics. As a consequence,
any reasoning we do using them is more readily understandable.
One specific outcome of the use of the unorthodox operators is
that the many cases where both the operands are indeed evaluated
have to be discovered by involved inferences. A better
solution is to have logical operators of the traditional kind,
reserving the McCarthy's operators for use when really needed.
To my mind, even when these McCarthy's operators are really
required , to spell them out as in

        if B1 then
              if B2 then
                 .....

is much more readily understandable. I suspect this to be the
main reason behind the warning " Tests which require a mixture
of &&, ¦¦, !, or parentheses should generally be avoided." of the
C-book(p61).

3.2 Assignments

The symbol denoting the assignment operator is = in C; it is rumored that this was a conscious choice as it means one less character to type. Pascal uses the conventional left arrow, written as :=. C allows assignments to simple (i.e., non-struct, non-array) variables only, at the moment; structure-to-structure and array-to-array assignments are among its promised extensions. The assignment statement has the same value as that assigned to the left hand side variable; thus, we can write conveniently,

$$i = j = 0;$$

Pascal allows assignments to whole arrays as well as records. However, the assignment is not an expression, and the above has to be expanded as:

$$i := 0;$$
$$j := 0;$$

3.3 Operator Precedence

C has over thirty "operators" (including (), [], ., the dereferencing operator *), and fifteen precedence levels, compared to Pascal's six arithmetic operators, four relational operators and four precedence levels. Because of the many levels, and also because some of them are inappropriately assigned, one learns to survive either by constantly referring to the C manual and eventually getting them by rote, or by over-parenthesising; for example,

```
x & 07 == 0      is equivalent to   x & (07 == 0)
*++argv[0]       is equivalent to   *++(argv[0])
```

The basic problem is that the operators like &, or && take any integers as operands, and a missing pair of parentheses will result in a meaningful but unexpected expression.

It is neccessary to parenthesise in Pascal also, but here the reason is different : there are too few levels, as arithmetic operators and boolean operators got merged in their priority. For example,

$$flag \underline{and} \quad a < b$$

would result in type incompatibility, which should be written as

or as,

$$\text{flag } \underline{\text{and }} (a < b)$$
$$(a < b) \underline{\text{ and }} \text{flag}$$

using commutativity of Pascal <u>and</u>.

3.4 The Semicolon

Pascal uses the semicolon as a statement separator, whereas C uses it as a statement terminator. It is well-known that statement separators are the cause of many syntax errors in beginner's programs [Nutt 1978]. But it rarely is a problem for the experienced; most of us have learned to use it as a terminator (with a null statement following).

4. Control Structures

Control structure is merely one simple issue, compared to questions of abstract data structure.

- D. E. Knuth (1974)

For the last ten years or so, the literature concentrated on control structures, and we have learned enough to cope with their abstraction. Some significant rules of thumb have emerged; e.g. use procedures extensively, keep them short, avoid <u>gotos</u>, never jump out of a procedure. As a result, control structures play a rather local role; they are important, but their effect can be localised to these short procedures. Data structure abstraction is not well-understood, in sharp contrast to their design and choice. Many of the remaining errors in large software systems, after an initial period of development, can be attributed to "interface problems" which can be roughly described as inconsistent assumptions about data structures in different places. With this perspective, we move on to the control structures of the two languages.

4.1 Looping

In C, loops are constructed using <u>while</u>, <u>do-while</u>, and <u>for</u>. To exit prematurely from a loop, a <u>break</u> is used; to terminate the current iteration but continue from the next, <u>continue</u> is used. Similar loop structures in Pascal are, respectively, while, repeat-until, and for; premature termination can be accomplished only by gotos. But there is a world of difference between the for statements of the two languages.

The C for statement duplicates what can be done by other structures with equal clarity;

        for (expr1; expr2; expr3) statement

is an abbreviation of

        expr1;
        while (expr2) {
            statement
            expr3;
        }

Note that the three general expressions can be arbitrarily complex. A missing expr2 is equivalent to specifying the constant 1 as expr2.

The Pascal for statement is an abstraction of an often occurring structure ;

        for i := first to last do statement

loops exactly last - first + 1 times, if first <= last, or not at all. The control variable i starts with a value of first, takes successive values up to last. The values last, first, and variable i are all of a scalar type. A downward for is constructed by using downto instead of to. There have been suggestions in the literature [Hoare 1972] that the variable i should be a read-only variable local to the body of the loop; Pascal compromisingly insists [Addyman et al. 1979] that the variable be local to the procedure/function/program block in which the for loop occurs.

4.2 Selection

The if statements of the two languages are very similar except that C uses general expressions, as in while-statements, instead of Boolean expressions, and the word then is omitted.

```
case expression of
      cl1  : S1;
      cl2  : S2;
      ...
      cli  : Si;
      ...
end;
T
```

The above case statement of Pascal transfers control to one
(say Si) of several statements whose constant case label cli
equals the value of the scalar expression. When the execution of
Si terminates, control is transferred to T. If the expression
value does not match any case label, the effect of case statement
is undefined in standard Pascal. A default label cannot be given
either; several implementors have felt the need for this, and it
is now allowed on most implementations. However, it should be
emphasised that in most well-written programs the expression
value belongs to an enumerated type which is exhaustively listed
by the case labels cli.

The switch statement of C is primarily used to create a
similar effect. However, control passes from Si to the next
Si+1, unless this flow is explicitly broken by a break :

```
switch (exp)  {
      case  L1  : S1
      case  L2  : S2
                       break;

            ...

      case  Li  : Si
      case  Li+1 : Si+1


            ...

      default   : Sn
}
T
```

The "usual arithmetic conversion" is performed on exp, if
necessary, to yield an integer value. The labels Li must be
manifest integer expressions. If exp matches no Li, it matches
the default and if the optional default label is absent, then
none of the statements in the switch is executed. Whereas a
default label is wanted in Pascal, it is needed in C as it cannot
be hoped that the case labels Li will exhaust the values that exp
can take.

Note also that C needs a break because the only way to group
cases is by falling through cases. For example, to combine more

than one case, say 2 and 4, you write

```
case 2   :
case 4   :
         ----
         ----
         break;
```

and in such situations Pascal does not need a break, as labels can be grouped. The C-book wisely cautions (p56), "...falling through cases is a mixed blessing....Falling through from one case to another is not robust, being prone to disintegration when the program is modified. With the exception of multiple labels for a single computation, fall-throughs should be used sparingly."

4.3 The Power of Control Structures

Loops with break/continue belong to the class DREC1, in the genealogy of control structures [Ledgard and Marcotty 1975]. Theorems by Kosaraju(1974) show that a DREC1 structure cannot be simulated by D-structures (D for Dijkstra), which are formed by any number of ifs, whiles, and concatenation using original variables, actions and predicates. In fact, some DRECi structures (which contain BLISS-like [Wulf et al. 1971] multi-level exit(i), exiting i enveloping loops, and cycle(i), continuing the next iteration of the i-th enveloping loop) are more powerful than any DRECi-1 structures.

With this background we make the following observations :

1. This does not mean that a given problem, for which we have a solution with break/continues, cannot be solved using D-structures only but with a different choice of data structures. In fact, most breaks used in the programs of C-book can be so avoided; some of them occur only because the array index cannot be negative.

2. Why stop at break and continue, which are equivalent to exit(1) and cycle(1) ? Certainly, for i > 1, exit(i) and cycle(i) add flexibilty and power. The primary function of control structures is to provide clarity by operational abstraction. Loops containing exits, and cycles are more difficult to understand. It is surprising how rarely one really needs exit(1) or higher exits. The need for control structures at higher levels than D-structures is still unproven.

3. But, if one feels a break is needed in a certain situation,

why not use a goto? Knuth(1974) argues that such use of goto
is not "unstructured", while a lot of others (like Ledgard and
Marcotty(1975)) would rather introduce a boolean variable, or
expand the range of values of an already existing variable, to
eliminate the break.

Both languages have the goto statement. In Pascal, the
labels need to be declared, and are always unsigned integers. C
allows arbitrary identifiers as labels, which are not declared.

5. Program Structure

Pascal and C both have a simpler program structure than
Algol 60. Pascal achieves simplicity by identifying blocks with
routines (procedures/ functions) and C does it by not allowing
nested routines. In spite of this, C program structure,
particularly the scope of variables, is more comprehensive than
that of Pascal. Successors to Pascal, such as Concurrent Pascal,
Modula, Pascal-Plus, have successfully blended into Pascal the
notion of Simula-classes, which structures programs far more
effectively.

5.1 Procedures and Functions

In Pascal, these are two distinct entities. A function
returns a scalar, real, or pointer value, but has no side-effects
when well-written. When a procedure is called, we expect the
environment to change; when a function appears in an expression,
we can evaluate it without at the same time worrying about side-
effects. This is how it should be in a statement-oriented
language.

C functions, on the other hand, may or may not return
values. In the latter case, they are equivalent to Pascal
procedures. But, C goes one step further, and permits a variable
number of parameters and the use of value-returning functions as
procedures. Certainly, it is more natural for some routines to
have a variable-number of parameters (e.g., Pascal's read and
write). But this should be the exception allowed only upon
explicit request.

Another surprise in C is all the parameters are passed by
value only. To achieve Pascal's var parameter, the address is
passed as a value parameter, and the function changes the content
of the cell pointed. Thus C depends too heavily on pointers,
providing a classic case of type confusion as in

```
char  *s ;
```

(Is s a pointer to a character, or a pointer to an array of
characters?)

5.2 Block Structure and Scope

C does not allow nested functions but the body of any
compound statement is a block and can contain declarations (of
struct, typedef, and variables). This feature, however, is
rarely used in practice, except in the outermost block of a
routine, or when register variables are needed. Such block
structure can be simulated in Pascal by calls to nested routines,
but this incurs the overhead of a call.

The names of functions in C are always global (unless
declared static) and available to routines in other source files.
Variables and new type names can be declared in between routines,
or before the very first one, and are visible to routines below
them in that file. To access variables declared in other files,
explicit extern declarations are required. Variables can be
declared, within a routine, to belong to the static storage class
(similar to own variables in other languages); such variables
retain their values between successive calls of that function and
are visible only within that routine. These features and the
ease of separate compilation make it possible to structure C
programs with as much clarity (but not security) as can be
achieved with the module concept. In contrast, such structuring
cannot be done elegantly in Pascal.

6. Language Support

It is clear to anyone involved in the production of
software that often the support given to a language plays a more
major role than the language itself. Supporting tools include
source language debugging packages, execution profilers, cross-
reference generators, macro (pre)processors, pretty printers, and
a host of other library programs. To be sure, none of these is
part of a language, but most users cannot distinguish them as
being separate entities because of their careful integration into
host languages.

C is a good example of this process. It uses a standard
preprocessor for handling constant definitions and file
inclusions. Many of these tools for C are written in C, and
hence available just as widely as the language itself. In

contrast, Pascal tools and separate compilation facilities [Kieburtz et al. 1978] are only now being developed by interested users. Some of these are written in non-standard Pascal and often integrate poorly with operating systems.

6.1 Preprocessors

Pascal programmers often get annoyed by the lack of some simple conveniences. Examples:

1. Expressions involving symbols defined at compile time cannot be used on the right hand side of a constant definition :

$$const \quad n = 10; \quad n1 = 11;$$

If we change n to, say, 20, then we should also change manually n1 to 21. The following is simpler and more informative :

$$const \quad n = 10; \quad n1 = n + 1;$$

but this is illegal.

2. Body substitutions for calls to (very short) functions and procedures cannot be specified. The grouping of short sequences of tests and other operations into functions and procedures is thereby discouraged.

Both situations are quite common in programming, and to argue that they can be done easily by hand, and that execution profiles often prove that body substitutions do not yield space/time gains is simply unrealistic.

C handles the above situations, as well as inclusion of text from other files, excellently through its standard macro preprocessor. Such a processor is easy to write for Pascal too, but as there is no standard syntax for it, too many different preprocessors are bound to mushroom [Comer 1979, Mateti 1979b].

7. <u>Efficiency</u>

"Don't diddle code to make it faster -- find a better algorithm."

- Kernighan and Plauger (1974)

We can distinguish between two kinds of efficiency improvements: of the algorithm, of the coding. The efficiency that complexity theorists discuss often deals with the asymptotic behaviour of the execution time of algorithms. When input data are of sufficiently large size n, an O(n) algorithm would in fact be faster than an O(n**2) algorithm. This may, however, not always be the case on small amount of input data. If you have only a five element array to sort, bubble sort may run faster on your machine than O(n log n) quick sort.

Also, the following appears to be the case, unless the algorithm in question is a well-studied one :

The lower the level of the language, the more afraid you are to use a more complex but significantly more efficient algorithm.

However, the practising programmer often appears overly concerned with improving efficiency only at the statement-level of coding. This penny-wise saving of micro-seconds has an apparently incurable side-effect that the resulting programs are harder to understand and often incorrect. Not uncommonly, more significant global improvements are not realized because of the unmastered complexity introduced at this statement-level. This is the direct result of incomplete analysis of the program written.

The benefits of a theoretical complexity analysis are very often substantial. But leaving this aside, one can further distinguish two kinds of efficiency improvements at the coding level :

1. measurable improvements
2. demonstrable improvements

For example, let us take a millisecond as the unit of measurement. Then, these are not always the same -- 1. implies 2., but not vice versa; for, you may be able to demonstrate that program A is faster than B by executing them a thousand times and comparing the total execution times, even though A is not measurably faster than B.

We should not ignore another observed phenomenon that programs spend most of their time in very small portions of the code. If this is true of the program in question, try to improve the efficiency of only these small segments of the code.

Correctness-preserving efficiency improvements, of whatever kind, should certainly be followed provided the required effort is not too great and the resulting code is equally easy to understand, maintain, enhance and modify. When this proviso is not satisfied a careful analysis of the benefits of efficiency improvements is necessary. For example, is it worthwhile to (demonstrably) improve a program that runs only a few times a day? Is not a millisecond too small a unit for distinguishing the two kinds of improvements for cost benefits?

By providing such things as register variables, and decrement and increment operations, C gives the impression of being an efficient language. We have, as yet no solid evidence that this is so, or if so, by what factor, in the domain of systems programming. For example, the absence of negative indices for arrays and the lack of sets induces more computation than is actually necessary. While it is true that i++ can be compiled straightforwardly into demonstrably faster code than i := i + 1, it is not clear if such things make programs measurably faster. On the other hand, there is the real danger of a slight slip turning such a statement into a major disaster (see Sections 9 and 10.1).

"It is very easy to exaggerate the need for efficiency and require a performance competitive with optimal hand coding."

- B. A. Wichmann(1978)

8. Portability

Perhaps the too restrictive nature of Pascal and the ease with which its compilers can be modified are the two factors that prompt many of its implementors to 'extend' the language and make it unportable. (Is giving rise to a host of suggested extensions a charactersitic of a superior language?) But programs in standard Pascal enjoy a considerable degree of portability (apart from problems caused in any language by the underlying character codes, ASCII or EBCDIC, or whatever).

This cannot be said of C. Even though most of the existing compilers are built by a rather close-knit group at Bell Labs and MIT, there are enough differences. One reason for this may be that the semantics of the language is often confused with what code the compilers produce in its Reference Manual.

Certainly, C programs have been and can be ported [Johnson and Ritchie 1978]. But this does not mean that they are portable as the word is generally understood. There is no clearly defined subset of it that would guarantee portability. A few example problems that the C Reference Manual cautions about are :

1. A pointer can be assigned any integer value, or a pointer value of another type. This can cause address exceptions when moved to another machine.

2. Integers can be assigned to chars and vice-versa.

To these we can add the problems caused by assumptions made in C programs about the addresses of variables (that they are a fixed distance apart ...). The unions of C and variant records of Pascal can both cause portability problems when misused.

9. Insecurities

"For the purpose of this discussion, an insecurity is a feature that cannot be implemented without either (1) a risk that violations of the language rules will go undetected, or (2) run-time checking that is comparable in cost to the operation being performed" [Welsh et al. 1977]. It may sound paradoxical but few or no insecurities need not always be a good thing. For, we observe that assembly languages have no insecurities whatsoever, according to the above definition, for the simple reason that it does not attempt to provide any security. It is only when a language purports to provide security, either explicitly or implicitly, and then fails that we should be upset by it. Thus, we modify (1) to read 'a risk that violations of the language rules and intentions will go undetected'. It is unlikely that a useful language without any insecurities can ever be designed. We can attempt to reduce their number, and explicitly identify them so that we are not lulled into believing that programs written in the language are safe.

9.1 Unsafe Features

An unsafe feature is an insecurity that generally causes havoc and is frequently the cause of evasive bugs.

The list of unsafe features of C is rather long : pointers to static as well as dynamic variables, address arithmetic, passing addresses as value parameters, treating an object pointed to as an array, all belong to this list. But what is more important is that they constitute the most heavily used features. Some of these exist in the language purely for the sake of statement-level efficiency. The use of pointers in accessing array elements is not only efficient, but has a certain elegance of its own. However, its setting is extremely unsafe, and provides much fuel to the "pointers considered harmful" debate (e.g. [Hoare 1975]). It is possible to control the use of pointers without any loss in efficiency [Mateti 1979a]. As they are now, they can be greatly misused, worse, an accidental slip can turn it into a very frustrating and harmful gremlin.

Not only is the list of unsafe Pascal features short -- variant records without tag fields, functions and procedures as parameters, dangling pointers to dynamic variables -- their relative frequency of occurrence is far lower.

9.2 Dirty Tricks

A dirty trick is an exploitation of an insecurity. The adjective "dirty" is used only to remind that such tricks often spring up as a nasty surprise to any one but their originators. Contrary to popular belief, dirty tricks can serve clean and legitimate purposes. This happens when the language is put to use in a way its designer has not foreseen or wished to forbid but could not. More often, however, they provide short-cuts. Two such examples follow.

1. Suppose we wish to access the exponent part e of the representation of a positive real number x. On the Interdata 8/32, this happens to be in bits 1 to 7. Thus, the function expo of Figure 1 would do the job in C.

2. Suppose we wish to produce the 32-bit concatenation of four 8-bit quantities, or vice versa. On some machines, characters are represented as 8-bit bytes and integers as 32-bit words. Thus, declare the 8-bit quantities as characters, and

```
var dummy :
    record case boolean of
        true  : (bits32 : integer);
        false : (bits8  :
            packed array [1..4] of char);
        end;
    ...
    ...
with dummy do begin
        bits8 [1] := first  8-bit quantity;
        bits8 [2] := second 8-bit quantity;
        bits8 [3] := third  8-bit quantity;
        bits8 [4] := fourth 8-bit quantity;
    end;
```

then dummy.bits32 is the required concatenation. Code similar
to this appears in some Pascal compilers. Pascal chose
deliberately to provide this flexibility at the expense of
security [Wirth 1975].

10. Psychological Effects

We are all p s y c h o l o g i s t s.

- from a book on psychology

It is with some trepidation that I write on these effects,
for I am a computer scientist. However, to shy away from this
"non-subject" would be to ignore the recognised importance
[Weinberg 1971] of the effects caused by our mental images of the
languages and by our human limitations. If you are sceptical of
what is said here, you are justified. But, I urge you to test
these hypotheses out and see how true/false they are.

10.1 Error Proofing

That the ratio of all "meaningful" constructs to all
syntactically legal constructs in any programming
language is almost zero

is a well-known fact. This is not because the said programming
language is defined in a context-free grammar rather than in a
more precise one such as vW grammar [Tanenbaum 1978].   (It is

possible, by technical trickery, to define a "programming language" where this ratio is unity; such a language would, however, have extremely limited "expressive power".) Let us recall the assumptions of Section 1.3. In addition, the following appear to be true, but are not well-tested:

> The number of errors in programs is proportional to the amount of detail that the writer had to handle in his program.

> The cost of debugging is a rapidly increasing function of the number of errors(bugs), which includes the extremely trivial ones.

It is therefore important to decrease the possibilities for (unintentional) misuse. Thus it is desirable to inform the compiler of our intentions.

> How can we expect a language to aid in avoiding mistakes, if it is even incapable of assisting in their detection.

> > — N. Wirth (1974)

10.2 Understandability and Compactness

> Programming is the art of writing essays in crystal-clear prose and making them executable.

> > — P. Brinch Hansen (1977)

It can justifiably be argued that the code is not a complete source of information about a program and that a programmer understands a program by successively refining guesses about how the program operates [Brooks 1978]. However, we confine ourselves here to the understanding gained through reading the code only.

Programs in expression languages are (to me) more difficult to understand than those in statement languages. In the latter, only the statements are active in modifying the values of variables. It is for this reason that we often discourage functions with side-effects. In understanding expression language programs we have to handle more details at different levels all at the same time. We need to remember not only what the expression value is so far, but also what variables have which new values. It is also true that expression language programs are more compact. Thus, we remark that

Readability is inversely proportional to compactness.

This is not to say anything verbose is readable. The word
compactness, as it is used here, needs explanation. Electronic
circuits can be made more compact by using integration. But this
does not make them less complex than their discrete component
counterparts. Compactness achieved in expression languages is of
this kind. Unlike in mathematics, where compact notation hides
detail irrelevant to a given level of discussion, expression
language programs while being compact still contain all the gory
details. The algorithm does not become simpler, nor is there any
reduction in the number of abstract operations except that in the
code generation some redundant load/store machine instructions
may be avoided.

In C, a programmer can certainly choose not to be compact but

the natural tendency of most programmers to write the
"best possible" code in a given language works against
writing readily understandable code.

Do give some thought to the qualification in the following quote.

C is easy to write and (when well-written) easy to
read.

McIlroy et al. (1978)

However, although we are all psychologists at
heart, not all of us are scientists.

- from the same book on psychology

11. Conclusion

The images that Pascal and C evoke are vivid. The strength
of C emanates from its identification of several practices used
in assembly programming that lead to very well-written, modular,

and efficient programs. In addition, C provides a modern syntax
for them adding the conventional wisdom of high-level languages,
notably automatic allocation of storage for variables and
recursion. Its fundamental flaw is that it failed to curb the
misuse of the very same features. While "misuse" is relative to
one's programming "morals", the failure to provide enough
redundancy to catch the accidental slip is unrealistic and can be
expensive.

Pascal, on the other hand, gives the impression that it may have
been designed by first synthesising all that has been put forward
in its time about "good and wholesome" programming, and
eliminating features that cannot be implemented efficiently
enough. Its promotion and exposition may have been, from a
psychological point of view, offensive : restrictions are often
resented, and rarely understood. It is true of nearly every
human endeavour that it takes far greater courage, training,
education and understanding to be disciplined, and computer
programming is no exception.

Optimism has not, apparently, worked in the past programming
projects. "Its [software] products have typically contained
other than what was expected (usually less, rather than more),
been delivered much later than scheduled, cost more than
anticipated, been poorly documented, and been poorly designed"
[Bersoff et al. 1979]. One should learn this lesson, and be
extremely careful at every step. Languages with convenient
features whose erroneous use cannot be detected by its compilers
should be avoided.

That excellent (as well as extremely ugly) programs can be
written in either language is clear. However, I am concerned
that it is all too easy to write incomprehensible programs in C.
Even more offending are the "features" such as unbridled
pointers, variable number of parameters in function calls,
absence of type checking and lack of Boolean variables... ; these
are a lot more troublesome than they are worth.

Finally, let me conclude by quoting Welsh et. al.(1977):

"Pascal is at the present time the best language in the
public domain for purposes of systems programming and
software implementation.

The discovery that the advantages of a high-level
language could be combined in such a simple and elegant
manner as in Pascal was a revelation that deserves the
title of breakthrough. Because of the very success of
Pascal, which greatly exceeded the expectations of its

author, the standards by which we judge such languages have also risen. It is grossly unfair to judge an engineering project by standards which have been proved attainable only by the success of the project itself, but in the interests of progress, such criticism must be made."

Acknowledgements

Many discussions with Paul Dunn, Robert Elz, Ken McDonnel, and Peter Poole prompted me to think about this topic and write this paper. However, they may not share my views as expressed here. I am grateful to the many authors who have influenced me and whose quotations I have so heavily used to make it clear that this paper is little more than a collage of their ideas.

12. References

[Addyman et al. 1979]
A. M. Addyman, et al., "A Draft Description of Pascal," Software - Practice and Experience, Vol. 9, No. 5, 381 - 424.

[Bersoff et al. 1979]
Edward H. Bersoff, Vilas D. Henderson and Stan G. Siegel, "Software Configuration Management : A Tutorial," IEEE Computer Magazine, Vol. 12, No. 1, 6 - 13.

[Brinch Hansen 1977]
Per Brinch Hansen, The Architecture of Concurrent Programs, Prentice-Hall.

[Brooks 1978]
Ruven Brooks, "Using a Behavioral Theory of Program Comprehension in Software Engineering," Proceedings of the Third International Conference on Software Engineering, IEEE, 196 - 201.

[Comer 1979]
Douglas Comer, "MAP : A Pascal Macro Preprocessor for Large Program Development," Software-Practice and Experience, Vol. 9, 203 - 209.

[Conradi 1976]
R. Conradi, "Further Critical Comments on the Programming Language Pascal, Particularly as a System Programming Language," SIGPLAN Notices, Vol. 11, 8 - 25.

[Flon 1975]
Lawrence Flon, "On Research into Structured Programming," ACM SIGPLAN Notices, Vol.10. No. 10, 16-17.

[Geschke et al. 1977]
Charles M. Geschke, James H. Morris Jr., and Edwin H. Satterthwaite, "Early Experience with Mesa," Communications of the ACM, Vol. 20, No. 8, 540-553.

[Habermann 1973]
A. N. Habermann, "Critical Comments on the Programming Language Pascal," Acta Informatica, Vol 3, 47 - 58.

[Hoare 1972]
C. A. R. Hoare, "A Note on the for Statement," BIT, Vol. 12, 334-341.

[Hoare 1975]
C. A. R. Hoare, "Data Reliability," ACM SIGPLAN Notices, Vol. 10, No. 6, 528-533.

[Jensen and Wirth 1974]
Kathleen Jensen and Niklaus Wirth, Pascal : User Manual and Report, 2nd ed., 4th printing, Springer-Verlag, pp 167.

[Johnson and Ritchie 1978]
S. C. Johnson and D. M. Ritchie, "Portability of C Programs and the UNIX System," The Bell System Technical Journal, Vol. 57, 2021 - 2048.

[Kernighan and Plauger 1974]
Brian Kernighan and P. J. Plauger, The Elements of Programming Style, McGraw-Hill.

[Kernighan and Ritchie 1978]
Brian Kernighan and Dennis M. Ritchie, The C Programming Language, Prentice Hall Software Series, pp viii + 228.

[Kieburtz et al. 1978]
R. B. Kieburtz, W. Barbash and C. R. Hill, "A Type-checking Program Linkage System for Pascal," Proceedings of the Third International Conference on Software Engineering, IEEE, 23 - 28.

[Knuth 1971]
Donald E. Knuth, "An Empirical Study of FORTRAN Programs," Software-Practice and Experience , Vol. 1, 105-133.

[Knuth 1974]
Donald E. Knuth, "Structured Programming with goto Statements," Computing Surveys, Vol. 6, No. 4, 261 - 301.

[Kosaraju 1974]
Rao Kosaraju, "Analysis of Structured Programs," J. Computer and System Sciences, Vol. 9, No. 3, 232 - 255.

[Lampson et al. 1977]
B. W. Lampson, J. J. Horning, R. L. London, J.G. Mitchell, and G. L. Popek, "Report on the Programming Language Euclid," ACM SIGPLAN Notices, Vol. 12, No. 2, pp ii + 79.

[Lecarme and Desjardins 1975]
O. Lecarme and P. Desjardins, "More Comments on the Programming Language Pascal," Acta Informatica, Vol. 4, 231 - 243.

[Ledgard and Marcotty 1975]
Henry F. Ledgard and Michael Marcotty, "A Genealogy of Control Structures," Communications of the ACM, Vol. 18, No. 11, 629 - 639.

[Liskov et al. 1977]
Barbara Liskov, Alan Snyder, Russell Atkinson, and Craig Schaffert, "Abstraction Mechanisms in CLU," Communications of ACM, Vol. 20, No. 8, 564-576.

[Mateti 1979a]
Prabhaker Mateti, "Enumerated Types and Efficient Access of Array Elements," in preparation.

[Mateti 1979b]
Prabhaker Mateti, "Specifications of a Macro Preprocessor for Pascal : A CS340 Project," University of Melbourne.

[McIlroy et al. 1978]
    M. D. McIlroy, E. N. Pinson and B. A. Tague, "Foreword (to
    the special issue)", The Bell System Technical Journal, Vol.
    57, No. 6, 1899 - 1904.

[Morris 1973]
    J. H. Morris, "Types are not Sets," Conference Record ACM
    Symposium on Principles of Programming Languages, Boston,
    Mass., 120 - 124.

[Nutt 1978]
    Gary J. Nutt, "A Comparison of Pascal and FORTRAN as
    Introductory Programming Languages," ACM SIGPLAN Notices,
    Vol. 13, No. 2, 57-62.

[Pascal News 197x]
    Pascal News, News letters of the Pascal Users Group, Andy
    Mickel (ed.), University of Minnesota.

[Plauger 1979]
    P. J. Plauger, A Review of Kernighan and Ritchie 1978 ,
    Computing Reviews, Vol. ?, 2 - 4.

[Sammet 1978]
    Jean E. Sammet, "Roster of Programming Languages for 1976-
    1977," ACM SIGPLAN Notices, Vol. 13, No. 11, 56-85.

[Shaw et al. 1978]
    Mary Shaw, Guy T. Almes, Joseph M. Newcomer, Brian K. Reid
    and Wm. A. Wulf, "A Comparison of Programming Languages for
    Software Engineering," Report CMU-CS-78-119, Carnegie-Mellon
    University.

[Tanenbaum 1978]
    A. S. Tanenbaum, "A Comparison of Pascal and Algol 68,"
    The Computer Journal, Vol. 21, 316 - 323.

[Weinberg 1971]
    Gerald Weinberg, The Psychology of Computer Programming, Van
    Nostrand Reinhold.

[Welsh and Bustard 1979]
    J. Welsh and D. W. Bustard, "Pascal-Plus - Another Language
    for Modular Multiprogramming," Australian Computer Science
    Communications, Vol. 1, No. 1, 49 - 62.

[Welsh et al. 1977]
    J. Welsh, W. J. Sneeringer and C. A. R. Hoare, "Ambiguities
    and Insecurities in Pascal," Software - Practice and
    Experience, Vol. 7, 685 - 696.

[Wichmann 1978]
    B. A. Wichmann, "Some Performance Aspects of System
    Implementation Languages," Constructing Quality Software, P.
    G. Hibbard/S. A. Schuman (eds.), IFIP, North-Holland, 46 -
    62.

[Wirth 1971]
    Niklaus Wirth, "The Design of a Pascal Compiler," Software
    -- Practice and Experience, Vol. 1, 309-333.

[Wirth 1974]
    Niklaus Wirth, "On the Design of Programming Languages,"
    (in) Information Processing 1974, J. L. Rosenfeld (ed.),
    North-Holland, 386-393.

[Wirth 1975]
    Niklaus Wirth, "An Assessment of the Programming Language
    Pascal," Proceedings of 1975 International Conference on
    Reliable Software, ACM SIGPLAN Notices, Vol. 10, No. 6, 23-
    30.

[Wirth 1977a]
    Niklaus Wirth, "Modula : A Language for Modular
    Multiprogramming," Software - Practice and Experience, Vol.
    7, 3-35.

[Wirth 1977b]
    Niklaus Wirth, "Programming Languages : What to Demand and
    How to Assess Them," (in the book) Software Engineering,
    edited by R. H. Perrott, Academic Press, 155 - 173.

[Wulf et al. 1971]
    W. A. Wulf, D. E. Russell, and A. N. Habermann, "BLISS : A
    Language for Systems Programming," Communications of the
    ACM, Vol. 14, No. 12.

[Wulf et al. 1976]
    W. A. Wulf, R. L. London, and M. Shaw, "An Introduction to
    the Construction and Verification of Alphard Programs," IEEE
    Transactions on Software Engineering, Vol. 2, 253-265.

PROCEEDINGS OF THE SYMPOSIUM ON
LANGUAGE DESIGN AND PROGRAMMING METHODOLOGY
SYDNEY, 10-11 SEPTEMBER, 1979

WHY RECURSION?

Jeffrey S. Rohl

Department of Computer Science
University of Western Australia

ABSTRACT

Recursion as a programming technique has been
with us for over two decades now, and yet it still
retains a certain mystery.   In this paper we consider
the objections to it and the claims for it.

1.   INTRODUCTION

Many programming texts use Euclid's algorithm for calculating the highest
common factor (HCF) of two integers p and q as one of their simple examples.
The description of the algorithm usually goes something like this: "To find
the HCF first divide p by q and calculate the remainder, r.   If $r = 0$ then
q is the HCF;   otherwise repeat the process with q and r taking the place of
p and q."   From this description an iterative solution along the lines of
Fig. 1 is usually presented (though if the example comes early it is expressed
as a program rather than a procedure of course).

```
function HCF(p,q : integer) : integer;
      var  r : integer;
      begin
      r := p mod q;
      while r <> 0 do
            begin
            p := q;
            q := r;
            r := p mod q
            end;
      HCF := q
      end
```

Fig. 1   A nonrecursive version of the HCF procedure

Yet the description given almost begs for the recursive procedure such as that
of Fig. 2.

```
function HCF(p,q : integer) : integer;
      var  r : integer;
      begin
      r := p mod q;
      if   r = 0 then HCF := q else HCF := HCF(q,r)
      end
```

Fig. 2   A recursive version of the HCF procedure

Why then does the first solution seem more natural to writers and teachers? The simple (simplistic?) answer is that most writers and teachers either learned to program in the fifties or early sixties when recursion was just beginning to appear, or were themselves taught by people reared in that period. There seems to be a collective feeling for iterative solutions as against recursive ones, though this feeling is certainly buttressed by cogent arguments.

2.   THE OBJECTIONS

What are these arguments against recursion?   There seem to be four, which we discuss in turn.

(a) It is expensive of space: This is quite a strong argument since each invocation of the recursive procedure requires an activation record consisting of links, parameters and local variables.   Let us make the simplifying assumption that all these quantities require a word each and that there are two links.   Then the recursive procedure for HCF gives $5n$ words, where n is the number of recursive invocations, whereas the non-recursive version requires a constant 3.   Whether this is important depends very much on the value of n. It so happens that for this example n must be small: if F_i is the ith Fibonacci number then it is bounded by $u-3$ where F_u is the largest Fibonacci number represented by a variable of type $integer$.   Similar statements apply to other numerical procedures such as that for factorial.

If on the other hand, the procedure is processing the elements of a list or an array, then n is usually related to the number of elements in this list or array, and this might be quite large; and in a program manipulating a small number of large lists it could be quite crucial.   The decision on whether or not to use recursion in this situation is quite a nice one especially where the non-recursive procedure requires a stack.

When we move onto more complex data structures such as a tree, the space required by activation records is less significant since n is generally related to the height of the tree which, for reasonably balanced trees, is a logarithmic function of the number of nodes.   The same is true but even more so for more general trees, including the search trees of combinatorial problems.

(b) It is expensive of time: This objection has in general lost much of its validity.   If a compiler writer implements procedure calls, not by a short sequence of open code but by a call to a subroutine, then calling procedures is expensive, and the complaints about the time penalty of recursion are based on experience with these compilers.

If we consider any procedure written both recursively and non-recursively we find that, in general, the same operations take place and that in general they take place in the same order.   The difference lies in the control structures: a recursive call or a traverse of a loop.   Although the procedure call is the more expensive, the significance of this becomes correspondingly less as the body of the procedure becomes more complex.   The HCF example is probably the most unsympathetic from the recursive point of view since the body is very small.   Fig. 3 gives an analysis, in terms of the number of iterations/recursions n, of the operations involved.

	Weight	Non-recursive (Fig.1)	Recursive (Fig.2)
Assignments	1	$3n + 2$	$2n + 2$
Mod	4	$n + 1$	$n + 1$
Comparisons	1	$n + 1$	$n + 1$
Procedure calls	5	1	$n + 1$
Parameters passed	1	2	$2n + 2$
Weighted figure		$8n + 14$	$14n + 14$

Fig. 3   An analysis of the HCF procedures

The weights used to produce the weighted average are rather arbitrary (and reflect the writer's feeling of what they should cost!)   On the CYBER they are reasonably accurate.   The times to calculate the HCF of F_{24} and F_{23}, so that $n = 21$, were 700 µsecs and 1120 µsecs respectively (to some rather variable accuracy).   This then sets an upper limit on the time penalty of recursion.

In more complex cases where the non-recursive procedure has to maintain a stack, the balance changes and the speed of the algorithms becomes more nearly equal.   Indeed there is evidence (Fike 1975), (Rohl 1976) that a recursive procedure can be the more efficient.

(c)   I can't understand it: There are those who have no need for recursion and for them the whole of this discussion is simply irrelevant.   There are many others, however, for whom recursion would be useful if only they could understand it.   Their inability to understand is a severe problem, and an indictment of those of us whose job it is to teach them and have failed.   It is perhaps significant that none of the introductory texts on Pascal (assuming here that Wirth [1976] and Alagic & Arbib [1978] are not introductory) give the subject more than a cursory treatment.

Once recursion is mastered, it is difficult to believe that some non-recursive procedures are easier to understand than their recursive equivalents. Consider a procedure for producing a copy of a list, assuming the definitions:

```
type listptr = ↑node;
     node = record
            item : itemtype;
            next : listptr
            end
```

where *itemtype* is left unspecified.

Fig. 4 gives a non-recursive version adapted from the function given by Alagic and Arbib.

```
procedure copy(l : listptr; var l1 : listptr);
      var  p, pred : listptr;
      begin
      if   l = nil then l1 := nil
      else
            begin
            new(l1);
            l1↑.item := l↑.item;
            pred := l1; l := l↑.next;
            while l <> nil do
                  begin
                  new(p);
                  pred↑.next := p;
                  p↑.item := l↑.item;
                  pred := p; l := l↑.next
                  end;
            pred↑.next := nil
            end
      end
```

Fig. 4   A non-recursive procedure for copying a list

Is this procedure really easier to understand than the recursive one
given in Fig. 5?

```
procedure copy(l : listptr; var l1 : listptr);
      begin
      if   l = nil then l1 := nil
      else
            begin
            new(l1);
            l1↑.item := l↑.item;
            copy(l↑.next, l1↑.next)
            end
      end
```

Fig. 5   A recursive procedure for copying a list

For those uninitiated in recursion it may be, so that it seems that the solution
is an educational one.   We must see to it that the mode of thought involved in
recursion is explained and that significant procedures are written using it.

(d) The language I use doesn't allow it: It is certainly true that Fortran
forbids recursion and that most assembly languages give no help in its
implementation.   However, the problem of mechanistically converting recursive
procedures to non-recursive ones has received a lot of attention.   (See
Griffiths [1975] for linear recursion, Knuth [1974] and Bird [1977] for binary
recursion, and Rohl [1977] for recursion in combinatorial problems.) Thus it
is possible to regard recursion as a design tool even where it may not be
available as an implementation tool.

3.   THE CLAIMS

The discussion so far has only been a partial answer to the four objections.
We consider now four advantages.

(a)   In appropriate situations it more naturally matches the problem: we have already given the example of a list copying procedure.   Since the recursive version of that procedure is vulnerable to the space argument, we give another example: that of adding an element to a binary search tree. Fig. 6 gives a recursive version assuming the definitions:

```
type treeptr = ↑node;
     itemtype = record
                key : keytype;
                info : infotype;
                end;
     node = record
            left : treeptr;
            item : itemtype;
            right : treeptr
            end;
```

where *infotype* is left unspecified.

```
procedure insert(newitem : itemtype; var t : treeptr);
    begin
    if   t = nil then
         begin
         new(t);
         with t↑ do
              begin
              item := newitem;
              left := nil; right = nil
              end
         end
    else with t↑ do
         if   newitem.key = item.key
              then writeln('item already on tree')
         else if newitem.key < item.key
              then insert(newitem, left)
         else {if newitem.key > item.key then}
              insert(newitem, right)
    end
```

Fig. 6   A recursive procedure for inserting an element in a tree

The recursive procedure enables us to avoid the *trailing pointer problem* and Barron's *protasis problem,* as a comparison with Fig. 7 graphically illustrates.

```
procedure insert(newitem : itemtype; var t : treeptr);
    var t1, t2 : treeptr;
        branch : (ℓ, ℛ);
        found : Boolean;
begin
new(t2); t2↑.right := t;
t1 := t; t := t2; branch := ℛ;
found := false;
while (t1 <> nil) and not found do
        with t1↑ do
            begin
            t2 := t1;
            if   newitem.key = item.key then
                 begin
                 writeln('item already on tree');
                 found := true
                 end
            else if newitem.key < item.key then
                 begin
                 t1 := t1↑.left; branch := ℓ
                 end
            else {if newitem.key > item.key then}
                 begin
                 t1 := t1↑.right; branch := ℛ;
                 end
            end;
    if   t1 = nil then
         begin
         new(t1);
         with t1↑ do
             begin
             item := newitem;
             left := nil; right := nil
             end
         if   branch = ℓ then t2↑.left := t1
              else t2↑.right := t1;
         end;
    t := t↑.right
end
```

Fig. 7   A non-recursive procedure for inserting an element in a tree

(b)   In many situations such procedures are easier to prove: For a linear recursive procedure, its proof is almost trivial, since the structure of the procedure mirrors directly the mathematical formulation. The proof process is essentially that of the induction used in the proof of the underlying mathematics.   Perhaps we are saying that it is the proof of the mathematics rather than the proof of the program that is important.

We give now a more difficult procedure, one for generating permutations in pseudo-lexicographical order, which we shall also use in later sections. We call the procedure *everyman* because every man and his brother seem to have discovered it.   It assumes the definitions:

```
type mark = {any enumeration or subrange};
     range = 1 .. max;
     marksarray = array[range] of mark;
```

where max is the cardinality of $mark$, and uses :=: as an interchange operator.

```
procedure everyman(m : marksarray; n : range);

        procedure perm(k : range);
            var i : range;
            begin
            for i := k to n do
                begin
                m[k] :=: m[i];
                if k = n-1 then {process}
                else perm(k+1);
                m[k] :=: m[i]
                end
            end;

        begin
        perm(1)
        end
```

Fig. 8   The *everyman* procedure for generating permutations

The proof is simple.   Suppose that a call $perm(k+1)$
  (i)   Leaves the marks in $m_1 \to m_k$ untouched;
 (ii)   Ensures that all permutations of the marks in $m_{k+1} \to m_n$ are
        produced in turn;
(iii)   Returns $m_{k+1} \to m_n$ to its original state.
This is trivially true when $k+1 = n-1$.

   Then a call $perm(k)$:
  (i)   Leaves the marks in $m_1 \to m_{k-1}$ untouched since the procedure does
        not reference them;
 (ii)   Ensures that all the permutations of the marks $m_k \to m_n$ are produced
        in turn because all possible choices for m_k (available in $m_k \to m_n$)
        are chosen and $perm(k+1)$ called after each choice;
(iii)   Returns $m_k \to m_n$ to its original state.

   Since *everyman* calls $perm(1)$ it follows that all permutations of the
marks in m are produced.

   The proof is not always so easy, of course.   We leave the reader to
prove a related algorithm due to Heap [1963] given in Fig. 9.

```
procedure Heap(m : marksarray; n : range);

    procedure perm(k : range);
        var i, p : range;
        begin
        if   k = n-1 then {process}
        else perm(k+1);
        for  i := k + 1 to n do
            begin
            if   odd(n-k) then p := i else p := n;
            m[p] :=: m[k];
            if   k = n-1 then {process}
            else perm (k+1)
            end
        end;

    begin
    perm(1)
    end
```

Fig. 9   Heap's algorithm for generating permutations

A non-recursive version of *everyman* is given in Fig. 10 and the reader is encouraged to prove it directly.

```
procedure everyman(m : marksarray; n : range);
    var i : array[range] of range;
        k : range;
        complete, downagain : Boolean;

    begin
    k := 1;
    i[1] := k;
    complete := false;
    repeat
        m[k] :=: m[i[k]];
        while k <> n-1 do
            begin
            k := k + 1;
            i[k] := k;
            m[k] :=: m[i[k]]
            end;
        process;
        downagain := false;
        repeat
        m[k] :=: m[i[k]];
            if   i[k] <> n then
                begin
                i[k] := i[k] + 1;
                downagain := true
                end
            else
                if k = 1 then complete := true
                else k := k-1
        until downagain or complete
    until complete
    end
```

Fig. 10   A non-recursive version of *everyman*

(c)   In many situations such procedures are easy to analyse: We illustrate this by reference to the *everyman* procedure again.   Let us ignore for the moment the details of what we choose to measure, and assume that:

a is the count inside the loop at level $n-1$
b is the count outside the loop at level $n-1$
c is the count inside the loop at the other levels,
d is the count outside the loop at the other levels.

If T_k is the count for a complete activation at level k then we have:

$$T_k = (n-k+1)*(T_{k+1}+c) + d \quad , \quad k \neq n-1$$
$$= 2 \times a + b \quad\quad\quad , \quad k = n-1$$

From this we can calculate T_1 as:

$$T_1 = n \times [a +$$
$$b \times \tfrac{1}{2!} \quad\quad\quad +$$
$$c \times (\tfrac{1}{2!} + \tfrac{1}{3!} + \ldots) +$$
$$d \times (\tfrac{1}{3!} + \tfrac{1}{4!} + \ldots) \;]$$
$$= n \times [a +$$
$$(b+c) \times \tfrac{1}{2!} +$$
$$(c+d) \times \tfrac{1}{3!} +$$
$$(c+d) \quad \tfrac{1}{4!} +$$
$$\vdots \;]$$

Fig. 11 gives an analysis of *everyman* with respect to some higher-level constructs.

	Weight	Parameters				Terms				
		a	b	c	d	a	$\frac{b+c}{2!}$	$\frac{c+d}{3!}$	$\frac{c+d}{4!}$	Total
Assignments	1	6	0	6	0	6	3	1	$\frac{1}{4}$	$10\frac{1}{4}n!$
Arithmetic	1	1	0	2	0	1	1	$\frac{1}{3}$	$\frac{1}{12}$	$2\frac{5}{12}n!$
Subscripts	1	8	0	8	0	8	4	$1\frac{1}{3}$	$\frac{1}{3}$	$13\frac{2}{3}n!$
Comparisons	1	1	0	1	0	1	$\frac{1}{2}$	$\frac{1}{6}$	$\frac{1}{24}$	$1\frac{17}{24}n!$
Loop entries	1	0	1	0	1	0	$\frac{1}{2}$	$\frac{1}{6}$	$\frac{1}{24}$	$\frac{17}{24}n!$
Loop traverses	3	1	0	1	0	1	$\frac{1}{2}$	$\frac{1}{6}$	$\frac{1}{24}$	$1\frac{17}{24}n!$
Parameters	1	0	0	1	0	0	$\frac{1}{2}$	$\frac{1}{6}$	$\frac{1}{24}$	$\frac{17}{24}n!$
Calls	5	0	0	1	0	0	$\frac{1}{2}$	$\frac{1}{6}$	$\frac{1}{24}$	$\frac{17}{24}n!$
Weighted		19	1	26	1	19	$13\frac{1}{2}$	$4\frac{1}{2}$	$1\frac{1}{8}$	$38\frac{1}{8}n!$

Fig. 11   An analysis of *everyman*

From a detailed analysis such as this we can determine the effects of proposed transformations on a procedure to improve its performance.   With *everyman*, for example, we could consider, among others, the following possibilities:

(i)   During all interchanges at one level the same element (the initial m_k) takes place in all interchanges, and reinterchanges.   We could save on both assignments and subscriptings by storing this value locally outside the loop so that the interchange within the loop required only two assignments instead of three.   Further we could avoid restoring m_k in the interchange sequence since on the next traverse it would be immediately overwritten.   That is, we could replace the loop of *everyman* by:

```
temp := m[k];
for   i := k to n do
      begin
      m[k] := m[i];   m[i] := temp;
      if    k = n-1 then {process}
      else perm(k+1);
      m[i] := m[k]
      end;
m[k] := temp
```

(ii) The interchange and reinterchange that takes place on the first traverse of each loop is redundant since it simply interchanges m_k with itself.   We could recognise this by dealing with it outside the loop and reducing the number of traverses by one.   Note that this means that a new derivation must take place.   The new result is:

$$T_1 = n! \times [(a+b+c) \times \frac{1}{2!}$$
$$+ \ d \times \frac{1}{3!}$$
$$+ \ d \times \frac{1}{4!}$$
$$\vdots$$
$$.]$$

Note, too, that the processing must now take place at two different places in the text, which itself may imply some cost.

(iii) The test for determining when the recursion is to terminate is constant within the loop.   It may be taken outside by splitting the loop into two and using the test to determine which loop is to be obeyed.   Further the loop at the bottom level is obeyed only once and can be replaced by its body.

(iv) We could stop the recursion one level later as in Wirth.   This involves a third analysis which we leave to the reader.

Fig. 12 gives the results of the analysis of the above suggestions together with times in msecs of running them on a CYBER 73 for $n = 6$.

	Weighted Parameters					
	a	b	c	d	Total	Time
Basic procedure	19	1	26	1	$38\frac{1}{8}n!$	130
Mod(i)	13	5	20	5	$30\frac{17}{24}n!$	108
Mod(i) → (ii)	13	14	14	15	$23\frac{5}{8}n!$	77
Mod(i) → (iii)	–	16	18	15	$20\frac{1}{8}n!$	67
Mod(i) → (iv)	–	1	18	14	$28\frac{11}{12}n!$	101

Fig. 12   An analysis of improvements to *everyman*

Furthermore, similar analyses (or the same ones stopping earlier) enable us to determine whether the same techniques are more or less efficacious if we want the permutations to be n at a time rather than n at a time.   This is relevant to adaptations of the procedure for, say, topological sorting or other procedures where inspection of the first n elements of a permutation may enable all $(n-n+1)!$ permutations starting with those n elements to be removed from consideration without being generated.

(d)   They are adaptable: This is rather a difficult claim to justify yet it is interesting to note how often workers express their amazement that minor changes to a program can produce a highly desirable variant.   Here we will simply illustrate by means of the classical *n-queens problem*: that is, the problem of determining how n queens may be placed on an $n \times n$ chessboard so that no queen is under attack from any other.   If we represent the solution as an array m where m_i gives the column in which the queen on row i is placed, then since there can only be one queen in each row and one queen in each column, it follows that m must be a permutation of the integers 1 to n.

Thus a permutation generation procedure can be adapted to solve the n-queens problem by testing each permutation to see whether it corresponds to a board in which no queen is under threat along the diagonals.   Further we can test partial permutations as they are generated to see whether the queen, represented by the latest element to be added to the permutation, is under attack since, if it is, there is no point building on the partial permutation.   Fig. 13 gives a procedure based on *everyman* which uses the traditional technique for testing the diagonals.

```
procedure queens(n : range);
    const max1 = {the value of max - 1};
          max2 = {the value of 2 × max};
    type  mark = 1 .. max;
    var   m : array[range]of mark;
          upl : array[-max1 .. max1] of Boolean;
          upr : array[2 .. max] of Boolean;
          i : integer;

    procedure perm(k : range);
        var  i, mi : range;
             temp : mark;
        begin
        temp := m[k];
        for  i := k to n do
            begin
            mi := m[i];
            if upl[k-mi] and upr[k+mi] := then
                begin
                upl[k-mi] := false; upr[k+mi] := false;
                m[k] := mi; m[i] := temp;
                if k = n-1 then
                    begin
                    if  upl[n-m[n]] and
                        upr[n+m]n]] then process
                    end
                else perm(k+1);
                m[i] := mi;
                upl[k-mi] := true; upr[k+mi] := true
                end
            end;
        m[k] := temp
        end;

    begin
    for  i := 1 to n do m[i] := i;
    for  i := 1-n to n-1 do upl[i] := true;
    for  i := 2 to 2 × n do upr[i] := true;
    perm(1)
    end
```

Fig. 13   The n-queens problem

4.   CONCLUSIONS

The reader will have noticed that the claims for recursion have generally been prefaced by the phrase "in many situations". The paper does not claim that recursion should be used for everything (though the author still nurtures the dream of teaching an introductory programming course this way). We simply want to say that recursion is a very powerful tool on the appropriate occasion and that it should not be dismissed as too esoteric for practical use.

5.   ACKNOWLEDGEMENT

I should like to thank M.S. Palm who tested, timed and instrumented all the procedures given here.

REFERENCES

1. ALAGIC, S and ARBIB, M.A. (1978): "The Design of Well-Structured and Correct Programs", Springer-Verlag.

2. BIRD, R.S. (1977): "Notes on Recursion Elimination", Comm. ACM, Vol.20, p.434.

3. FIKE, C.T. (1975): "A Permutation Generation Method", Computer Journal, Vol. 18, p.21.

4. GRIFFITHS, M. (1975): "Requirements for and Problems with Intermediate Languages for Programming Language Implementation" (Lecture notes for the NATO International Summer School, Marktoberdorf, W. Germany).

5. HEAP, B.R. (1963): "Permutations by Interchanges", Computer Journal, Vol. 6, pp 293-4.

6. KNUTH, D.E. (1974): "Structured Programming with Goto Statements", Computing Surveys, Vol. 6, p.261.

7. ROHL, J.S. (1976): "Programming Improvements to Fike's Algorithm for Generating Permutations", Computer Journal, Vol 19, p. 156.

8. ROHL, J.S. (1977): "Converting a Class of Recursive Procedures into Non-recursive Ones", Software - Practice & Experience, Vol. 7, p.231.

9. WIRTH, N. (1976): "Algorithms + Data Structures = Programs", Prentice-Hall.

PROCEEDINGS OF THE SYMPOSIUM ON
LANGUAGE DESIGN AND PROGRAMMING METHODOLOGY
SYDNEY, 10-11 SEPTEMBER, 1979

ON THE PRIME EXAMPLE OF PROGRAMMING

Paul Pritchard

Department of Computer Science
University of Queensland

ABSTRACT

The problem of finding prime numbers has been much
favoured by expositors of modern programming methodology.
In this paper the problem is tackled once more, but from
a broader view of the programming process than has
previously been taken. The initial steps toward a solution
parallel those in the well-known presentations of Dijkstra
and Wirth. However a general program transformation is
shown to capture the clever "inventive step" in Dijkstra's
solution, and another is employed to lead naturally to
an alternative program. Complexity analyses of the two
programs show that the latter is significantly more
efficient.

1. INTRODUCTION

The problem of finding prime numbers enjoys a special status
as an exemplary exercise for modern programming methods. Dijkstra[1]
chooses it as his "first example of step-wise program composition"
in what is probably his most widely read essay, "Notes on Structured
Programming"; Wirth (1973) develops a variant of Dijkstra's program
for the problem as a key example in his "Systematic Programming";
Hoare (1972) employs a given abstract algorithm for the problem to
illustrate the transition from abstract data structures to their
realizations in a programming language.

We choose herein to tackle the problem once more, with a view
to exemplifying the total programming process. For our purposes
we take this to encompass the following stages:

1. problem specification;
2. design of an initial solution;
3. creation of alternative solution(s);
4. evaluation and comparison of the solutions.

The numbering of these stages is not meant to suggest a rigid
chronological order; considerable interaction would be expected
in the later stages.

As with Dijkstra and Wirth, program correctness is the dominant
concern in all but the fourth stage. In this respect, we show that
the dependence on a "deep" theorem of number theory of Dijkstra's
(and Wirth's) program can easily be removed; we also bring to light
a subtle verification condition for Wirth's program. This condition
is a complicated number-theoretic assertion whose validity is unclear.

---

1. Dijkstra (1972), p.26.

We hope to show that program transformations have an important role to play in both the creation of an initial solution and subsequent solutions. We show that a general optimising transformation gives a much better account of the "inventive step" in Dijkstra's solution. Furthermore, another general transformation is the crucial step in the development of an alternative program. Our final concern is with analysing the time and space complexity of the two solutions; we reference results which clearly demonstrate the superior efficiency of the second program.

2. THE PROBLEM, AND THE DEVELOPMENT OF AN INITIAL SOLUTION

We choose the following formulation of the problem:

find all primes not greater than a given integer N > 1.

Dijkstra and Wirth actually find the first n primes, but this is not an important difference (Dijkstra is uncharacteristically concrete with n = 1000).

Our initial design steps parallel those of Dijkstra and Wirth; p_i is used to denote the i'th prime.

Step 1: accept 2 as the first prime, then examine successive odd integers 3, 5, 7... for primeness, stopping when the next candidate exceeds N.

Step 2: (refining the test for primeness): since an odd number x is prime if and only if it has no odd prime factors other than itself, we decide to divide x by p_2, p_3,... successively until a factor is found or no candidate factors remain. So it is decided to store p_i in an array (as p[i]) when found, in order that primes be available for the primality test.

Step 3: (deciding when to stop testing): if x is composite, its smallest (prime) factor must be $\leq \sqrt{x}$. So we must stop testing if

(i)   a factor is found, or
(ii)   we run out of primes < x, or
(iii)   the next prime p to be tried satisfies $p^2 > x$.

Hence, if k primes have been found thus far, the upper bound lim on the index of primes to be tried is given by

$$lim = \begin{cases} k+1, \text{ if } p[k]^2 \leq x, \\ l+1, \text{ where } l \text{ is the smallest index such that} \\ \quad x < p[l+1]^2, \text{ otherwise.} \end{cases} \qquad \dots (1)$$

It is incumbent on the programmer to ensure that (1) is invariantly true before doing the primality test on x. Since lim is a function of x only, we seek to adjust its value for each new value of x. So suppose (1) holds with x, k and lim equal to x1, k1 and lim1 respectively, just before testing x1. Let x2 and k2 be the new values of x and k after completing the test and incrementing x. Suppose lim1 > k2. This can only happen if lim1 = k1+1 and k2 = k1 (because x1 was composite). So by (1), $p[k2]^2 \leq x2 = x1 + 2$, so lim should not be changed. The remaining case is lim1 ≤ k2. Here lim must be increased if $p[lim1]^2 \leq x2$, and it can only increase by 1 since k and l (in(1)) can increase by at most 1. The resulting program is given in Figure 1.

```
const N=?; pbound =?;
var p: array [1..pbound] of integer;
    i,x,k,lim : integer;
    prim: Boolean;
begin p[1]:=2; k:=1; lim:=1; x:=3;
      while x ≤ N do
          begin if lim ≤ k
                then if p[lim]² ≤ x then lim:=lim+1;
                i :=2; prim:= true;
                while prim and (i < lim) do
                    begin prim:=<x is not divisible by p[i]>;
                          i:=i+1
                    end;
                if  prim
                    then begin k:=k+1;
                               p[k]:=x
                         end;
                x:=x+2
          end
      end
end.
```

FIGURE 1.

The Dijkstra and Wirth programs differ from our program only in omitting the test lim ≤ k. Since p[lim] is not defined for lim>k, the correctness of their programs depends on showing that lim ≤ k is invariantly true. They do this by appealing to what Knuth calls "a deep result of number theory, namely .... we always have

$$p_{n+1} < p_n^2\text{".}\ [2]$$

2. D. Knuth, quoted in Dijkstra (1972), p.34.

This is unfortunate in a pedagogical example chosen because "its mathematical background is so simple and familiar".[3] We have shown above that the programmer who is unaware of this fact is not disadvantaged (at this stage), as it is only of very minor importance.

We now proceed to step 4 (refining <x is not divisible by p[i]>): the obvious choice here is

$$(x \underline{\text{div}} \ p[i]) \ * \ p[i] \neq x.$$

Dijkstra and Wirth surprisingly (to the reader) do not stop at this point, and give rather strange reasons for continuing the process of refinement - Dijkstra: "to give the algorithm an unexpected turn we shall assume the absence of a convenient remainder computation"[4]; Wirth: "Let us, however, assume that the program is to be developed without the availability of an explicit division operator"[5]. We feel these invitations are unconvincing; what is hardware division for if not to divide?

But it is not difficult to motivate the move. It is in fact an example of a general optimizing transformation we might express as follows:

if, in a loop, x is incremented by $\delta(x)$ before calculating $f(x)$, and $f(x + \delta(x)) = g(f(x), \delta(x))$ where $g(c,y)$ is easily calculated for small values of y, then save the (previous) value of $f(x)$ in fx and compute with $g(fx,\delta(x))$.

(Dijkstra actually addresses this same phenomenon later in his essay.) Furthermore, a healthy respect for the cost of division and multiplication is sufficient stimulus to look for this situation in our example.

In our program, given fx = (x $\underline{\text{div}}$ p[i]) * p[i],

$$(x+2 \underline{\text{div}} \ p[i])^* \ p[i] = \begin{cases} fx+p[i], & \text{if } fx+p[i] \leq x, \\ fx, & \text{otherwise.} \end{cases}$$

Since the above is clearly easy to compute, we decide to introduce an array of multiples m[i] of p[i] for i < lim. This amounts to keeping the maximum multiple of p_i not greater than x; Dijkstra's "unexpected turn" is a slight variation - m[i] is the minimum multiple of p[i] not less than x. The natural place to adjust m[i] is in the loop for the primality test, which Wirth codes as follows:

```
i:=2; prim:= true;
while prim and (i<lim) do
     begin if m[i] < x then m[i]:=m[i] + p[i];
           prim:= (x ≠ m[i]);
           i:=i+1
     end
```

---

3. Dijkstra, op.cit., p. 27.
4. Ibid., p.37.
5. Wirth (1973), p.140.

But there is a trap here! If $m[i]$ is only calculated when needed, we must be sure it cannot lag too far behind x. Dijkstra solves this with

> while $m[i] < x$ do $m[i] := m[i]+p[i]$,

which is guaranteed to preserve the appropriate invariant. Wirth's program has an implicit verification condition VC, on whose validity the correctness of his program stands or falls.

> VC: In any interval $n \cdot p_i < x < m \cdot p_i$, $n \geq p_i$, n and m coprime
> to all p_k with $k < i$, there are distinct integers x_j,
> $1 \leq j \leq m-n-1$, such that for each j, x_j is coprime to all
> p_k with $k < i$ and $x_j > (n+j-1) \cdot p_i$. (Pritchard, 1979a)

We know of no proof of VC, and expect a proof would be quite complicated. Note that if VC is not valid, it is still possible that Wirth's program finds the expected prime numbers. A counter-example to VC demonstrates the incorrectness of the asserted program, which means that correct input/output behaviour of the program would essentially be fortuitous and undemonstrated.

3. THE DEVELOPMENT OF AN ALTERNATIVE PROGRAM

The purpose of the inner loop in our first solution/program is to check if x is equal to (at least) one of a number of values $m[i]$, which, when computed, satisfy

$$m[i] = \text{the least multiple of } p[i] \geq x. \qquad (2)$$

Now at an abstract level there is an obvious transformation applicable here, viz. to regard the primality test as a test for membership of x in the set $M = \{m[i] \mid 1 \leq i < \lim\}$. Furthermore, it is easy to specify the value of M for the next value of x - it is just

> $M - \{x\} \cup \{x + p[i] \mid m[i] = x\}$.

It is clear that this adjustment ensures that (2) is invariantly true.

The information in M is not sufficient to perform the adjustment; it is necessary to associate with each member m the set $I(m) = \{i \mid m[i] = m\}$. Given this information, the primality test and its dependent actions can be written abstractly as

> if $I(x) \neq \emptyset$ {i.e. $x \in M$}
>> then $\forall i \in I(x)$ do $I(x+p[i]) := I(x+p[i]) \cup \{i\}$
>> else begin $k := k+1$;
>>> $p[k] := x$
>> end

This algorithm ensures that the relation

> $I(x) = \{i \mid x = \text{the least multiple of } p_i \geq x\}$

holds invariantly before the test $x \in M$ (provided x is incremented by 1; alternatively, see the second remark in §5).

We now look for a suitable implementation of the above algorithm. We write $\Pi(y)$ for the number of primes not greater than y, and $\lfloor y \rfloor$ for the integer part of y. Since from (2)

$$M \subseteq \{m \mid x \leq m < x+p[\text{lim}-1]\},$$

and $\text{lim}-1 \leq \Pi(\sqrt{N})$, a circular array $C[0..\lfloor\sqrt{N}\rfloor]$ seems appropriate, since

$$|M| \leq p_{\Pi(\sqrt{N})} \leq \lfloor\sqrt{N}\rfloor.$$

Also, the elements of this array can be (pointers to) lists representing the sets $I(m)$. An index xp defines the current position of x, so that

$$I(m) \text{ is-represented-by } C[(xp + m - x) \bmod (1 + \lfloor\sqrt{N}\rfloor)]$$

is the appropriate invariant for the data structure. Figure 2 is a typical snapshot of this data structure. It is now easy to implement the abstract operations used above.

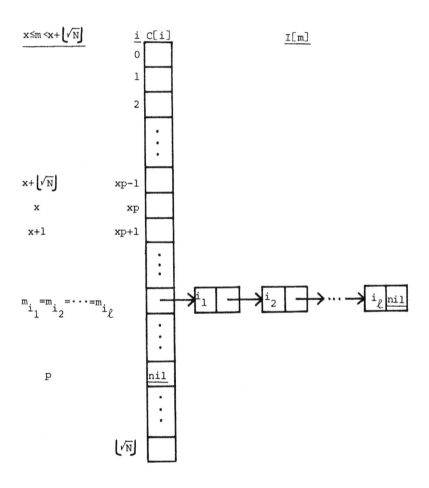

FIGURE 2: A SNAPSHOT OF THE DATA STRUCTURE FOR THE SET OF MULTIPLES

At this point the programmer would likely want to obtain a
feeling for the (absolute and relative) space and time efficiencies
of the two algorithms. We consider such analyses to be an important
part of the programmer's task. They are essential for comparing
alternative algorithms, and as a check on intuitions. The latter
use is well illustrated by McMaster (1978), whose analyses show that
a series of refinements performed by Dijkstra to speed up a certain
algorithm have almost no effect. Also, absolute analyses of
complexity can be a useful guide to the "distance" of an algorithm
from the best possible; i.e. as to whether it is worthwhile seeking
a more efficient algorithm.

Given the derivation of the current algorithm, a relative analysis
with respect to program 1 is not difficult, and indicates an increase
in time-efficiency. The operations used to mark composites (i.e. form
the sets I(m)) in the transformed program are done implicitly in the
original because $m[i]$ steps through the multiples of p_i. But extra
operations are incurred when $m[i]$ is tested without being incremented.
The results referred to in the next section substantiate this informal
argument. However it is apparent that space is wasted with nil pointers,
because at most $\Pi(\sqrt{x}) \leq \Pi(\sqrt{N}) = 0(\sqrt{N}/\log N)$ primes are "active". So it
is worth investigating whether the second algorithm can be transformed
to increase its storage efficiency (it needs $0(\sqrt{N} \log N)$ bits at present).

A fertile source of program transformations is the procedure of
abstracting away from inessential time-ordering of operations (this
is a strong motivating factor in the recent work of Dijkstra (1976)).
In the algorithm under consideration a case in point is the process of
adding i to $I(x+p[i])$ for all $i \in I(x)$ before considering further value(s)
of x. It seems a good idea to avoid numerous list operations by marking
$x+n \cdot p[i]$ as composite for $n=1,2,\ldots$, and only adding i to $I(x+n \cdot p[i])$
when $x+(n+1) \cdot p[i]$ falls outside C. This process can then be repeated
for the remaining values $i \in I(x)$. When all members of $I(x)$ have been
processed, successive values of x can be examined and accepted as primes
if unmarked, until the first value with $I(x)$ non-empty is found, and/or
lim needs to be increased to "activate" a new potential factor. The
processing of all $i \in I(x)$ is then repeated.

Given this new time-ordering of operations, it is not difficult to
see that the data structure of Figure 2 is no longer appropriate, because
only elements near the bottom of the (virtual) array are used for
(pointing to) lists of indices of active primes. Furthermore, if the
circularity of the array is removed, so that numbers x are processed in
successive intervals of length $\lfloor \sqrt{N} \rfloor$, the first multiple of $p[i]$ outside
the current interval can be stored in an array as $m[i]$. Then, when the
next interval is to be processed, the marking of all composites $m[i]+n \cdot p[i]$
can be done in any order of the indices i. Now each element of the array
C need only be a Boolean (one bit) which records whether or not the
corresponding value was marked as a composite. The program we have
arrived at is given in Figure 3.

```
const N = ?; rootN = ⌊√N⌋ ; pbound = ? ; mbound = ? ;
var p : array [1..pbound] of integer;
    m : array [2..mbound] of integer;
    C : array [1..rootN] of Boolean;
        i, x, k, lim, xp : integer;

procedure mark (var m: integer ; p : integer);
{N.B. m is changed}
{marks C[m + n·p] as composite for n=0, 1, ...
 and stores next multiple of p in m}
begin while m ≤ rootN do
        begin C[m] := true;
              m:= m+p
        end;
        m:= m-rootN
end;

begin {initialise}
        p[1] :=2; k:=1; lim:=1;
        x:=3 ; xp:=3;
        for i := 1 to rootN do C[i] := false;
        while x ≤ N do
        begin {process the interval x..x+rootN-1}
              i :=2;
              while i < lim do {mark multiples of pᵢ}
              begin mark (m[i], p[i]); i := i+1 end;
              while xp≤ rootN do
              begin if lim ≤ k
                      then if p[lim]² ≤ x
                              then {a new active prime}
                                  begin i:=lim;
                                        lim:=lim+1;
                                        if i ≠ 1
                                            then {mark the multiples}
                                            begin m[i]:=xp;
                                                  mark(m[i], p[i])
                                            end
                                  end;
                      if C[xp] {x∈M }
                      then C[xp] := false
                      else begin k:=k+1; p[k]:=x end;
                      xp := xp+2 ; x:=x+2
              end;
              xp := xp - rootN
        end
end.
```

FIGURE 3 : PROGRAM 2

The bounds on the arrays p and m can be determined when the time- and
space- complexities of programs 1 and 2 are calculated. Further
transformations can be done to obtain local increases in efficiency
in program 2, which is essentially the "segmented sieve of Eratosthenes"
of Bays and Hudson (1977). This seems to be the best practical

algorithm for very large values of N, although we have given
algorithms with lower bit complexities in Pritchard (1979b, 1979c).

4. COMPLEXITY ANALYSES

In order not to burden the reader with undue mathematical detail,
we simply state the results of our complexity analyses in the time
domain. These analyses can be found in Pritchard (1979a). The
space requirements of the two programs are much easier to calculate,
and we proceed to do so. It is only necessary to know that $\Pi(y) \sim y/\log y$.

Program 1 takes $O(N\sqrt{N}/\log^3 N)$ additions, and this estimate is
tight. As for storage, it requires $\Pi(\sqrt{N})$ multiples and $\Pi(\sqrt{N})$ primes
(the rest need be printed only). The multiples can each be stored
in $\log_2 N$ bits, and the primes each take $\frac{1}{2}\log_2 N$ bits since they are
not greater than $\sqrt{N}$. So the storage requirement is $\sim 3 \log_2 e\sqrt{N}$ bits.

Program 2 requires $O(N \log \log N)$ additions, which is much better
than the $O(N\sqrt{N}/\log^3 N)$ additions required by program 1. What is its
storage requirement? Well, 3 arrays are used: p, m and C. pbound = $\Pi(N)$,
but only the first $\Pi(\sqrt{N})$ primes need to be kept, requiring $\Pi(\sqrt{N}) \cdot \log_2 \sqrt{N}$
bits. mbound is also $\Pi(\sqrt{N})$, so another $\Pi(\sqrt{N}) \cdot \log_2 \sqrt{N}$ bits are needed
for m. Lastly, C takes $\lfloor \sqrt{N} \rfloor$ bits. Hence the total storage requirement
is $\sim (2\log_2 e + 1)\sqrt{N}$ bits, which is slightly smaller than that of program 1.
These figures unequivocally show the superior efficiency of the alternative program.

5. FINAL REMARKS

The importance of _refinement_ in the development of clear and
correct programs is indubitable. This recognition is due in large
part to the efforts of Dijkstra and Wirth. Our point in re-examining
their primes problem is to show the importance of program _transforma-
tions_ in the development of efficient programs; they add an extra
(lateral) dimension to the programming process.

Dijkstra (1972), in a postscript to his development of program 1,
notes that m[i] can in fact be increased by $2 \cdot p[i]$ because only odd
values of x are tested, and hence only odd multiples of p_i are needed.
This move carries over directly to the transformed algorithm - i is
added to the set I(x + 2·p[i]) instead of I(x + p[i]). No increase
in storage results because C need only contain odd values in the
interval $x \le m < x + 2 \cdot p[\text{lim}-1]$, and there are at most $\lfloor \sqrt{N} \rfloor$ of these.

Finally, we note that an attempt is made to formally capture and
certify the original (and fundamental) transformation of program 1
in Pritchard (1978), where two other examples of this high-level
transformation are also examined.

REFERENCES

BAYS, C., and HUDSON, R.H. (1977): "The Segmented Sieve of
    Eratosthenes and Primes in Arithmetic Progression to 10^{12}".
    B.I.T., Vol. 17, pp 121-127.

DIJKSTRA, E.W. (1972): "Notes on Structured Programming".
    In "Structured Programming", Academic Press, New York, pp. 1-82.

DIJKSTRA, E.W. (1976): "A Discipline of Programming".
    Prentice-Hall, Englewood Cliffs, New Jersey.

HARDY, G.H., and WRIGHT, E.M. (1965): "An Introduction to the
    Theory of Numbers". Fourth edition, O.U.P., London.

HOARE, C.A.R. (1972): "Notes on Data Structuring".
    In "Structured Programming", Academic Press, New York, pp.83-174.

MCMASTER, C.L. (1978): "An Analysis of Algorithms for the Dutch
    National Flag Problem". Comm. ACM, Vol. 21, No. 10, pp. 842-846.

PRITCHARD, P.A. (1978): "Program Design Via Multiple-Pass Algorithms".
    Typescript, Canberra, dated May 1978.

PRITCHARD, P.A. (1979a): "On the Prime Example of Programming".
    In "Variations on a Scheme of Eratosthenes", Tech. Report No. 8,
    Dept. of Computer Science, Univ. of Queensland, pp. 1-21.

PRITCHARD, P.A. (1979b): "On a Proposed Method of Generating Prime
    Numbers". In "Variations on a Scheme of Eratosthenes",
    Tech. Report No. 8, Dept. of Computer Science, Univ. of
    Queensland, pp. 22-28.

PRITCHARD, P.A. (1979c): "A Fast Linear Sieve for Finding Prime
    Numbers". In "Variations on a Scheme of Eratosthenes",
    Tech. Report. No. 8, Dept. of Computer Science, Univ. of
    Queensland, pp. 29-41.

WIRTH, N. (1973): Systematic Programming: An Introduction.
    Prentice-Hall, Englewood Cliffs, New Jersey.

PROCEEDINGS OF THE SYMPOSIUM ON
LANGUAGE DESIGN AND PROGRAMMING METHODOLOGY
SYDNEY, 10-11 SEPTEMBER, 1979

DESCRIBING THE COMPLETE EFFECTS OF PROGRAMS

Ria Follett

Department of Computer Science
University of New South Wales

ABSTRACT

It is important to consider the total effect of program in
order to produce correct software. If the effects of the
program are formally considered, it is usually done by
describing the invariants and predicate transformers of
program segments. Instead of using predicate transformers, a more powerful concept of a passback pair is introduced. Passback pairs allow the effects of a program to
be described to a level suitable for the problem at hand.
Methods of automatically deriving passback pairs of various degrees of refinement are discussed. These methods
are then applied in an automatic program synthesis system,
PROSYN.

1. INTRODUCTION

The complete effects of programs must be considered in any system which either uses the program or attempts to prove facts about
the program. The complete effects of a program can be characterized
by the way any relation (such as a relation on the values of variables) is altered by the execution of the program. Knowledge of the
effects of any given program segment is especially vital to any program verification system, and to any automatic programming system,
as 'intuition' cannot be used. These effects must be described formally, so they can be used mechanically, or derived automatically.
A method of describing the complete effects of a program is discussed here, together with methods of analysing programs to discover
these effects. This analysis may be done either automatically or
manually. These descriptions can then be used in program verification or program synthesis. An automatic program synthesis system
which uses these descriptions of the effects of a program, and analyses programs for their effects, is discussed.

2. PRECONDITIONS

Most program verifiers, (King 1969, and Deutsch 1973), and some
automatic program synthesis systems, (Waldinger 1975) use predicate
transformers to describe the effects of a program segment. The
predicate transformers calculate the preconditions of any given relation. The preconditions are those relations whose truth guarantees that a given relation is valid after the associated program
segment is executed. Thus to achieve (or verify) the relation R
after the program segment, it is sufficient to achieve (or verify)

its preconditions before the segment.

The precondition is calculated using a predicate transformer. The predicate transformer is usually given as a rule or function on the relation R. For example, for the program segment
    v:=a
the relation R is true after the segment if its precondition is true before the segment. The precondition is the relation obtained by substituting a for v in R.

The predicate transformer describes the effects of a program segment. If the precondition of R is the same as R, then the program does not affect R. If the relations are not identical, then the predicate transformer gives the complete effect of the segment on the relation R.

The main problem with this method is that it is extremely difficult to generate the predicate transformers of complicated program segments such as loops. The study of predicate transformers for loops is usually limited to finding invariants of the loop. An invariant is a relation whose precondition is identical to itself, thus unaltered by the predicate transformer. (Manna 1974, Dijkstra 1976)

However in order to synthesise programs automatically, it is not sufficient to find only the invariants of loops. The preconditions of the loop for other specific relations are required so that those relations may be achieved and verified. This means that predicate transformers of program segments must be obtained to a varying degree of generality.

In program synthesis, it is fortunately not usually necessary to find predicate transformers applicable to all relations. For example, it may be sufficient for the above assignment statement to consider only the predicate transformers for R where R does not contain v. The precondition will then be R itself. In other circumstances, the preconditions for other relations are required. To allow the predicate transformers to be generated at the appropriate level of generality for the relations to which it may be applied, the concept of predicate transformers is generalised to the passback pair.

3. THE PASSBACK PAIR

A passback pair is an ordered pair (D,f) of a predicate D, and a function f, on an arbitrary relation R. It is a description of the effects of a particular program segment p on a relation R. The second element of the ordered pair, f, denotes the function which calculates the precondition of R. The first element, D, is the domain of relations on which f is defined. If D(R) is satisfiable, then f can modify R, thus giving the precondition of R. If D(R) is not satisfiable, then the precondition of R cannot be calculated using f. There is a range of passback pairs valid for any program segment. The passback pair (FALSE,I) is valid for all program segments, where I is the identity function, meaning that no relation will be passed back over this segment to produce a precondition.

Two possible passback pairs for the assignment statement v:=a are

(v is not contained in R , I)

and (TRUE , substitute a for v in R).

The first means that only relations R, where R does not contain the variable 'v', may be passed back. These relations will be passed back unaffected by the assignment statement.

The second means that all relations R may be passed back by replacing all the occurrences of 'v' in R by 'a'.

The process of obtaining a more precise passback pair is called refining the passback pair. Refining the passback pair implies enlarging the domain, with a corresponding modification to f. It is the refining process which gives the passback pair more power than the usual concept of predicate transformers. For many, especially complex, program segments, it is difficult to obtain a complete predicate transformer. For these segments, a passback pair with a limited domain may be easily derived. If this description is sufficient for the problem at hand, no further work need be done. However, if the description is not sufficiently precise, the passback pair may be refined (either by an automatic system, or manually) to increase the size of the domain. The amount of work thus required for program verification (or synthesis) is reduced without affecting the validity of the resulting program.

4. DERIVING PASSBACK PAIRS

The passback pairs for primitive program segments (called PRIMITIVES) must be supplied initially by the user. The primitives required depend on the particular programming domain, but may be limited, say, to the assignment statement. The passback pair for any other program segment can be derived only by combining the passback pairs of basic program segments. This can often be done automatically.

The control structures which will be analysed consist of straight line programs, the branch statement (IF - THEN - ELSE) and the insertion of recursive procedure calls. The automatic programming system discussed in Section 5 is also limited to these constructs. The programs are then analysed in stages. First, a passback pair is found for the program segment. If it is sufficient for the current purpose, then it is used. Otherwise the passback pair is refined to produce a more accurate description.

In the following examples, the two program segments P1 and P2 are described by the passback pairs (D1,f1) and (D2,f2) respectively. These program segments may be primitives, or segments which have already been analysed.

4.1 Combining Straight Line Programs

The program segment formed by processing the first primitive before the second, denoted by P1;P2 may be described by the passback pair (D2 ∧ D1.f2, f1.f2). The passback pair description means that, for a goal R to be passed back using the function f1.f2, it must be possible to satisfy both D2(R) and D1.f2(R) simultaneously.

4.2 Branches

Branches are in the form IF A THEN P1 ELSE P2. The following description assumes that the test A has no side effect and can be computed as often as desired. The passback pair for the branch may be described as

$\quad$ (D1 ∧ D2 ∧ (f1(R) ≡f2(R)) , f1(R))

or$\quad$(D1 ∧ D2, f1(R) ∧ f2(R))

or$\quad$(D1 ∧ D2, IF A THEN f1(R) ELSE f2(R)).

The first passback pair is obtained by allowing only the relations which satisfy both D1 and D2, and are altered in an identical manner along both branches, to be passed back over the branch.

The second passback pair is a refined version of the first and is obtained by passing the relation back over both paths. The program needs to achieve both f1(R) and f2(R), to ensure that the relation R is true after the branch.

However, the relation f1(R) is required only if A is true, and otherwise f2(R) is required. This means that the second passback function may be simplified, giving the complete passback function of
$\quad$ IF A THEN f1(R) ELSE f2(R).
Note that the value of A cannot be used in the domain on which the passback function is defined as A may have been modified by P1 or P2. Thus (A ∧ D1) OR (~A ∧ D2) is not a valid domain.

For _example_ - consider a program segment that sorts two numbers x and y. The program segment generated may be
$\quad$ IF x≤y THEN NIL
$\qquad\qquad$ ELSE BEGIN temp := x;
$\qquad\qquad\qquad\qquad$ x:=y;
$\qquad\qquad\qquad\qquad$ y:=temp
$\qquad\qquad$ END

Let this new subprogram be called SORT2(x,y). As the test x≤y has no side effect the above discussion applies. A possible passback pair is (temp ∉ R ∧ x ∉ R ∧ y ∉ R , I), where ∉ denotes "is not contained in". This passback pair is derived from using the passback pair of "v:=exp" as (v ∉ R,I). This passback pair allows only relations in which neither temp nor x nor y occurs, to be passed back. Although valid, it is unnecessarily restrictive in its domain. It does not allow relations such as x<z AND y<z to be passed back even though this relation is in fact unaltered by SORT2(x,y).

If a refined version of the passback pair for "v:=exp" such as (TRUE,substitute exp for v in R) is used, then the else branch can

be described (using Section 4.1 for combining straight line programs) as (TRUE, R''')
 where R''' is obtained by substituting x for temp in R''
 and R'' by substituting y for x in R'
 and R' by substituting temp for y in R.

The passback pair for the THEN section is (TRUE,I). These may
be combined giving
 (R'''≡R , I).

This passback pair means that whenever x and y can be interchanged in the relation without altering the relation, the relation
can be passed back unaffected. If this description is not sufficient for the problem at hand, the passback pair may be further refined giving the passback pair
 (TRUE , IF x⩽y THEN R ELSE R''')
where R''' is defined as above.

4.3 Recursive Procedures

Recursive procedures cannot easily be analysed for the associated predicate transformer. This is because the number of procedure
calls is usually unknown a priori. It is here that the passback
pair simplifies the description. For any recursive procedure a
non-trivial passback pair can be obtained in the following manner.

Firstly, consider the procedure obtained by deleting all the
recursive procedure calls from the procedure. A passback pair can
be constructed for this procedure with an identity passback function. For example, the passback pair could have as its domain the
relations which do not contain any variables that may be set by the
procedure. This passback pair can then be generalised over all the
recursive procedure calls, to give a valid passback pair for the recursive procedure.

For example, consider the procedure MAX, which places the maximum element of an array in the zeroth element of that array:
 MAX <= IF n<1 THEN NIL
                 ELSE BEGIN SORT2(x(0),x(n));
                            MAX(n-1)
                      END

A passback pair for the procedure obtained by deleting the recursive procedure call, MAX(n-1), is
        (x(0) ∉ R ∧ x(n) ∉ R , I).

Generalised over the recursive procedure calls, a passback pair
for MAX(n) is
        (FORALL i=0,n x(i) ∉ R , I).

4.4 Refining the Passback Pair

The passback pair defined above corresponds to a loop invariant. It is clearly not the most precise passback pair. In many
cases this passback pair suffices in program synthesis or verification but there are a number of refinements that may be applied.

4.4.1 The Domain of the Passback Pair may be Widened by Using Invariants

A loop invariant is a relation among the program variables which is unaltered, at a given point in the loop, by executing the loop. A relation which is an invariant both at the start and end of the loop may enlarge the domain of a passback pair.

Given any such invariant N, it is possible to refine the passback pair (D,I) to (D ∨ N,I) which increases the size of the domain over which f is defined. Some methods of automatically generating invariants are given by Elspas(1974), Wegbreit (1974) and Katz and Manna(1976).

4.4.2 Passback Functions may be Derived

The above discussion leads to passback pairs for recursive procedures of the form (D,I) where I is the identity function. Invariants can be used to increase the size of the domain D, but still lead to an identity passback function. However, it is usually possible to derive a passback function where the segments also have a non-identity passback function. From Section 4.1 it is possible to combine passback functions as
$$f1.f2.f3. \ldots .fn$$

The problem is to find a general function (possibly in terms of commutative operators FORALL and EXISTS) describing this sequence.

In the previous example, MAX, a possible passback pair for SORT2(x,y) is
(TRUE , R AND (R with y and x interchanged)).

For the case where i=n=1, the relation R may be passed back over MAX resulting in the relation R1, where R1 is
R1 : R AND (R with x(1) x(0) interchanged).

This means that the relation R1 must be achieved before SORT2(x(0),x(1)) in order to achieve R after the SORT2 procedure call.

For the case n=2 the relation which needs to be achieved is
R2 : R1 AND (R1 with x(2) x(0) interchanged).

This may be generalised as
R AND FORALL k≤n FORALL j ≤k (R with x(k) x(j) interchanged).
The passback pair for the loop then becomes
(TRUE , R AND FORALL k≤n FORALL j≤k (R with x(k) x(j)
            interchanged)).
Stated plainly, this means that R is valid after MAX(n) if all relations obtained by the various permutations of interchanging x(k) and x(j) are valid before MAX(n).

5. USING PASSBACK PAIRS IN PROGRAM SYNTHESIS

The concept of passback pairs has been applied to program synthesis. The implementation, called PROSYN, takes a list of goals and achieves these in turn. Goals may be passed back through previously achieved program segments as appropriate. This effectively reorders the initial list of goals. Once achieved, goals are protected. Passback pairs are also used to ensure that the insertion of program steps does not interfere with protected goals. Recursive procedures may be synthesised, and passback pairs are derived and refined where appropriate.

The passback pairs have been very useful in program synthesis, as they ensure that the program produced is valid. As the synthesiser automatically derives the passback pairs from simple primitives, a simple passback pair can be derived and used as required. Usually quite simple passback pairs resulted in quite complex programs. This meant that only a simple analysis of the program segments was required to produce valid programs. Some automatic refining methods were used if the simple analysis failed.

This approach has succeeded in synthesising a wide variety of programs. Various domains such as BLOCKS, LISTS and numerous NUMBER domains have been used. In the NUMBER domain (augmented to include arrays) the programs synthesised include
- SORT2
- MAX
- SUM of an array
- solving two simultaneous equations
- REMAINDER from dividing two numbers
- moving elements up and down arrays
- sorting arrays
- adding, multiplying and transposing matrices
- inverting matrices
- finding eigenvectors of matrices
- finding the zeros of a function
- solving a set of linear simultaneous equations.

Note that, in all the above cases, a program to achieve the result was obtained.

6. EXAMPLE

As a simple example to illustrate the use of passback pairs in automatic program synthesis, consider the problem of shifting elements down an array. In this example, unless the elements are shifted in the correct sequence, the side effects of the program will alter the values of the array itself. The problem may be expressed by the goal
FORALL i=2,n v(i-1)=s(i)
where v is the array and s is the initial value of that array.

This example is one of many synthesised by the automatic program synthesiser PROSYN. Both the synthesis of the program and the analysis of the relevant effects occur automatically. The following is an informal description of the steps which took place in the synthesis.

PROSYN may have the array v predefined with the initial values s, or this may be supplied by the user. The user then requests PROSYN to synthesise a program to achieve the goal. The goal is currently specified in prefix notation, being
(NEWGOAL "(FORALL (i 2 n) (EQUAL (v (i-1)) (s i)))).

PROSYN then synthesises the subroutine to do this, together with the main program calling this subroutine. A complete description of the subroutine is also produced, allowing that subroutine to be used in other contexts. For ease of understanding, the general subroutine name generated by PROSYN for the subroutine has been altered to "SHIFT".

Given this goal, PROSYN attempts induction, as FORALL is defined in the current domain to operate on a set of values, in this case with i ranging from 2 to n. The problem is split into two subproblems,
v(n-1)=s(n) AND FORALL i=2,n-1 v(i-1)=s(i).

The problem can be split into these two subproblems only if n>2. This condition must first be synthesised, giving the program segment with the set of values (2,n) generalised to (m,n) as :
SHIFT(m,n) <- IF n<m THEN NIL
                    ELSE ...

PROSYN then attempts the split goals in turn. The first goal v(n-1)=s(n) can be achieved using the assignment primitive
VAR:=EXP.
As s(n) is a value instead of a variable, PROSYN must find a variable with that value. As no variable has yet been altered, it finds that initially s(n)=v(n). This results in the primitive
v(n-1):=v(n).

As no other goal has yet been achieved the primitive can be simply inserted without interfering with any goal, giving the program segment:
SHIFT(m,n) <- IF n<m THEN NIL
                    ELSE 0 BEGIN
                         50 v(n-1):=v(n)
                        100 END.

The relations that have been developed, either to achieve the goal, or used in achieving the goal are then protected. These are
s(n)=v(n)   is protected from step 0 to step 50
v(n-1)=s(n) is protected from step 50 to step 100.

The goal remaining to be accomplished at step 100 is
FORALL i=m,n-1 v(i-1)=s(i).

This is an instance of the original goal, so a recursive call is attempted. Firstly termination is established. Then the effect of the function is calculated in the form of a passback pair. Using the methods in Section 4.3 a passback pair of SHIFT(m,n-1) is calculated to be (FORALL i=m-1,n-2 v(i) ∉ R , I).

As this does not interfere with the protected relation v(n-1)=s(n), it may be inserted. However the precondition of the function SHIFT(m,n-1) is calculated to be
FORALL i=m,n-1 v(i)=s(i).
This precondition cannot be achieved as v(n-1)=s(n) is protected. This causes the insertion of the recursive function call to fail.

The failure resulted from the order in which the goals were attempted. Induction was first attempted on n rather than on m. If induction on m were attempted first the procedure would have resulted in success. This ordering was chosen on purpose to illustrate the use of passback pairs in the program synthesis.

PROSYN then attempts to pass back the goal
FORALL i=m,n-1 v(i-1)=s(i)
over the program step v(n-1):=v(n). The goal may be passed over this by replacing v(n-1) by v(n) in that goal, but as v(n-1) is not in the goal, the goal will be passed back unaffected. This results in the goal to be achieved before 50 as
FORALL i=m,n-1 v(i-1)=s(i).

Once again a recursive function call may be inserted. The preconditions are true by the initial conditions, so the resulting program is:
```
SHIFT(m,n) <- IF n<m THEN NIL
                 ELSE   0 BEGIN
                       25 SHIFT(m,n-1)
                       50 v(n-1):=v(n)
                      100 END
```

with the protected goals:-

FORALL i=m,n-1 v(i)=s(i)	from 0 to 25
FORALL i=m,n-1 v(i-1)=s(i)	from 25 to 100
v(n)=s(n)	from 0 to 50
v(n-1)=s(n)	from 50 to 100.

The initial program written simply consists of a subroutine call SHIFT(2,n).

The description of the function generated was

name:	SHIFT(m,n)
goal:	FORALL i=m,n v(i-1)=s(i)
precondition:	FORALL i=m,n v(i)=s(i)
passback pair:	(FORALL i=m-1,n-1 v(i) ∉ R , I).

The above subroutine was synthesised with only a simple description of the passback pair relating to that function. Most subroutines that were synthesised required only a simple description such as the one derived here. In some cases, the simple description was not adequate. Only these cases need a more completed analysis of the overall effects, thus saving in effort for the other cases. However, any passback pair derived is sufficient to verify the completed program.

7. CONCLUSION

Using the passback pair has given more flexibility in the description of programs than the use of simple predicate transformers. The correctness of a program in the sense that a particular goal is achieved can be proved using passback pairs without the need to discover the details of all the possible effects. This has been particularly useful in automatic program synthesis, where only the effects of a program on given relations need to be derived, and where complicated recursive procedures then need to be analysed, if possible automatically. For recursive procedures predicate transformers cannot be easily derived. The process of refining a passback pair means that valid programs can be synthesised with a minimum of analysis for the complete effects of the program. Further analysis of its effects occurs only if this is required for the problem currently being attempted. This has resulted in the automatic synthesis and analysis of a wide variety of programs.

The problem of deriving predicate transformers, considered in the context of refining passback pairs, is still very difficult. Some strategies for refining passback pairs exist, but there is no general algorithm for arbitrarily complicated programs, in the same way that there is no general algorithm for discovering invariants and predicate transformers. However, the generalisation of predicate transformers to passback pairs means that complete analysis is not usually required to synthesise the required program.

REFERENCES

Deutsch L.P. (1973) 'An Interactive Program Verifier', PhD Thesis, Dept of Computer Sci., University of California, Berkeley.
Dijkstra E.W. (1976) 'A Discipline of Programming', Prentice-Hall, NJ.
Elspas B. (1974) 'The Semiautomatic Generation of Inductive Assertions for Proving Program Correctness', Research Rep, Stanford Research Institute, Menlo Park, Calif.
Katz S. and Manna Z. (1976) 'Logical Analysis of Programs', Comm ACM Vol 19 No 4.
King J. (1969) 'A Program Verifier', PhD Thesis, Dept of Computer Science, Carnegie-Mellon Uni., Pittsburgh, Pa.
Manna Z. (1974) 'Mathematical Theory of Computation', McGraw-Hill Book Co.
Waldinger R. (1975) 'Achieving Several Goals Simultaneously', Stanford Research Institute A.I.Center Technical Note 107.
Wegbreit B (1974) 'The Synthesis of Loop Predicates', Comm ACM 17,2 p102-112.

PROCEEDINGS OF THE SYMPOSIUM ON
LANGUAGE DESIGN AND PROGRAMMING METHODOLOGY
SYDNEY, 10-11 SEPTEMBER, 1979

PATTERN-MATCHING COMMANDS

Jan B. Hext

Basser Department of Computer Science
University of Sydney

ABSTRACT

The paper investigates the following question: what happens
if we try to embed the pattern-matching facilities of Snobol4
in a more conventional language? It shows that the facilities
can be improved in some significant ways. However, the control structures that underlie pattern-matching operations are
radically different from the usual ones, and this creates difficulties if the full power of the Snobol4 system is to be
retained.

1.   SNOBOL4

Snobol4 is well known as a significant and useful programming language and is widely taught for its ability to handle non-numeric computations (Griswold et al., 1971). Indeed, for some applications it makes
most other languages appear crude and primitive. At the same time, it
must be admitted that Snobol4 itself is open to criticism in some respects. For example, its notation is rather obscure, its control facilities are very limited, and its data structures have certain unorthodox
aspects which constitute a definite health hazard. It is therefore reasonable to ask whether the best features of the language might be transferred to some other environment, where they could shine to better advantage. Our purpose in this paper is to investigate the factors which
would be involved in such an enterprise. Some of the proposals have
been implemented using BCPL as the host language; but any other general-
purpose language could be considered for the purpose.

Although Snobol4 has many facilities, our only concern will be with
its most distinctive and interesting feature, namely the pattern-
matching statement. This has the form

$$< label> \quad < subject> \quad <pattern> \quad = \quad <object> \quad : \quad <goto>$$

Its effect is to scan the string $<subject>$ for an occurrence of the
$<pattern>$ and, if the search is successful, to replace the matching
substring by the string $<object>$. The $<goto>$ part consists of one or
two clauses of the form ($<label>$), S($<label>$) or F($<label>$). These
cause transfer of control to the specified labels, the last two being
conditional on the success or failure of the scan. For example, the
statement

$$L1 \quad TEXT \; 'GREAT' \quad = \quad 'BIG' \quad : \quad S(DONE)$$

will scan the value of $TEXT$ for the first occurrence (if any) of the
string $'GREAT'$ and will replace it by the string $'BIG'$. If successful,

it transfers control to the statement labelled *DONE;* otherwise it continues to the next statement.

The power of this facility lies in the great range of patterns which the programmer can specify and in the fact that various other operations can be executed during the pattern-matching process. The following are some simple examples of the available patterns:

NULL	:	the null string
LEN(5)	:	any string of length 5
ANY('ABC')	:	any one of the letters A, B, C
SPAN('ABC')	:	any sequence of the letters A, B, C (such as *CAB,* or *ABBA,* or *CCCCC).*

Strings and other basic patterns may be combined into pattern structures by means of *alternation* and *catenation.* Snobol4 denotes the former by '|' and the latter by actual concatenation (as in BNF). However, we shall use a more explicit notation:

P1 alt P2	:	any string that matches either *P1* or *P2*
P1 cat P2	:	any string that consists of a substring that matches *P1* followed by a substring that matches *P2.*

These are familiar as the first two operations of regular expressions. The third operation, namely repetition, is provided by the pattern *ARBNO(P),* which matches nought, one or more occurrences of the pattern *P.* There are obvious counterparts in the basic control structures of programs, namely *if*-statements, sequencing and loops. However, as we shall see later, the analogy needs to be treated with caution.

There are two facilities for executing operations during the pattern-matching process. The first of these is *value assignment,* which allows a matching substring to be assigned to a variable. In the simplest case, a variable *V* can be associated with a pattern *P* in such a way that, whenever a search for *P* is successful, the matching substring is immediately assigned to *V.* This applies even when *P* is part of a larger pattern and even if *P* is matched several times during the complete operation.

The second facility is the use of "pseudo-patterns". These may be defined as patterns whose primary role is not to match particular strings but to produce specific side-effects. For example, the expression @*X* is defined to be a pattern structure that matches the null string; but its real purpose is to assign to the variable *X* the position of the cursor (the pointer that is used for the scanning operation). For example, if *TEXT* has the value *'THE GREAT AUSTRALIAN BYTE',* the statement

> *TEXT   'GREAT'   @X*

matches *'GREAT'* followed by the null string. As a side-effect, it assigns *X* the value *9,* indicating the position that was reached after *'GREAT'.*

The programmer can define his own functions and have them called as pseudo-patterns in a similar way. This enables him to execute arbitrary operations during the pattern-matching process. The use of pseudo-patterns is rather artificial, but the underlying facility adds greatly to the power of the language.

2.   A SCAN COMMAND

If we embed the above pattern-matching command in some other language, we may prefer to make it more explicit:

<string variable> _match_ <pattern> := <string expression>

The _match_ operator may be understood as designating a substring of the variable; the substring (if found) is replaced by the value of the <string expression>. A flag may be set to indicate whether or not the matching was successful.

This transliteration is an obvious starting point. Unfortunately, though, it preserves one of the main deficiencies of the Snobol4 system. The trouble is that it does not allow for more than one _match_ operation to be executed during a single scan of the string. To illustrate the resulting drawbacks, we may extend the GREAT-BIG substitution problem so that it requires _every_ occurrence of 'GREAT' to be replaced by 'BIG'. The technique commonly used in the textbooks is to use the following loop:

LOOP   TEXT 'GREAT' = 'BIG'   :   S(LOOP)

This certainly solves the problem. However, for each substitution that it makes, it requires (a) that the string be reconstructed and (b) that the next scan start afresh from the first character. If TEXT is more than a few lines long, this is clearly very inefficient. There are ways of speeding it up - e.g., by using the '@' operator to record the current position - but none can be regarded as satisfactory.

To avoid this inefficiency, we can take a cue from conventional text editors. They operate on an input string S1 and produce an output string S2, carrying out an arbitrary sequence of operations within a single scan. This suggests that the previous command be rewritten in the following form:

S2   :=   _scan_ S1 _do_ <statement sequence>

Within the <statement sequence> we provide the ability to search for patterns starting from the current position of the scan. The GREAT-BIG substitution problem can then be programmed as follows:

```
text  :=  scan text do
              repeat
                  match 'great' := 'big'
              until endstring;
```

The condition _endstring_ is automatically set to _true_ when the scanner reaches the end of the string. The resulting statement expresses what we want to do in an elegant and efficient way.

Within the _scan_ command we could include many other special operations. For example, we could copy characters, skip characters, insert characters, and so on. Text editors provide a wealth of facilities which deserve consideration in this regard. However, the precise details would doubtless be a matter of some controversy and it is not our intention to discuss them here. Besides these special operations, though, the body of the scan may include all the ordinary statements of the language. Thus assignments, procedure calls, etc. may be interspersed with pattern-matching commands in an arbitrary fashion.

3.   PATTERNS WHICH ACTIVATE COMMANDS

If we implement the above proposal, one of the deficiencies of Snobol4 will immediately disappear - namely, its inability to do several *match* operations in a single scan. On the face of it, we might expect another problem to disappear also - namely, the need for pseudo-patterns. The point is that we can insert ordinary statements between pattern-matching commands; so why bother to insert them into the patterns themselves? All we need do is convert a pattern of the form *P1 alt P2* into the two branches of an *if*-statement and a pattern of the form *P1 cat P2* into two sequential statements; then, surely, we can insert side-effects quite freely.

Unfortunately, the conclusion does not follow quite so easily. The *alt* and *cat* operators cannot be equated with conventional control mechanisms in such a simple manner. The trouble is that a pattern such as

   (P1 alt P2) cat P3

has the following implication. If we succeed in matching *P1* but then fail to match *P3*, we must go back and try *P2* instead. In fact, if there are alternatives within *P1*, we must try them also. This means that a pattern has the nature of a semi-coroutine: after matching it successfully, we must be able to resume it later in order to look for alternatives. In general, therefore, a pattern-matching statement cannot be transformed into a more primitive sequence of statements except by introducing some rather elaborate apparatus. As a result, it would be more convenient if some other method were provided for including arbitrary statements within the pattern-matching process.

From the above observations, we may conclude that the natural thing to do is to allow statements to be specified *within the pattern itself*. As we have seen, Snobol4 provides two facilities for this, namely value assignments and pattern functions. Both of these have a rather *ad hoc* flavour. As an alternative, we might therefore consider the possibility of allowing an arbitrary statement to be attached to a pattern or subpattern. Taking the notation from Snobol's *<goto>* field, we can express the idea by means of the following pattern extensions:

   <pattern>   :   *(<statement sequence>)*
   <pattern>   :   *S (<statement sequence>)*
   <pattern>   :   *F (<statement sequence>)*

The first executes the *<statement sequence>* whenever a match against the *<pattern>* is attempted. The other two execute it conditionally, depending on whether the match succeeds or fails.

As an example, let us consider the problem of counting the number
of vowels and consonants in the string *text*. Using the above facility,
we can proceed as follows:

```
vowel       :=  any ('aeiou');
consonant   :=  any ('bcdfghjklmnpqrstvwxyz');
vcount      :=  0;
ccount      :=  0;
scan text do
    repeat
        match vowel : S(vcount  :=  vcount + 1)
          alt consonant : S(ccount  :=  ccount + 1)
    until endstring;
```

This is much neater than matching *vowel alt consonant* and then having
to determine which of the two (if either) was successful. The facility
also provides a natural context for doing value assignment. We could
introduce a quantity *pat* (say) that represents the matching substring;
it can then be assigned to a variable using an ordinary assignment
statement.

4. PATTERN-MATCHING PROCEDURES

If we adopt the above policy, it is clear that patterns can no
longer be regarded simply as templates for matching strings. Instead,
they have developed into a special sort of procedure. The procedure
is characterized by a control structure which is based on the *alt* and
cat operators and which executes related statements according to the
progress of the scan. Snobol4 recognizes the special nature of this
control structure by introducing four pseudo-patterns which can further
alter its course - namely, *ABORT, FENCE, SUCCEED* and *FAIL*. We might
therefore incorporate these as special directives within our new facility. They would have a status similar to the *exit, loop* and *return*
commands which are sometimes found in ordinary programming languages.

In order to regulate the use of such facilities, there are advantages in introducing explicit *pattern procedures*. Their declaration
might take a form similar to that of other procedures:

pattern P (<parameter list>) ; ...

The use of the special control facilities could then be restricted to
this context. Instances of P could be generated in the context of the
match command or as procedure parameters. Like other functions and procedures, though, they would not normally be assignable to variables.

As in Snobol4, the use of pattern procedures enables patterns to
be defined recursively. This has the attraction that it opens up the
whole area of syntax analysis, with each category of the syntax being
represented by a separate pattern procedure. The prospect is appealing. However, it should be noted that the pattern-matching algorithm
could prove rather slow for the purpose and it would run into difficulties with left-recursive categories.

5.   CONCLUSION

The above proposals embody two basic principles for the inclusion
of pattern-matching commands within the framework of a general-purpose
language. They show that the provision of a useful string-processing
facility is not simply a matter of adding a few operators. Indeed, the
difficulty of the enterprise may explain why conventional languages
pay such scant attention to this area of need.

It will be appreciated, of course, that neither of the two principles is at all original. As already remarked, the sequential scanning operation is familiar enough in text editing and it has an earlier
ancestry in the updating of sequential files. The concept of associating statements with patterns goes back to the first syntax-directed
compilers (Irons, 1961). More recently, it has appeared in AI languages
such as QLisp, Planner and Conniver, where it is known as "the pattern-
directed invocation of commands" (McDermott and Sussman, 1972).

As far as the implementation is concerned, it will be clear that
strings must be given the type *sequence of char* rather than *array of
char*. A recent report by A.H.J. Sale (1978) argues the case for doing
this in the context of Pascal and makes specific recommendations for the
necessary language changes.

Space precludes a presentation of the basic algorithm for implementing the pattern-matching command - that is, for matching a string
against a pattern with *alt* and *cat* operators. Since no easy-to-follow
description appears to have been published in the literature, the author
has prepared an elaboration of the outline given by Harrison (1973) and
would be happy to supply copies of it on request. Griswold (1977)
discusses language facilities for implementing such algorithms at a
higher level.

REFERENCES

Griswold, R.E. (1977) : "Language facilities for programmable backtrack-
    ing", Proceedings of the Symposium on Artificial Intelligence and
    Programming Languages, SIGPLAN Notices, Vol.12, No.8, and SIGART
    Newsletter, No.64.

Griswold, R.E., Poage, J.F. and Polonsky, I.P. (1971) : *The Snobol4 Pro-
    gramming Language,* 2nd edition, Prentice-Hall, Englewood Cliffs, NJ.

Harrison, M.C. (1973) : *Data Structures and Programming,* Scott Foresman
    and Co., Glenview, Illinois.

Irons, E.T. (1961) : "A syntax directed compiler for Algol 60", Comm.ACM,
    Vol.4, pp.51-55.

McDermott, D.V. and Sussman, G.J. (1972) : "From Planner to Conniver - a
    genetic approach", Proc. FJCC, 1171-1179.

Sale, A.H.J. (1978) : "Strings and the sequence abstraction in Pascal",
    Report R78-4, Department of Information Science, University of
    Tasmania.

PROCEEDINGS OF THE SYMPOSIUM ON
LANGUAGE DESIGN AND PROGRAMMING METHODOLOGY
SYDNEY, 10-11 SEPTEMBER, 1979

A LANGUAGE FOR DESCRIBING CONCEPTS AS PROGRAMS

Claude Sammut and Brian Cohen

Department of Computer Science
University of New South Wales

ABSTRACT

A learning program produces, as its output, a boolean function which describes a concept. The function returns true if and only if the argument is an object which satisfies the logical expression in the body of the function. The learning program's input is a set of objects which are instances of the concept to be learnt. A compiler/interpreter has been written which performs the reverse of the learning process. The concept description is regarded as a program which defines the set of objects which satisfy the given conditions. The interpreter takes as its input, a predicate and produces as its output, an object which belongs to the set.

1. INTRODUCTION

In the field of pattern recognition, there has been increasing interest in structural description languages. These are formal languages which are used to describe objects and the concepts (or patterns) to which they belong. Of further interest is the ability of programs to learn the description of concepts in terms of such description languages.

This paper describes such a language currently under development. The compiler which exists is intended to be used in conjunction with a learning algorithm similar to that developed by Cohen (1978). Although intended primarily for use by another program, the language illustrates many features included in new languages for Artificial Intelligence. We will discuss these features, comparing them, in particular, with similar features in QLISP (Rulifson et al, 1972) and PROLOG (Kowalski, 1974).

The syntax of the language is quite simple, being a form of predicate logic. An object description is passed as a parameter to a predicate function. If the conditional expressions which make up the body of the function are satisfied then the object is said to be recognized by the concept that the predicate represents.

For example, if we represent a binary number as a string of 1's and 0's (with no leading 0) then we define "number" as follows:

```
define number =
  [x: x.head = nil & x.tail = 1 | number(x.head) & digit(x.tail)]
```

where "x" is the object passed to the function, and digit is the concept:

$$[x:\ x = 0\ |\ x = 1]$$

The recognition of a number is equivalent to parsing the string left to right. It is a recursive concept with the termination condition given in the first disjunct. Although recursive functions are not new to programming languages, few concept description languages include this important feature.

Concept descriptions are closed sentences. That is, the only variables known to a function are those passed as parameters. An object is described in terms of its properties. A physical object, say, may have properties such as size, shape, colour, etc. The description of such an object would consist of a set of property/value pairs, for example:

box : <shape: cube; colour: red; size: big>

The number 2 may be described as:

<head: one; tail: 0>

where one is:

<head: nil; tail: 1>

Values may be atomic (e.g. 1 and "nil") or structured (e.g. one).

2. QUANTIFIED VARIABLES

A learning program, such as Cohen's CONFUCIUS, takes as its input a number of objects as instances of a concept which is to be learnt. From these examples, a concept description is formed. That is, the output of the process is a predicate which is true if and only if the argument is an object which satisfies the logical expression.

The description of complex concepts may require a language with more expressive power than simple expressions joined by "and" or "or" operations. For example, the existential quantifier may be used in the description of the concept of "maximum number in a list":

```
define maximum =
[list, max:
    list.tail = nil & max = list.head                (1)
    | [E x: maximum(list.tail, x) &                  (2)
        (
            lt(list.head, x) & max = x               (3)
            | le(x, list.head) & max = list.head     (4)
        )
    ]
]
```

("list" and "max" are the two arguments to "maximum". "lt" is the relation "less than" and "le" is "less than or equal").

However, the introduction of quantifiers raises many propblems in the evaluation of an expression. How do we test a statement which claims the existence of an object? It would be impossible to search for such an object since the set of all possible objects may not be specified and may not even be finite. This leads us to ask, is it possible to construct an object which will satisfy the given conditions? Thus, the task of our language is to take as input a predicate and attempt to produce, as output, an instance of the concept. This is the reverse of the learning process.

Let us consider briefly how we might find the maximum number in a list. The following statement may be used:

$$[E\ x:\ maximum(L,\ x)]$$

For this example, let us assume L = (1 5 3 2 4). The value of "L" is passed to "maximum"; a special "quantified variable" is created to represent x.

Initially, the tail of the list is not nil, therefore line (1) in the definition above is false, causing the second part of the disjunction to be evaluated. Now a new quantified variable is created in order to represent the maximum of the tail. On line (2) "maximum" is called recursively until list.tail = nil. At this point we test max = list.head. "max" is a quantified variable which has no value, yet. When an equality test involves an undefined quantified variable, the operation becomes an assignment rather than a boolean expression. Thus max is temporarily assigned the value of list.head, which happens to be 4.

The call, "maximum((4), 4)" now returns. Since x = list.head, line (3) fails, but line(4) is true. The function exits. The overall effect is that 4 is passed back as the maximum of the tail until the recursion returns to the level where list = (5 3 2 4). Whereas, in previous activations max = x was executed, now max = list.head is executed (i.e. the maximum is changed to 5). In fact this will be the final result.

3.   BACKTRACKING

So far, we have quite a straightforward evaluation process. However, there is no guarantee that the learning program will construct the concept with the statements in the order written down above. Suppose the body of maximum is:

```
list.tail = nil & max = list.head
| [E x:
        ( lt(list.head, x) & max = x
        | le(x, list.head) & max = list.head
        )
        & maximum(list.tail, x)
  ]
```

The expression "lt(list.head, x)" is encountered before the call to maximum so the system would attempt to construct an "x" greater than list.head. Since the first element is 1, the number 2 might be constructed, then maximum is called again. In this call, the system would be required to construct an "x" greater than 5. However, no such construction would be successful since the number constructed must belong to the list but there is no number greater than 5 in the list. In the disjunction, the second disjunct should have been chosen rather than the first.

These considerations require the implemention of the system to include backtracking facilities. Each simple logical expression may be considered as a goal to be achieved. Our problem is to find a set of goals which, together, satisfy the overall goal without conflicting, as happened in the example above. A conflict between two goals must be resolved by choosing an alternative if one exists. If one does not then the object cannot be constructed, therefore the quantified statement is false.

Execution is controlled by a queuing system:

1. When a simple expression is first encountered, a new goal is created and put on a "ready" queue.

2. The first goal in the "ready" queue is attempted. The effect of such an attempt is either to test the value of an object (or its properties) or, if no value exists, to give it one.

3. An expression which has given a symbol a value is said to control it. If it is found that a quantified variable is already controlled then the current value is checked. If this goal agrees with the controller, then the current goal is put on a queue associated with the variable. This queue contains all the controlling expressions.

4. If two goals are found to conflict then the current goal must temporarily be considered false. Therefore, it and the goals which belong to the same conjunct must be suspended. They go into a second queue associated with the variable, the "conflict" queue.

It is possible that, later on, a choice will be found to be incorrect. Therefore, the work of the expressions controlling the offending variable must be undone. A new value is then assigned to it by a set of goals taken from the conflict queue.

An example best illustrates this scheme.

```
[E x y z:
    (x = 0 | x = 1) &
    (x = 0 & y = 0 | x = 1 & y = 1) &
    (x = 1 & z = 0 | x = 1 & z = 1)
]
```

This is not a particularly useful statement, but it does demonstrate the need for backtracking quite well.

Let us briefly consider the execution of the concept. We may first choose "x" to be zero. This enables us to choose $y = 0$ also. However, with $x = 0$, no alternative in the last disjunct can be satisfied. Therefore, a new choice for "x" must be made since this is the variable which caused both conflicts. Since the value of "x" is to be changed, all statements depending on the old value must be considered false. Thus, the choice of $y = 0$ must also be undone. Now $x = 1$. The goals which govern the choice of alternatives are now reactivated. These result in $y = 1$ and either $z = 0$ or $z = 1$. (Since both values will satisfy the predicate, the choice depends only on the order in which the goals are attempted).

Initially our system contains no knowledge. It does not even have "integer" as a basic data type. A concept of "number" must be learnt. However, given a powerful description language, the program can learn many useful concepts. "maximum" has already been described. Another is the concept of the sum of two numbers:

$$sum(x, y, z) \text{ is true if } x + y = z$$

Once a definition of sum has been learnt it may be used as a program to perform an addition. For example:

$$[E \ z: sum(x, y, z)]$$

causes a "z" to be constructed such that it is the sum of x and y. A new concept may be learnt which has, in its description, a previously learnt concept. Thus, the language can be extended to include many useful concepts.

4. COMPARISONS WITH SOME AI LANGUAGES

It must be remembered that the initial intent of this language is that it be used by a learning program. It is very much a "computer language" since programs will be written by the learning system and executed without human intervention. Thus, the complete system represents a new approach to automatic program synthesis. Nevertheless, the language contains features that are useful in artificial intelligence and common to several high level languages. We will now consider some examples in PROLOG and QLISP.

The "maximum" program used before may be expressed in PROLOG as:

```
maximum(cons(x, nil), x).
maximum(cons(head, tail), x) :- maximum(tail, y),
                                swap(head, x, y).
swap(x, y, y) :- lt(x, y).
swap(x, x, y) :- le(y, x).
```

The left hand sides of the clauses above are goals. A goal can be achieved only if the expressions on the right hand side of the clause are true. When a function is called, and there is more than one occurrence of the goal expression (e.g. both "maximum" and "swap" occur twice on the left) then the occurrence whose arguments match those in the call is executed. Thus, if the list has a null tail, the first clause describing "maximum" is chosen. The choice of goal statements involves pattern matching. Note that in the example above "cons" is a list constructor as in LISP.

Although the notation here is somewhat different to that used in our language, the concept of using a goal directed form of programming is present. It also suffers from the problem that although, logically, the order of expressions in a clause is irrelevant, in practice the order can greatly affect efficiency. PROLOG is also based on predicate logic. It aims to provide a way of specifying a solution to a problem in a completely machine independent way. Thus, the first decision in developing the language was to choose a convenient representation for humans rather than for computers.

QLISP is a language derived from LISP. It is intended to be used to write problem solving and theorem proving programs. Although it is a procedural language it also exhibits goal directed behaviour in its "GOAL" expression:

(GOAL goal-class goal)

Here the programmer asks the system to attempt some goal. For example, a robot planner might have an expression of the form:

(GOAL $DO (INROOM BOX1 ROOM4))

The system maintains a list, "goal-class", of programs which might help to achieve this goal. One such program is chosen . If it is not successful, the system backtracks and tries another alternative. If no alternative is left, a failure occurs.

These examples have in common the fact that a program tells the system what is to be done, but says very little about how it is to be done. That is left to the interpreter. That is, a statement in the language is regarded as a command to a problem solver. The ability to construct objects allows our system to solve problems also. For example, a concept may describe how a robot arm is to move a block from one place to another. The object which is produced then describes the state of the system after such a movement. The change in state may be interpreted by machinery resulting in a real block actually being moved.

It is hoped that work in the area of structural description languages such as the one described in this paper will result in powerful learning and programming systems, an important goal in artificial intelligence research.

5. <u>REFERENCES</u>

COHEN, B.L. (1978): "A Theory of Structural Concept Formation and Pattern Recognition". Ph.D. Thesis, Dept. of Computer Science, University of N.S.W.

KOWALSKI, R.A. (1974): "Predicate Logic as a Programming Language". 1974 IFIP Congress.

RULIFSON J.F., DERKSEN J.A., WALDINGER R.L. (1972): "QA4: A Procedural Calculus for Intuitive Reasoning". S.R.I. Artificial Intelligence Center, Technical Note 73. (Note: QLISP was originally known as QA4).

A HUMAN MOVEMENT LANGUAGE FOR COMPUTER ANIMATION

Don Herbison-Evans

Basser Department of Computer Science
University of Sydney

ABSTRACT

Seven different methods used for specifying human movement
are considered: ideographic notation, animation chart,
specialised dance languages, natural language, numerical
description, demonstration and muscle tension. The pro-
spects of adapting each of them for computer input are
discussed. The NUDES language (Numeric Utility Displaying
Ellipsoid Solids, version 3) is described and related to
this discussion. Current problems with movement specification are also discussed.

1.   INTRODUCTION

From time immemorial humans have sought to represent pictorially
their shape and movements. With the advent of computer graphics,
there have been a number of attempts to draw human figures with devices
controlled by computer. The simple reproduction of outline and tonal
value pictures by computer graphic devices allows manipulation of the
shape and representation of the figure. Some results have shown great
artistic skill, e.g. "Transformations" by Csuri and Shaffer (Franke,
1971), but these types of manipulation do not easily allow natural articulation of the figure.

Attempts to represent all or part of human figures which can art-
iculate have been made for car crash simulation (Bartz, 1973) ergonomic
(Fetter, 1964) and choreographic (Noll, 1967) studies.

The present study was initiated by the choreographer Phillipa
Cullen. She indicated that the general problem of describing human
movement in an economic, explicit, unambiguous, easily comprehensible
fashion, especially as a linear string of conventional symbols was far
from solved. To examine this problem, the seven current methods of
describing human movement require analysis.

2.   TYPES OF LANGUAGE

2.1   Ideographic Notation

For several hundred years, dancers and choreographers have realised
that the constraints of movement on the parts of a human body have an
analogy with the constraints of syntax on language, and have sought a

language to describe human movement. Hutchinson (1968) reviews 23 notation languages published over the last four centuries for this purpose, starting with Arbeau (1589). Generally these languages are two
dimensional and show either a vertical (plan) view of the movements
of the figure, e.g. Feulliet (Savage and Officer, 1978) or a series
of horizontal views of an abbreviated figure (e.g. Zorn, 1905), or
both, e.g. Benesh (Causley, 1967). Typically, they have a complex
alphabet of special characters whose size, position, orientation and
juxtaposition are part of the language. They all suffer from the problem of trying to reduce a multiple four dimensional continuum (space
plus time for each joint/limb) onto a two dimensional piece of paper.
This can only be done by quantisation of at least two dimensions, and
this accounts for the proliferation of symbols, e.g. Laban notation
uses 1421 different symbols.

The two main notations in common use are Laban (Hutchinson, 1970)
and Benesh (Causley, 1967).

Laban is probably the most widely taught dance notation. It was
originated by Rudolf Laban in 1928 in the USA. It has a vertical stave
of several columns with time notionally running upwards. Different
columns of the stave are reserved for movements of the different parts
of the body: the legs, arms, torso, head, etc. Motions for each part
are marked for those time periods in which they occur, i.e. time is
treated in a continuous analog   fashion. Various symbols placed on
the stave represent the various directions and amounts of movement.
Thus space is quantised. There are 27 main directions, and intermediate directions are specified by additional symbols. Laban notation
is propagated by the Dance Notation Bureau in New York, who maintain
a library of the scores of many dances, and ensure its standardised
application.

Benesh notation is probably the most widely used notation in professional dancing. It was devised by Joan and Rudolf Benesh in the
UK in 1947. It is drawn on a horizontal musical type of stave. Time
runs left to right as in music, which facilitates synchronisation of
movement with the music, as the music can be placed above the notation.
At appropriate intervals along the stave are drawn symbolic pictures
of the figure and its movements since the last picture. The bottom
line of the stave represents ground level. Thus positions in the plane
of the figure are recorded in an analog fashion but time is quantised.
The third spatial dimension is communicated by the foreshortening of
the parts of the body, up to an ambiguity about whether they are in
front of or behind the plane of the figure. By using special symbols
for these two possibilities, Benesh effectively manages to show analog
representations of all three spatial dimensions on a two dimensional
piece of paper.

Benesh notation is propagated by the Institute of Choreology in
London, who also maintain a library of the scores of many dances.
Many professional ballet companies now have staff choreologists who
record and interpret the dances at rehearsals including the Royal
Ballet at Covent Garden, and also the Australian Ballet.

Both Benesh and Laban require a three year learning course although shorter courses are offered for those only wishing to read

the notation. Neither notation can be written in real time, and in both cases the preparation of the final score is an arduous task.

2.2 Animation Chart

This is used by makers of animated cartoons. The cartoon frames are generated by a series of overlapping transparent celluloid sheets with parts of bodies or scenes painted on them. These are called cels. Every cel is given a separate identifier. The animation chart has a set of columns, one column for each part of the body or scene which moves. Across these columns are rows representing each frame of the film. Specifications are written in each row of the cels that are in use for that frame. For example in cheaper cartoons the same set of cels may be used several times to show the legs moving in a walk cycle. The set of cels would be written into its column at the several appropriate places in the chart.

The animation chart has some similarities to Laban notation, with time running vertically and body parts spaced horizontally.

2.3 Specialised Dance Language

For several styles of dancing, specialised technical terms have evolved that describe the movements and positions of that style, e.g. square dancing, ballroom dancing (Moore, 1936), classical ballet (Vaganova, 1969). A sequence of these terms serves to describe fully a dance of the appropriate style.

2.4 Natural Language

To describe human movement, a variety of nouns, adjectives, verbs and adverbs are available which can describe the spatial disposition and movements of the body. It has been estimated that 20% of the words of English are concerned with spatial position (Hall, 1969).

Many words describe movement by specifying contact with some other part of the body or external surface, e.g. grasp, kick, kiss. Even more powerful are the words which describe bipedal locomotion: walk, run, skip, strut, tiptoe, shuffle, sneak (Blair, 1949).

2.5 Numerical Description

By this is meant a prescription of the positions and orientation angles of the parts of the body in every frame of an animated sequence. One of the published ideographic dance notations approaches this form (Eshkol and Wachmann, 1958).

2.6 Demonstration

This is the usual method employed in professional dance for comm- unication of human movement (Tomkins, 1970). When a company adds a new dance to its repertoire, either the choreographer or a principal

dancer from a previous production elsewhere is imported to teach it
to the company. Each dancer is then shown the movements usually in
segments of a few seconds duration. These must be remembered and concatenated by each dancer. A full ballet lasting over an hour involving perhaps 30 or more dancers can require rehearsal times of several
months for this process.

2.7 Muscle Tension

This is the body's own language. Given the masses and moments
of inertia of the parts of the body, and the distances between joints
and points of insertion of the muscles on the skeleton, the forces and
couples generated by the muscles serve to determine completely the motions of the body in accordance with Newton's laws of motion (Wells,
1971). Hence movements can be notionally specified by a sequence of
muscle tensions.

3. Computerisation

In principle any of the seven types of language can be adapted
and used to communicate with a computer which has as its output a
graphic display of an animated human figure. Each method has advantages and drawbacks.

Several attempts have been made to use some of the ideographic
notations.

A subset of Massine notation has been successfully implemented
and used in dance teaching (Savage and Officer, 1978). Regrettably
the computer system on which it was implemented has been superseded
and the software has proved impossible to transfer to the replacement
hardware. The system allowed the interactive generation and editing
of a small score and it then played this back as a stick figure performing a dance. The system was confined to movements on the spot:
locomotion was not implemented.

A substantially complete editor has been implemented for Laban
notation (Brown et al., 1978). It uses a storage tube display which
limits selective erasure and makes it somewhat difficult to use.
The system is being rewritten for a refresh display, and the group
also plans to drive a figure with the stored score.

A project of this type was also proposed for Benesh notation
(Mendo, 1975). This involved the input of existing scores by tracing
them with a digitiser. They were then to be analysed and a dancing
figure generated from them. Although the system has been designed
down to the data representation and analysis stage, it has not yet
been implemented.

All three above systems use the two dimensions of the screen/
page. This contrasts with the normal mode of computer input which is
a character string: one dimensional and quantised. Attempts have
been made to transliterate ideographic notations into this form.

An early attempt devised such a transliteration for Laban notation but did not translate it (Keen, 1973). A complete transliteration and translation has subsequently been implemented (Calvert and Chapman, 1978). Only a small subset of Laban was implemented, but this has been made to drive a gesturing stick figure. Again, locomotion was not translated.

Similarly a subset of Benesh has been transliterated and translated and used to drive a multiellipsoid figure (McNair, 1979). This was outstanding in that locomotion was included. However only the general position signs of the body and limbs were implemented. The movement signs and more detailed symbols were not included.

The complexity of extending the systems to include both locomotion and movement details has so far proved a barrier for all the ideographically based systems.

The animation chart has been implemented for the computer generation of cartoons (Catmull, 1978), but has not proved very successful. Nevertheless, the concept of applying a number of sets of actions over a series of possibly overlapping quantised time periods is valuable. It gives very flexible time control of complex actions.

An attempt is being made to translate the specialised terms of classical ballet (Hunt, 1978). The interfacing of adjacent movements, which is normally left to a dancer's common sense, is a serious but not insuperable problem. Certain aspects of specialised language map well into a computer language. Each technical term can be viewed as a subroutine/macro call. This deals well with complex action sequences but gives only simple timing control. A more serious drawback is the limited types of movement that can be produced by a system that is tied to a specialised style of dance.

This can be overcome by using full natural language which gives useful facilities such as command verbs, body part names, adverbs for acceleration control and named sequences of actions. The disadvantage of natural language is its lack of precision in the specification of timing and position, except for the case when movement ends in touching a surface.

Demonstration has been used in the past for communication with computers. This has taken several forms:

A. A human wearing an exoskeleton with potentiometers at the joints. Readings are fed back to the computer and stored (Toscas, 1971). This is useful for generating specific movement sequences, but is rather cumbersome for general movement synthesis.

B. Cine films of moving humans taken from different points of view have been measured frame by frame and the measurements used to reconstruct a moving stick figure (Shigeru Ohe, 1969).

C. A virtual puppet visible on a screen has been provided which can be manipulated by conventional interactive devices (Withrow, 1970). The movements are recorded and played back as required. The figure used was a stick figure, and only gesturing, not locomotion was implemented.

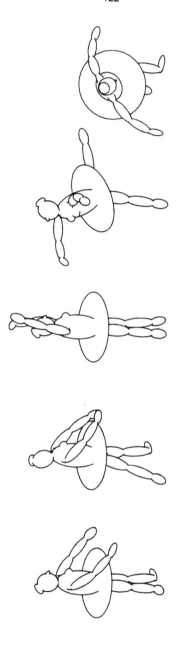

FIGURE 1 SAMPLE NUDES3 OUTPUT

This last technique is potentially very useful to a choreographer, and the problems of extending it are discussed later in the paper.

Numerical description was tried by the author at an early stage (Herbison-Evans, 1974). It is a tedious error-prone method of programming anything substantial. It is however a necessary intermediate language in the translation of more sophisticated human movement languages.

Muscle tensions may be useful for kinesic and physiological studies but is a difficult mode for controlling figure activity. Some indication of the difficulty of using this language for figure control may be gleaned from an observation of the time required to generate, say, a sequence for walking by a normal human naturally, namely about two years.

3. NUDES3

This Numeric Utility Displaying Ellipsoid Solids (version 3) is a procedural language that attempts to combine the generality of natural language with the temporal control of the animation chart and the precision of numerical language. Like natural language the user gives and uses names for the figures, body parts, joints and action sequences. Also a vocabulary of words is predefined for use in commands and acceleration control. It is like an animation chart in that every action is specified by a set of frames in the resulting film. These are identified by their frame numbers. It is numerical in that the sizes of the body parts (ellipsoids), the relative positions of the joints, and the displacements and rotations in the actions must all be specified numerically.

3.1 Implementation

The NUDES3 language program is processed by a suite of five programs. Four are written in ANSI FORTRAN IV. The fifth is in IMLAC assembler. The first converts the NUDES3 program to a numerical sequence of three dimensional positions and orientations. The second projects these into two dimensions and works out which outline arcs are obscured. The third draws these on a printer page or Calcomp plotter. The fourth compresses the two-dimensional data numbers to two digit base sixty numbers which are implemented as ASCII characters for transmission down a low speed data line to an IMLAC PDS4. The fifth generates from this compressed data a 16 mm movie using a computer controlled stopped frame animation camera attached to the PDS4.

A sample plotter output is shown in Figure 1.

The current limitations of the suite are a maximum of 41 ellipsoids and 300 actions.

3.2 Layout

All commands have a free format with the space character used as a separator between words, values, etc. An asterisk is used as a signal to ignore the rest of a line/card. This allows commentary to be included among the commands.

Each action keyword has an expected set of parameters following it. The order of these parameters is predefined, and hence the position of a parameter determines its type.

Variables may be used in place of values or in place of the names of figures, joints, ellipsoids, axes, or subroutines.

All keywords and names may be arbitrarily abbreviated by using only the first one or more characters. It is however unwise to abbreviate to the point of ambiguity with other names or keywords. Names may be any length but only the first six characters are used by the compiler. It is also unwise to use a name which is the same as the beginning of any other name or keyword.

A NUDES3 program is divided into two parts: a set of declarations and a set of action specifications.

3.3 Declarations

Each figure must be declared by using the keyword FIGURE followed by a name for the figure, then the number of body parts, and then a list of the names of those parts.

The actual implementation of the drawing routines assumes that the body parts are ellipsoids, so each of these parts must then be defined by using the keyword ELLIPSOID followed by its name and by the lengths of the x, y, and z semi-axes.

Each joint must be defined by using the keyword JOINT followed by its name and the names of the two ellipsoids that it joins. Each of these ellipsoid names must be followed by the relative x, y, z coordinates of the joint with respect to the ellipsoid centre. The ellipsoids may only be simply connected by the joints.

The names of all variables and subroutines must be declared using the VARIABLE and DECSUB keywords respectively. In each case the keyword must be followed by the number of names in that declaration and then by the names themselves. Any number of VARIABLE and DECSUB declaration statements may be used.

The various declarations can occur in any order provided only that the ellipsoid names are declared as part of a figure before being dimensioned or jointed.

3.4 Actions

Action commands begin with a keyword and two frame numbers. The keyword is one of: REPEAT, LINEAR, QUADRATIC, ACCELERATE, or DECELERATE, depending on how the action is required to be distributed over the specified frame sequence.

Actions can be specified to be limited to one figure or to apply to all figures. The available actions are:

GROALL, GROFIG: these cause all dimensions of all or of one of the figures to be multiplied by a scaling factor.

MVALTO, MVALBY, MVFGTO, MVFGBY cause absolute or relative translation of all or of one of the figures by the amounts specified in the command in the x, y, z directions. Absolute movements are specified by nominating an ellipsoid whose centre is moved to the point specified.

GRNDAL, GRNDFG: these cause one or all of the figures to be moved vertically (in the y direction) so that the lowest point of the figure(s) just touches y = 0.

The coordinate axes used are left handed: x is from left to right; y is up; z is away from the observer.

RTALPT, RTFGPT, RTALEL, RTFGEL cause rotation about a specified point or about the centre of a nominated ellipsoid of all or one of the figures by a specified angle about a specified axis (x, y, or z).

BENDBY, BENDTO cause articulation of the figure containing a nominated joint at that joint, moving a nominated ellipsoid. The bend can be specified as relative by using the BENDBY command, or absolute using the BENDTO. For a relative bend the rotation of the moving subfigure (attached to the moving ellipsoid) is specified by an angle and axis fixed in a nominated reference ellipsoid. For an absolute bend, the required Eulerian angles of the nominated ellipsoid are specified with respect to a nominated reference ellipsoid.

In both the rotation and the bend commands, angles are specified as positive if they are anticlockwise when viewed from the reference origin along the axis of rotation. They are specified in degrees.

SUBROUTINE, END, and CALL allow a sequence of actions to be named, and for that sequence to be called from elsewhere. The minimum and maximum frame numbers used inside the subroutine are purely formal, and are offset to match the actual frame numbers in the call of the subroutine.

SET assigns a value to a variable for every frame between the specified pair of frame numbers. The value may be that of another variable, which can be that of another variable, etc. to any depth up to the maximum number of allowed variables. Any variable may hold a value that is a specification of a displacement, angle, growth factor, ellipsoid, figure, joint, or subroutine. The user is encouraged to use types in a consistent manner.

VIEW and SPEED allow checking of animated sequence without generating all of it. VIEW allows a subsequence of frames to be generated. SPEED allows extra frames to be interpolated or all but every nth frame to be deleted. Both may be used once only in a

NUDES3 program. If both are used, then the frame numbers in the
VIEW command refer to those numbers before the effect of the SPEED
command is applied.

The frame with the lowest frame number is not drawn, and is purely
formal.

4.   CURRENT PROBLEMS

A major problem is the specification of rotations in the rotation
and bend commands. The NUDES3 numerical method is very error prone,
particularly the specification of the sign of the required rotation
angle. The BENDTO command is also a difficult concept to understand
and use. Possibly the commands should be altered to use verbal descriptions of the signs of the angles and of the required axes, with words
like "up", "down", "left", "right", "forward", "back". The difficulty
with this is that in naming a direction relative to some other part of
the body, if that part is already oriented abnormally, then the description will again be very unnatural, e.g. what direction is "forward"
for the arms when the torso is twisted 90 degrees at the waist?

Another major problem is how to specify and to determine the complex motions required to bring one part of a figure into some specified
position by moving other parts, e.g. move the hand to a specified position by bending the arm at the shoulder. This is exacerbated by the need
to forbid parts of the body to interpenetrate and also by the limited
angular movement available at the joints.

An extension of this problem is the general need for commands for
motion until some part of the figure contacts a specified surface. Such
contacts are essential for serious dance work, for example when two figures are dancing together. Even in natural language the importance of
contact can be understood, e.g. in such a film classic as "Holstering
his gun, he leapt onto his horse, tipped his hat, and galloped off into
the sunset". Calculating such contacts appears to require time-
prohibitive iterative techniques. An analytic algorithm for finding
the rotation that will cause two nominated ellipsoids to touch is required.

One overall basic problem with NUDES3 however is that it is designed for working in a batch environment. What is needed is not a programming language but an interactive command system.

A choreographer or animator needs a set of three dimensional puppets each with appropriate store and recall facilities for movement sequences, plus a set of simple manipulation commands to generate and edit
such sequences. Then directions of rotation and the generation of contact can be determined visually.

The puppets must be notionally solid. The stick figures used in
most systems to date give some three dimensional cues by foreshortening but do not resolve the in front/behind ambiguity. Only apparently
solid figures can do this by the removal of hidden lines. Doing this
in still somewhat expensive (Watkins, 1970; Herbison-Evans, 1979).

5. REFERENCES

ARBEAU, T. (1589): "Orchesographie". Jehan des Preyz, Langres.

BARTZ, J. (1973): "Modelling People in Car Crashes". New Sceintist, 23 Aug. 1973, p.447.

BLAIR, P. [c 1949]: "Animation". Foster Art Service Inc., Calif., p.24.

BROWN, M., SMOLIAR, R.W., and WEBBER, L. (1978): "Preparing Dance Notation Scores with a Computer". Computers and Graphics, Vol.3, pp.1-7.

CALVERT, T.W., and CHAPMAN, J. (1978): "Notation of Movement with Computer Assistance". Proc. Annual Conf. A.C.M., pp.731-736.

CATMULL, E. (1978): "The Problems of Computer Assisted Animation". Computer Graphics, Vol.12, No.3, pp.348-353.

CAUSLEY, M. (1967): "An Introduction to Berest Movement Notation". Man Parrish, London.

ESHKOL, N., and WACHMANN, A. (1958): "Movement Notation". Weidenfeld and Nicolson, London.

FETTER, W.A. (1964): "Computer Graphics in Communication". McGraw-Hill, New York.

FRANKE, H.W. (1971): "Computer Graphics Computer Art". Phaidon, London, p.32.

HALL, E.T. (1969): "The Hidden Dimension". Anchor, New York, p.93.

HERBISON-EVANS, D. (1974): "Animated Cartoons by Computers Using Ellipsoids". Proc. 6th Australian Comp. Conf., pp.811-823.

HERBISON-EVANS, D. (1979): "Algorithms for Real Time Animation of Drawings of the Human Figure with Hidden Lines Omitted". Sydney University: Basser Dept. of Computer Science, Technical Report 148.

HUNT, F. (1978): Department of Computer Science, University of Utah, Private Communication.

HUTCHINSON, A. (1968): "Experiences of Dance Notations". Dance Magazine, pp.304-308.

HUTCHINSON, A. (1970): "Labanotation", Oxford University Press, London, Second Edition.

KEEN, J. (1973): "Movement". Sydney University, Basser Dept. of Computer Science, Honours Report.

McNAIR, B. (1979): "Benesh Movement Language", Sydney University, Basser Dept. of Computer Science, M. Sc. Reprot.

MENDO, G., (1975): "Computer Choreology Project", Institute of Choreology, London.

MOORE, A. (1936): "Modern Ballroom Dancing". Ritman, London.

NOLL, A.M. (1967): "Choreography & Computers".

SAVAGE, G.J., and OFFICER, J.M. (1978): "Coreo: an Interactive Computer Model for Dance". Internat. J. Man-Machine Studies, Vol.10.

SHIGERU OHE (1969): "Computer Animation", Film, Moore School of Elec. Eng., University of Pennsylvania.

TOMKINS, C. (1970): "An Appetite for Motion" in "The Dance Experience", Edited by Nadel M.H., and Nadel C.G., Praegar, New York, p.257.

TOSCAS, G. (1971): "Instant Animation from a Magic Box". International Photographer, February.

VAGANOVA, A. (1969): "Basic Principles of Classical Ballet". Dover, New York.

WATKINS, G.S. (1970): "A Real Time Visible Surface Algorithm", Dept. of Computer Science, University of Utah, Report UTEC-CSC-70-101.

WELLS, K.F. (1971): "Kinesiology". Fifth Edition, Sanders, Philadelphia.

WITHROW, C. (1970): "A Dynamic Model for Computer Aided Choreography", Dept. of Computer Science, University of Utah, Report UTEC-CSC-70-103.

ZORN, F.A. (1905): "Grammar of the Art of Dancing". Franklin, New York.

PROCEEDINGS OF THE SYMPOSIUM ON
LANGUAGE DESIGN AND PROGRAMMING METHODOLOGY
SYDNEY, 10-11 SEPTEMBER, 1979

ALGEBRAIC SPECIFICATIONS AND TRANSITION GRAPHS

Norman Y. Foo

Basser Department of Computer Science
University of Sydney

ABSTRACT

A simple connection between transition graphs and algebraic specifications of data types is explained and its use in extracting equations for data abstraction is illustrated.

1. INTRODUCTION

The algebraic specification to data abstraction has been advocated by several researchers including Guttag [G1], Liskov and Zilles [L1], and ADJ [A1]. In this approach a data type is abstracted by exhibiting a finite set of equations (axioms, identities, or laws) which hold between pairs of finite sequences of data operations. For a complete specification this set must be satisfied by the data operations and every conceivable equality between two operation sequences must be implied by it. Mathematically, as is argued in Guttag [G1] for example, an algebraic specification of a data type is really a heterogeneous algebra in the sense of Birkoff and Lipson [B2] which captures the data type semantics. ADJ [A1] further argues that correct specifications must be initial objects, i.e. they must uniquely represent data types up to isomorphism; this was also advocated from a different viewpoint [F1] where the equivalent model-theoretic notion of categoricity was used.

A plausible strategy for the correct abstraction of data types could proceed as follows. Using some easily understood but quite possibly partial or semi-formal semantic description of a data type, one attempts to extract (operation sequence) equations consistent with the description. One could then use an automated initial-object or categoricity prover to verify that the extracted specification is correct. Efficient realization of this strategy is a long-term goal.

This and related papers [N1] report some techniques which are proving to be helpful at different stages of our investigations. The main topic

addressed here is a relationship between the state-transition
graphs of data types and the equation sets which make up
algebraic specifications. The semi-formal semantic description
used is therefore the state behaviour of the data type. In
almost all non-trivial data types the state space is unbounded,
so a complete description of state behaviour is not possible in
any pictorial representation of a transition graph. In some
cases finitary descriptions are possible, e.g., using primitive
recursive schemes, and these are in turn translatable into transition graphs. It will be seen that the relationship mentioned
above can be used on partial representations of transition
graphs to help extract equations (or suggest remedies when this
proves to be difficult) for at least those data types where the
operations are unary over a homogeneous domain. We will later
indicate how this last restriction can be removed by re-inter-
preting standard transition graphs; the difficulties appear to be
more notational than conceptual.

With these remarks the data types which will be primarily
discussed in the sequel can be abstracted as homogeneous algebras as
treated by Birkhoff [B1], or in a more model-theoretic vein by
Tarski [T1], to which the reader is referred for some results
which are quoted here. The little graph theory and algebra that is
presumed here can be found in Seshu [S1] and Birkhoff [B1] respectively, and the automata-theoretic terminology is more than adequate-
ly covered by Booth [B3]. We also presume familiarity with the
basic notions of algebraic specifications as presented in, say, the
introductory portions of the reference cited at the beginning of
this section. We introduce the notation required in the next
section.

2. GRAPH ALGEBRAS

An algebra $\mathcal{A} = (A, \theta)$ is a pair where A is the domain (carrier)
of the algebra and θ is a finite set of operations on A.
Since we are restricting consideration to operations which are
at most unary the arity (rank) of each operation f in θ is 0 or 1.
The 0-arity operations are effectively constants in A and
correspond to fixed states of the data type, e.g., an initial

state or an error state. The remaining unary operations represent
the usual operations of the data type (operations of higher arity
will be briefly considered when we discuss the removal of these
restrictions). The kind of algebra which we use here to describe
data types is a graph algebra deriving from the state-transition
graph of the data type. Let $G = (Q,E)$ be such a graph, where
the vertex set Q is the extended state space of the data type, and
E the set of labelled directed edges represents the state transition
function $\delta : \theta \times Q \rightarrow Q$ (θ being the operation set) in the usual
way, viz., an edge labelled by f goes from q to r if and only if
$\delta(f,q) = r$. The extension to the state space of the data type
merely consists in adding a special element denoted by # to it.
This is done so that all operations can be uniformly represented
in G: a 0-ary operation f_0 will both name a state f_0 in G as well
as label an edge from # to state f_0. G can be interpreted as an
algebra in the obvious way. Every operation sequence on the data
type corresponds to a directed path in G and is a word (term) of
the algebra. An equation is a pair of (α,β) such words, normally
written $\alpha = \beta$, denoting functional identity and interpreted in G
as path pairs which form circuits of a special kind - the
e-circuits defined below.

Having explained what a graph algebra is we now review a
completeness theorem proved by Birkhoff [B1] about syntactic
inference rules which can be used to generate equations from a
base set of equations. The formal language used in this proof-
theory has the equality symbol and names for all operations in θ.
A term in this language is any legal string of operation symbols,
i.e., if a 0-ary name occurs it must only be rightmost in a
string (composition is interpreted as left composition). In this
latter case we call the terms type 1, all other terms being of
type 2. Formulas are of the form $\alpha = \beta$ where both α and β are terms.
A formula is of type 1 if both its terms are type 1, and is type 2
otherwise. The meaning of formulas is given in G by the
following interpretations. A type 1 formula $\alpha = \beta$ is true in G
if $\delta(\alpha,\#) = \delta(\beta,\#)$; a type 2 formula $\alpha = \beta$ is true in G if for
all $q \in Q$ $\delta(\alpha,q) = \delta(\beta,q)$ or $\delta(\alpha,q) = \delta(\beta,\#)$. We write $G \vDash \sigma$ to
mean the formula σ is true in G. T(G) is the set $\{\sigma | G \vDash \sigma\}$.

A basis for $T(G)$ is a subset Σ of formulas such that $G \vdash \sigma$ iff $G \vDash \Sigma \Rightarrow \sigma$, i.e. Σ logically implies σ in G. This is a semantic concept whose syntactic counterpart was formalized and proved complete by Birkhoff in the above cited paper. The result states that Σ is a basis for $T(G)$ iff $T(G)$ is the closure $\overline{\Sigma}$ of Σ under the following derivation schema:

(i) $\Sigma \subset \overline{\Sigma}$ (ii) $\alpha = \alpha$ is in $\overline{\Sigma}$ for all terms α

(iii) if $\alpha = \beta$ and $\beta = \gamma$ are in $\overline{\Sigma}$ then so is $\alpha = \gamma$

(iv) if $\alpha = \beta$ is in $\overline{\Sigma}$ then so is $f\alpha = f\beta$ for all f in θ

(v) equals may be substituted for equals. If σ is derivable from Σ we write $\Sigma \vdash \sigma$. The completeness of this schema is to say that Σ is a basis for $T(G)$ iff $\Sigma \vdash T(G)$. An algebraic specification, as understood in the literature, exists for a data type with graph algebra G precisely when $T(G)$ has a finite basis Σ.

Lemma 1

   Rules (iii) and iv) can be replaced by rule (vi) below:

   (vi) $\alpha\mu\beta = \gamma$ and $\nu = \mu$ in $\overline{\Sigma}$

   imply $\alpha\nu\beta = \gamma$ in $\overline{\Sigma}$

The proof of this lemma is easy and therefore omitted. We shall consider rules (i), (ii), (v) and (vi) to be the schema for obtaining $T(G)$. We wish to interpret each of these rules into G assuming that Σ is a basis for $T(G)$. To do this easily we make use of the following definition.

Definition

   An e-circuit at q in G is a pair $(q,\{\alpha,\beta\})$ such that $\delta(\alpha,q) = \delta(\beta,q)$ and a pseudo e-circuit is a pair $(q\{\alpha,\beta\})$ such that $\delta(\alpha,\#) = \delta(\beta,q)$ or vice versa.

   The interpretation of the derivation rules depends on the type of equation, but in any case rule (i) interprets into G as a set Σ of e-circuits. The essential difference between type 1 and type 2 interpretations is simply that type 1 equations $\alpha f_0 = \beta g_0$, where the 0-ary operations have been written explicitly, denote e-circuits at $\#$, i.e., $(\#,\{\alpha f_0, \beta g_0\})$, while type 2 equations $\alpha = \beta$ really denote a global set of e-circuits $\{(q,\{\alpha,\beta\}) \mid q \in Q\}$. The latter however is not strictly mathematically correct and to be rigorous we should be really faking quotients - but this turns out to be unnecessary since a rule like (iii) simply asserts that in G if $(q,\{\alpha,\beta\})$ and $(q,\{\beta,\gamma\})$ are e-circuits in $\overline{\Sigma}$ for every $q \in Q$ then $(q,\{\alpha,\gamma\})$ is also an e-circuit in $\overline{\Sigma}$ for every $q \in Q$. This last assertion is obviously true in G. Likewise the remaining rules are also true in G, as would have been expected from completeness.

The interesting rule is (vi). What this asserts is that a special kind of ring-sum of e-circuits is also an e-circuit. Recall [S1] that subsets of the directed circuits of directed graphs form an abelian group under the ring-sum addition of edges where these are counted modulo 2. In fact if one regards the integers modulo 2 as a field the system of circuits is a vector space. E-circuits are directed circuits of a particular form which in general are not closed under arbitrary ring-sums: a counterexample is suggested by Figure 1. To be more precise suppose that in rule (vi) $\mu = \nu$ is of type 1. Then β must be null in $\alpha\mu\beta = \gamma$, hence this equation is also of type 1 and may in fact be written $\alpha\mu = \gamma$. By the interpretation into G the assumption of rule (vi) is that $(\#,\{\alpha\mu, \gamma\})$ and $(\#,\{\mu,\nu\})$ are e-circuits in $\overline{\Sigma}$, from which the conclusion is $(\#,\{\alpha\nu, \gamma\})$ is an e-circuit in $\overline{\Sigma}$. A pictorial representation of this is in Figure 2 showing the ring-sum interpretation of the rule.

The remaining cases are explained similarly and left to the reader. We say that an e-circuit $(q,\{\alpha,\beta\})$ translates to r if $(r,\{\alpha,\beta\})$ is also an e-circuit. Restating the definition of Σ being a finite basis for $T(G)$ in terms of the e-circuits of G we may now say that a finite set Σ of e-circuits generates (is a basis for) all e-circuits whenever Σ decomposes into $\Sigma_1\Sigma_2$, the e-circuits in Σ_2 translate to all of Q, and every e-circuit in G is a ring-sum of those in Σ_1 and the translates of those in Σ_2. The sets Σ_1 and Σ_2 correspond to equations of type 1 and 2 respectively. This observation is recorded as:

Theorem 1

A data type has an algebraic specification iff its transition graph has e-circuits which are finitely generated.[1]

As it stands the result is not very useful because it says nothing about how one might search for such a basis in graphs. To remedy this we will now analyse operation equations (and hence e-circuits) to expose some simplifications. Specifically it will be shown that we need only consider the following forms of equations for any basis Σ (a) $\alpha = \lambda$ where λ is null (b) $\alpha = \beta$ where no proper suffixes α^1, β^1 of α, β are such that $\alpha^1 = \beta^1$ (c) $\alpha\mu = \mu$, where no proper suffix α^1 of α is such that $\alpha^1\mu = \mu$, and (d) $\alpha\mu = \beta\mu$ where no proper suffixes α^1, β^1 of α, β are such that $\alpha^1\mu = \beta^1\mu$. Interpreted as e-circuits these forms are shown in figure 3.

Definition

An e-circuit $(q, \{\alpha, \beta\})$ such that for no proper suffixes α, β^1 of α, β is $(q, \{\alpha, \beta\})$ an e-circuit is called simple. A path concatenated with a simple circuit is called p-simple.

The e-circuits denoted by equations in (b) above are simple. The loops in (a) are also simple. Those in (c) and (d) are paths concatenated respectively with loops and simple non-loops and therefore p-simple. Once this result is established the search for candidate e-circuits which can be used as basis sets Σ_1 and Σ_2 above will be considerably amplified. We proceed to do this.

By the index of an equation $\alpha = \beta$ we mean the following. Let α be $\mu\gamma$ and β be $\nu\gamma$ where γ is the longest common suffix of α and β, possibly null. Denoting the length of a word η by $|\eta|$ the index of $\alpha = \beta$ is $|\gamma| + |\alpha| + |\beta|$. If γ is null this is simply $|\alpha| + |\beta|$. The proof of the assertions above is by induction on the index of equations. Consider first an equation $\alpha = \beta$ of index 1. This must be of form (a) so our assertion is trivially

---

(1)   In fact the graph-theoretic version of vector space bases for directed circuits can be shown to imply the Birkhoff completeness theorem and hence the two are equivalent. But we do not pursue this issue here.

satisfied. Assume that the assertions are true for all equations of
index less than n and let $\alpha = \beta$ have index n. Either α and β have a
common suffix or they do not. Suppose they do not, and let α^1, β^1 be
the shortest suffixes of α, β respectively such that $\alpha^1 = \beta^1$. If
these are not proper suffixes then $\alpha = \beta$ is of form (b). If they are,
we may replace $\alpha = \beta$ by the equations $\alpha^1 = \beta^1$ and $\mu\alpha^1 = \nu\alpha^1$ (where α
is $\mu\alpha^1$ and β is $\nu\beta^1$), the first being of form (a) or (b), and the
second has smaller index than $\alpha = \beta$ whence by the induction hypothesis
it may be replaced by equations of forms (a) through (d). Suppose
then that α and β do have a common longest suffix γ and let α be $\mu\gamma$,
β be $\nu\gamma$. Either μ, ν have shortest proper suffixes μ_1, ν_1 such that
$\mu_1\gamma = \nu_1\gamma$ or not. If not, $\alpha = \beta$ is of form (d). If μ_1 and ν_1 are
proper then $\alpha = \beta$ may be replaced by the equations $\mu_1\gamma = \nu_1\gamma$ which
is of form (c) or (d), and $\mu_2\mu_1\gamma = \nu_2\mu_1\gamma$ which is of smaller index
than $\alpha = \beta$.

Two observations are made about the above proof. First, the
replacements are valid via an appeal to the derivation rules. Second,
the type of the equation $\alpha = \beta$ is preserved in the replacing equations.

Let us say that type 1 equations are irredundant in Σ if $\Sigma_1 \neq \emptyset$
and $\Sigma_2 \nvdash \Sigma_1$. Type 1 equations are not irredundant in Σ iff there
exists an equivalent basis with only type 2 equations. Thus, if type 1
equations are irredundant in a given basis Σ they must also be present
in all bases. Otherwise there is a basis Σ^1 having only type 2
equations, and by the above construction Σ^1 may be assumed to be of
the forms (a) through (d). Since $\Sigma \vdash \Sigma^1$, $\Sigma^1 \vdash \Sigma$ and $\vdash$ preserves equation
type, Σ is of type 2, contradicting the assumption. We restate the
preceding results in terms of e-circuits.

Theorem 2

The e-circuits of a transition graph are generated by basic sets
consisting only of simple and p-simple e-circuits.

Corollary

A data type is algebraically specifiable iff its transition
graph e-circuits are finitely generated by simple and p-simple
e-circuits.

Theorem 3

Type 1 e-circuits (i.e. of the form $(\#, \{\alpha, \beta\})$) are irredundant
in one basic set iff type 1 e-circuits are irredundant in all basic sets.

3.   EXAMPLES AND APPLICATIONS

Some simple examples and applications of the preceding characteriz-
ations are discussed in this section. A few cautionary remarks are in
order. It should not be concluded that the use of transition graphs will
yield easy and complete procedures for extracting equations for data
types, but rather that they suggest what equations might be necessary and
provide insight into the process of abstraction. Graph descriptions have
obvious limitations if they are finite (in which case they will usually
be only partial descriptions). Even when finitary descriptions are available things are not easy because the existence of algebraic specifications
may not be decidable.

Theorem 4.

If the state transition graph of a data type is described by primitive recursive fractions there is no algorithm to decide if the data type
has an algebraic specification.

The proof of this will be merely outlined since the details are tedious. We show that if there is such an algorithm the Halting Problem for
Turing machines is solvable, which is a contradiction. Without loss of
generality we can modify the halting states to go into small loops. From
Minsky [M2] we know that a Turing machine with a (say, given) input tape
the next configuration (i.e. instantaneous description) function is primitive recursive. This function determines an autonomous transition graph
in which we could trivially label every edge by a fixed operation symbol
to define a graph algebra. Now, there are two possibilities — either the
graph is an infinite path or else it is a path concatenated with a loop.
In the first case there is no algebraic specification for the corresponding data type. In the second case there is an algebraic specification
consisting of one type 1 equation of the form (c) in the previous section.
So there is an algebraic specification iff (i) the machine loops around a
modified halting state or (ii) the machine loops in other states. But for
looping machines there are computable upper bounds on the number of steps
which will reveal the nature of the loop. Hence an algorithm for deciding
the existence of algebraic specifications in this case will yield one for
deciding halting.

In [M1] Majster raised the question of hidden operations and algebraic specifications. In the present context hidden operations are new labelled edges in a transition graph which are consistent with the old edges. Consistency really means that it is not possible to derive a contradiction from the implied new set of equations and is equivalent to saying that the transition graph is deterministic.

Definition

A transition graph G which has another graph G^1 as a subgraph is an inessential extension of it if the vertex sets of G^1 and G are identical; it is a consistent extension if G^1 is deterministic (and hence G too).

A data type may have a graph algebra without a finite basis and yet admit consistent inessential extensions which do have finite bases. Since we are only interested in reasonable extensions (although hidden states could be considered in an alternative treatment) we will simply say extension in the sense to mean consistent and inessential ones. As a good example of the preceding theory we consider a partial transition graph of the data type TOY-STACK which was proved by ADJ [A2] to be not algebraically specifiable but which was shown by them to have an algebraically specifiable extension. TOY-STACK was intended as a simplification of a traversing stack data type introduced by Majster [M1]. Its functional specification as given by ADJ is:

(1)   Error ( )   =   *
(2)   Empty ( )   = $\langle 0,0 \rangle$
(3)   Down (*)   =   Push (*)   =   *
(4)   Down $\langle p,s \rangle$ =   if p>o then $\langle p-1,s \rangle$ else *
(5)   Push $\langle p,s \rangle$ =   if p=s then $\langle p+1, s+1 \rangle$ else *

This does not have a finite basis, but on adding

(6)   Shove (*)   =   *
(7)   Shove $\langle p,s \rangle$ = $\langle p,s+1 \rangle$

the new data-type has a finite basis. Using primes to denote the extension, Figure 4 shows partial transition graphs of these data types. To keep things simple we have abbreviated the operations and repeated the * state at various positions. We now argue for the non-existence of a finite basis of e-circuits for TOY-STACK from its transition graph to illustrate how such graphs could be used.

It can be seen that PD = Er (it is perhaps more intuitive but somewhat misleading to write this as PD = *) denotes the only global set of
e-circuits in the graph. These happen to be pseudo e-circuits. Now consider the set of e-circuits denoted by the equations $\{PD^n\ P^n\ Em = DD^n\ P^n$
$Em\ |\ n>1\}$. These are the downward paths concatenated with the horizontal
ones ending in simple circuits in the figure. They are all independent
in that none are generated by the others. Further, the pseudo e-circuits
cannot be used in ring sums with the paths since this results in disconn-
ection. Hence the e-circuits corresponding to these equations do not
have a finite basis and TOY-STACK is not algebraically specifiable. By
extending TOY-STACK to TOY-STACK[1] with the introduction of the hidden
operation "shove" the new data type was shown by ADJ to be algebraically
specifiable. An examination of the transition graph of TOY-STACK[1] reveals
its increased regularity over that of TOY-STACK. This is to be expected
since the graphs with finite bases are precisely those with a finite number of type 1 e-circuits and a finite number of type 2 e-circuits such
that every e-circuit is the ring-sum of the former and (translates of)
the latter.

To illustrate the process of extracting this information from typical
graphs we use TOY-STACK[1] as an example. Any such process using graph
descriptions cannot, of course, be completely algorithmic on account of
theorem 4, but it is not inconceivable that such extraction heuristics
combined interactively with an automated initial object or categoricity
prover could indeed yield a correct set of equations. It is convenient
to tabulate the various rules in the heuristic as follows: (1) for constant states, i.e. those which are "named" by 0-ary operations, list the
global pseudo e-circuits which lead into these states; (2) for all states,
list the global simple and p-simple e-circuits; (3) other residual simple
and p-simple e-circuits which are not ring-sums of (translates of) those
in (1) and (2) are listed as type 1 e-circuits using paths from # if
necessary.

In looking for global e-circuits absorbing states can be ignored. A
state is called an absorbing state in automata theory when no exit from
it is possible; in such a case every pair of words $\{\alpha,\rho\}$ are suitable
labels for e-circuits at that state. Applying these rules to TOY-STACK[1]
we extract the following equations. Since * is the only constant state

and the only global paths that lead into it are named by the words PS and
PD, equations PS = Er and PD = Er will suffice. This completes rule 1.
For the other states the simple e-circuit which is global is the one denoted by the equation SD = DS, depicted in the figure by the parallelo-
grams. The right angled triangles (e.g. $\langle o,o \rangle$, $\langle 1,1 \rangle$, $\langle o,1 \rangle$) apply
precisely to states which are reached by a P operation, and hence become
global if they are denoted by the equation D P P = SP; these are in fact
p-simple e-circuits. Next one may write down all the equations which
say that * is an absorbing state, e.g., D Er = Er etc. This completes
rule (2). The residual e-circuits which are not ring-sums of the preceding are those at #. These are specified by the equations D Em = Er
and D P Em = S Em. This completes rule (3). In fact ADJ shows that this
set of equations is categorical and hence correct for TOY-STACK[1]. We
have produced here one more equation than was used by them, namely PD = Er
which turns out to be redundant, but this is not of great consequence in
the light of our objectives.

Some additional remarks may be helpful. Since the graphical representation of state transitions is important for this heuristic, visual
clues (or their automated pattern matching equivalents) are necessary.
To this end let us recall concepts from classical automata theory [B3].
A homing sequence is a word which leads to a unique state from any arbitrary state. If we relax this definition to say that a homing sequence μ
is a word which leads to a subset of states in which a certain e-circuit
label $\{\alpha, \beta\}$ is global then $\alpha\mu = \beta\mu$ is an equation for the data type denoting p-simple e-circuits. Similar remarks hold for pseudo e-circuits.
Hence what we are after in the applications of rules (1) through (3)
above is really a (not necessarily disjoint) decomposition of the state
space into homing sets identified by homing sequences, such that within
each homing set the graph looks uniform with regard to its simple or
pseudo e-circuits.

4.   CONCLUSION

We have presented a connection between transition graphs and algebraic specification of data types. Rules were given for the extraction
of equations from transition graphs but we also indicated that even if
the information contained in the transition graph is finitary these rules

cannot be algorithmic. We believe that the techniques discussed here are useful aids in the abstraction of data types starting from intuitive state descriptions, and envisage that further development would combine automated versions of these with automated provers as software tools.

5. REFERENCES

[A1]   ADJ (Goguen, Thatcher & Wagner) - "An Initial Algebra Approach to the Specification, Correctness and Implementation of Data Types". Current Trends in Programming Methodology, Vol.IV, Data Structuring (Ed) R. Yeh, Prentice Hall, 1978.

[A2]   ADJ (Thatcher, Wagner & Wright) "Data Type Specification and the Power of Specification Techniques". Proceedings SIGACT 10th Annual STOC.

[B1]   Birkhoff, G. "On the Structure of Abstract Algebras". Proc. Cambridge Phil. Soc. Vol. 31, part 4, Oct. 1935.

[B2]   Birkhoff, G. & Lipson, D. "Heterogeneous Algebras". J. Combinatorial Theory, 8, 1970.

[B3]   Booth, T. "Sequential Machines and Automata Theory". Wiley, 1968.

[F1]   Foo, N. & Nolan, G. "Correctness of Algebraic Specifications for Data Structures". Aust. Univ. Computer Science Seminar, 1978.

[G1]   Guttag, J. "The Specification and Application to Programming of Abstract Data Types". Univ. of Toronto, CSRG Tech. Report 59, Sept. 1975.

[L1]   Liskov, B. & Zilles "Formal Specifications for Data Abstraction". Current Trends in Programming Methodology, Vol II, (ed) R. Yeh, Prentice Hall, 1977.

[M1]   Majster, M. "Limits of Algebraic Specifications". SIGPLAN Notices, 12, 1977.

[M2]   Minsky, M. "Computation: Finite and Infinite Machines" Prentice Hall, 1967.

[N1]   Nolan, G. "DASIM1: A Practical Exercise in Data Abstraction".

[S1]   Seshu, S. & Reed, M. "Linear Graphs and Electric Networks".
          Addison-Wesley 1961.

[T1]   Tarski, A.   "Equational Logic and Equational Theories of Algebras".
          Contributions to Mathematical Logic (ed) Schutte, K.
          North Holland, 1968.

Figure 1 - Non-closure of ring sums

Figure 2 - Closure of ring sums

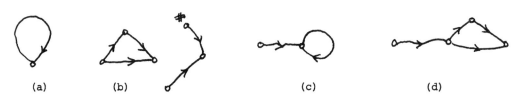

| (a) | (b) | (c) | (d) |

Figure 3 - Example e-circuits and classification

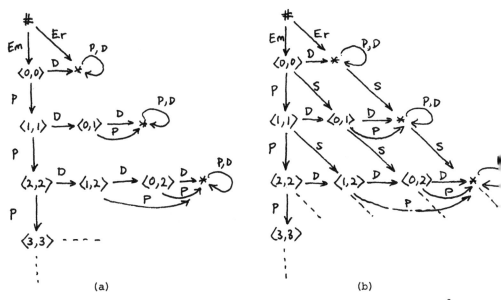

| (a) | (b) |

Figure 4 - Transition graphs for TOY-STACK and TOY-STACK[1]

PROCEEDINGS OF THE SYMPOSIUM ON
LANGUAGE DESIGN AND PROGRAMMING METHODOLOGY
SYDNEY, 10-11 SEPTEMBER, 1979

DASIM1: A PRACTICAL EXERCISE IN DATA ABSTRACTION

Geoffrey J. Nolan

Basser Department of Computer Science
University of Sydney

ABSTRACT

The program DASIM1 accepts an axiomatic specification for a
data structure, then constructs an instance of the structure
thus defined and executes operations upon it. This paper
explains how such a specification is developed, indicating
some of the problems which may be encountered. The manner
in which DASIM1 employs the axioms in the simulation of the
structure is described. Finally, certain correctness proofs
concerning the axioms are discussed.

1. INTRODUCTION

Data Abstraction is the process of 'correctly' specifying the
properties of a data structure without regard to details of implementation. We regard a 'correct' specification as one which provides all
relevant details about the structure (and no irrelevant details), and
which contains no ambiguities, contradictions or redundancies. Or, in
model theoretic terms, we wish our specification to be complete, consistent and independent [Foo and Nolan, 1978].

Such specifications may be expressed in many different fashions,
but we have chosen an equational axiom system. The construction and
application of such a system is discussed in the following sections.

The program DASIM1 accepts an axiom system as input, and provides
a simulation of the corresponding data structure. Simulation is
perhaps not the appropriate word to use in this case, as the program
actually constructs and executes operations on an instance of the
structure arising from the axioms.

The program as it stands does perform various syntactic checks on
the axioms as they are read. However, future versions of the program
will also check the axioms for incompleteness, inconsistency, redundancy, and other semantic errors. The test for consistency (and independence) is particularly efficient because of the axiom system used
by the program. This test will be described later.

The program is also limited to those structures which can be expressed using axioms of one particular form. At present, such structures consist primarily of linear and circular (i.e. non-branching)
structures which are well-behaved, in the sense that the operations
performed on them have the same effect, in general, on each instance
of the structure.

2.   CONSTRUCTING AN AXIOMATIC SPECIFICATION

Clearly, before any simulation can take place, we must specify to the program exactly the type of structure we require. DASIM1 expects this information in the form of a list of axioms, the exact nature of which will be described in the following sections.

The task of constructing an axiomatic specification is a complex one, so we will illustrate the process throughout with a sample structure. The so called 'peek-stack' [Majster, 1977] will be used for this purpose, since while being fairly simple conceptually, it poses most of the problems normally met in this area.

The peek-stack may be considered to be a normal stack equipped with a 'pointer'. The pointer can be moved down the stack by a special operation (DOWN), and reset to the top-of-stack by another (RETURN). The READ operation, instead of returning the top element of the stack, returns the element currently indicated by the pointer. Any PUSHing or POPing attempted while the pointer is not at the top-of-stack results in an error condition.

In order to establish a specification for any data structure, we must first state the operations with which we wish to equip the structure. Thus, for our peek-stack, we need the operations PUSH (an item onto the stack), POP (an item off the stack) and READ (an item). In addition, we will need the operations DOWN and RETURN described above.

Finally, we need at least one structure to act as a reference point. In this case, we choose two: NEWPS returns a new (empty) peek-stack, while ERROR is a distinguished structure which results from any illegal combination of operations. Note that we may regard NEWPS and ERROR either as constant elements of the set of peek-stacks, or as nullary functions which map into that set. Conceptually, the former definition is closer to our true intention, but we can use the same techniques on all the operations if we regard them all as functions.

Now that we have defined the operations we wish to use, we can express any peek-stack by combining these operations. For example, the peek-stack consisting of the elements '2' and '6', with '6' at the top-of-stack and the pointer indicating '2' would be expressed in the form

    DOWN.PUSH(6).PUSH(2).NEWPS

The operations are performed from right to left and are separated by a dot. Henceforth, we will refer to such a string of operations as an op-sequence. The value of the above op-sequence is the peek-stack just described.

As another example, the value of

    READ.DOWN.PUSH(6).PUSH(2).NEWPS

is '2'. Note that the value of an op-sequence is an element of the set mapped into by its leftmost operation (see next section).

3. FUNCTIONALITY

As stated above, the operations we wish our structure to possess may be considered as mappings. In the case of the peek-stack (and all other structures compatible with DASIM1), such mappings involve two sets. These will be referred to as D, the set of structures (in this case peek-stacks), and I, the set of items (DASIM1 uses integers).

While operations of any functionality are possible, the current version of the program recognises only the following four cases :

```
1 : D x I -> D    (PUSH)
2 : D     -> D    (POP, DOWN, RETURN)
3 :       -> D    (NEWPS, ERROR)
4 : D     -> I    (READ)
```

It is this factor which is chiefly responsible for the limitation on the type of data structure that DASIM1 is capable of representing. The reason for this restriction will become apparent later.

4. HIDDEN OPERATIONS

We have already stated that many data structures cannot be specified at all using operations with only the above four functionalities. It is also true that many structures would require an infinite number of axioms, if only the desired operations are used in the axioms. The peek-stack is such a structure [Thatcher et al., 1978].

However, by using additional operations in the axioms, finite axiom systems can be developed in some cases. The addition of an operation SHOVE (D x I -> D) is sufficient for the construction of a finite axiom system to represent the peek-stack. SHOVE has the effect of adding an item to the top of the stack irrespective of the current position of the pointer.

Of course, we may not wish the user to have access to SHOVE. It is possible within DASIM1 to specify that certain operations found in the axioms should not be available during simulation. We call such operations 'hidden' operations.

5. THE AXIOM SYSTEM

In the context of data abstraction, the term 'axiom' usually refers to a statement asserting the equivalence of seemingly dissimilar structures (i.e. op-sequences). Thus the statement "a PUSH followed by a POP is equivalent to the identity operation" could be considered an axiom. A more common form for such an axiom would be POP(PUSH(A,B)) = A .

The notation used in DASIM1 is POP.PUSH(X).\$ = \$, where the dollar sign is a variable representing any element of D.

The axioms which define the peek-stack to DASIM1 are :

```
PS1  : PUSH(X).#ERROR = #ERROR
PS2  : PUSH(X).#SHOVE(Y).$ = #ERROR
PS3  : #SHOVE(X).#ERROR = #ERROR
PS4  : POP.#ERROR = #ERROR
PS5  : POP.NEWPS = #ERROR
PS6  : POP.PUSH(X).$ = $
PS7  : POP.#SHOVE(X).$ = #ERROR
PS8  : DOWN.#ERROR = #ERROR
PS9  : DOWN.NEWPS = #ERROR
PS10 : DOWN.PUSH(X).$ = #SHOVE(X).$
PS11 : DOWN.#SHOVE(X).$ = #SHOVE(X).DOWN.$
PS12 : RETURN.#ERROR = #ERROR
PS13 : RETURN.NEWPS = NEWPS
PS14 : RETURN.PUSH(X).$ = PUSH(X).$
PS15 : RETURN.#SHOVE(X).$ = PUSH(X).RETURN.$
PS16 : READ.#ERROR = !E
PS17 : READ.NEWPS = !N
PS18 : READ.PUSH(X).$ = X
PS19 : READ.#SHOVE(X).$ = READ.$
```

The '#' before ERROR and SHOVE indicates the hidden nature of these operations. '!E' and '!N' are distinguished elements of I which are defined in the axioms to indicate the empty and error conditions; they are not normally available to the user during simulation. X and Y are arbitrary elements of D.

The axioms are used in the following manner. As stated earlier, each op-sequence corresponds to some peek-stack (or element of I). We apply an axiom to such a sequence by trying to match the left-hand-side (LHS) of the axiom to some right subsequence of the operations. If a match occurs, we substitute the RHS of the axiom. This produces a new string which represents the same structure. If the axioms above are repeatedly applied to any op-sequence representing a peek-stack, the sequence will be transformed into its 'Standard Form' (see below).

We will refer to an axiom system such as the one above as an NASF (Non-Associative Standard Form) equational axiom system.

The axioms are non-associative in that where more than one axiom could conceivably be applied to an op-sequence, the axiom whose LHS matches the smallest possible right subsequence of operations is always chosen. Contradictions can quite easily be forced if the axioms are applied in any other order. For example, READ.PUSH(2).#ERROR would take the value '2' if PS18 were applied first. However, the NASF system ensures that PS1 (which matches the smallest right subsequence: PUSH(2).#ERROR) is applied first, then PS16 is applied to give the correct result ('!E').

Since any given instance of a data structure can in general be represented by a number, possibly infinite, of different op-sequences, it is useful to be able to choose a unique sequence to represent each instance. We call such a sequence the 'Standard Form' (or SF) of the structure.

For example, the standard form chosen for the peek-stack is #SHOVE*.PUSH*.NEWPS + #ERROR . That is "a NEWPS followed by zero or more PUSHes, followed by zero or more SHOVEs, or an ERROR by itself".

Each axiom is of the following form :

OP1.OP2. ... .OPM.DS = op1.op2. ... .opN.DS

where OPi and opi are operations, DS is either a nullary operation or $, and the following restrictions apply :

       (1) OP1.OP2. ... .OPM.DS is not in SF.
       (2) OP2.OP3. ... .OPM.DS is in SF.
       (3) M >= N   and   N >= 0   and   M > 0.
       (4) If M = N, then op2. ... .opN.DS is not in SF.

(1) and (2) imply that the LHS of each axiom is of the form 'OP1.S' (where S is an SF sequence). This reflects the fact that axioms must always be applied to the smallest non-SF right subsequence.

(3) and (4) tell us that when the axiom has been applied, either SF is restored, or a new axiom can be applied to a new and smaller right subsequence.

The use of the NASF system has a number of advantages. Perhaps the most important is that the nature of the axioms follows directly from the SF. For once we have obtained the SF, we form the LHS of our axioms by prepending the operations to various SF sequences.

Another advantage of NASF is that the axioms are much more amenable to proofs of completeness, consistency etc. This is because only one axiom is normally applicable to any given op-sequence. Finally, of course, no proofs for associativity of axioms are necessary (or possible).

A possible disadvantage of the NASF system is that it may not be capable of representing certain classes of data structures. Although this possibility is mentioned in Thatcher et al. [1978], the exact extent of such restrictions is still an open problem.

6.   CORRECTNESS

Once the axioms have been established, it is highly desirable to be able to prove them 'correct'. By 'correctness', we do not mean that the axioms specify the 'intended structure', since without a pre-existing specification it is impossible to determine what the 'intended structure' is. (Of course, it may be possible to prove two specifications equivalent, but that problem is beyond the scope of this discussion.)

We will describe an axiom system as 'correct' if it gives rise to exactly one type of data structure. A correctness proof can be divided into two parts. Firstly, the axiom system must contain no internal contradictions (i.e. it must be consistent). Secondly, the effect of every possible combination of operations must be clearly defined by the axiom system (i.e. it must be complete).

A third property we may wish our axioms to possess is independence. That is, no two axioms must apply to the same op-sequence. While not strictly necessary, independence is a desirable property as we avoid the complications of unnecessary axioms and simplify other proofs concerning the axioms.

Now, the NASF system requires that axioms be applied only to the smallest possible right subsequence, and that the axioms are repeatedly applied until SF is reached. Therefore, inconsistency and redundancy can only be present when two or more axioms can be applied to the same op-sequence, and hence to the same right subsequence. This condition can only occur when the LHS of one axiom is the same as, or a left subsequence of, the LHS of another axiom. Note that in this case we ignore any '$' in the LHS. By applying this simple test to all the axioms, we can determine whether any inconsistency or redundancy is present.

The second phase of the correctness proof is to ascertain that every legal op-sequence can be converted to SF by repeated application of the axioms. If this is the case, we call our axioms 'complete'. Moreover, since on any computer we can only generate finite op-sequences, we can say that for all practical purposes a complete system is also categorical (i.e. can only generate one type of structure).

Completeness proofs for individual axiom systems suggest that a testing algorithm would rely on induction on the lengths of op-sequences. However, at the time of writing, no general completeness algorithm had been perfected.

7.   THE PROGRAM 'DASIM1'

DASIM is being written in two stages. Stage 1 accepts correct axioms as input and thereafter acts as a "black box" containing the data structure. Stage 2 (currently being designed) will accept axioms and the nature of the SF. The axioms will be checked for compatibility with the SF, and for any semantic errors (incompleteness, inconsistency etc.). Thereafter, the simulation is as before.

DASIM1 is written in standard PASCAL [Jensen and Wirth, 1975] (future versions may be written in SNOBOL4). The program accepts NASF axioms, whose operations are of the four functionalities described above. This purely arbitrary restriction ensured that the essential features of the prototype program were not submerged in the morass of implementational details associated with more general data structure simulation.

However, it is hoped that future versions of the program will accept operations of a much wider (and perhaps even arbitrary) range of functionalities. In addition, the restriction on using only the sets D and I may be lifted. This will correspondingly widen the range of data structures that DASIM is capable of representing.

A brief summary of the program's operation follows :

The program operates in two modes, an axiom gathering mode and a simulation mode. Initially, the program reads a file containing axioms written in the form :

    AXNAME : LHS = RHS ; COMMENT

Each axiom is then checked for syntactic errors (such as functionality conflicts and incorrect syntax).

The axioms are then stored on a linked list, each axiom itself pointing to linked lists of operators (LHS and RHS). There is a separate list in which is stored the details of the various operations.

The axiom gathering mode is terminated by an escape character which also indicates how much of the internal workings of the structure are to be displayed.

After the axioms have been verified, the program enters the simulation mode during which it interactively accepts input lines consisting of single operations (or commands such as "clear the current structure" etc.). The program maintains a circular list on which the current SF of the structure is stored. Note that a circular list is used for convenience only, a linear list is sufficient to store circular structures. When an input line is received, the appropriate operation is added to the list. The axioms are now applied to the list as follows.

Successively larger right sublists are compared with the LHS of each axiom in turn. If a match occurs, the RHS of the axiom is substituted for the sublist. The process is repeated until no further matches can be found (i.e. SF is achieved). However, if the most recent operation returns an item, the whole structure is duplicated and the axioms are applied to the duplicate. This is because the process of extracting an item invariably has a destructive effect on the stored structure. The integer value of the operation is then displayed and the original structure is left intact.

8. THE CONCEPTUAL NATURE OF 'DASIM1'

We have variously referred to the operation of DASIM1 as 'construction' and 'simulation' of data structures. In fact, DASIM1 embeds data structures onto an internal structure, namely the linked list in which instances of the structure are stored. If we allowed the operators to have more general functionalities, they would have to be stored in a more general data structure. For example, the operations necessary for a finite axiomatisation of tree-like structures would themselves have to be internally stored on a tree (or more general structure).

Taking this concept to its logical conclusion, we should be able to simulate any data structure below a certain level of complexity by designing a suitably general internal structure for our simulating program. However, each such increase in generality entails a substantial increase in the size and complexity of the simulating program. Nevertheless, it should be possible to write programs operating on the same principles as DASIM1 for a number of general applications.

REFERENCES

FOO, N. Y. and NOLAN G. J. (1978):
    "Correctness of Algebraic Specifications for Data Structures".
    Proceedings Australian Universities Computer Science Seminar,
        Feb. 1978.

JENSEN, K. and WIRTH, N. (1975):
    "PASCAL User Manual and Report" (2nd Edition).
    Springer-Verlag, New York.

MAJSTER, M.E. (1977):
    "Limits of the 'Algebraic' Specification of Abstract Data Types".
    ACM SIGPLAN Notices, 12(10), Oct. 1977.

THATCHER, J.W., WAGNER, E.G. and WRIGHT, J.B. (1978):
    "Data Type Specification: Parameterization and the Power of
        Specification Techniques".
    Proceedings 10th STOC Conf., May 1978.

PROCEEDINGS OF THE SYMPOSIUM ON
LANGUAGE DESIGN AND PROGRAMMING METHODOLOGY
SYDNEY, 10-11 SEPTEMBER, 1979

THE DESIGN OF A SUCCESSOR TO PASCAL

Ken Robinson

Department of Computer Science
University of New South Wales

ABSTRACT

A new programming language intended as a contribution to the
development of Pascal is discussed.

* The language supports all of the type constructs of Pascal
  except the variant record.

* A class construct has been provided to allow the implementation of abstract data types and the hiding of the actual
  implementation.

* A type union replaces the variant record.

* Parameterized types allow procedures to operate on wider
  classes of conformable data types than Pascal.

* Predefined data types of "complex" and "string" have been
  added.

* A new concept called a "selector" has been added.

* The var parameter has been discarded. Parameter modes are
  now const, value, result and value result.

* Functions are generalized to any type and additionally may
  return more than one value.

* The assignment statement is replaced by the concurrent
  assignment statement.

* The if-, while- and repeat-statements are replaced by
  Dijkstra's if- and do-statements.

* A pipeline facility is provided for communication and synchronization of sequential processes.

This work was initiated while the author was visiting the Computer
Studies Group, Department of Mathematics, Southampton University.

1. INTRODUCTION

The design of a new programming language frequently is approached with a great deal of trepidation and announced with apologies for the introduction of "yet another programming language". The trepidation is understandable - there are too many existing examples of bad language design or bad language implementation - yet the apologies are not appropriate - apologies cannot cover up a bad design and only other programmers and time can pass judgement on a language. Perhaps there is a need to apologize in advance for the fact that should the language gain substantial acceptance then it is destined to outstay its original welcome. Despite the existence of so many programming languages this author feels that there are not enough good languages with good compilers widely available on a large number of machines. Pascal is one such language and having now established itself in many areas of computing it can justifiably claim to be the most influential language of the last decade. Pascal is now in the process of being standardized and this inevitably gives rise to much argument. Pascal has probably achieved all that its designer Wirth (1971) ever hoped for it and yet there are many programmers who want and require more. Thus there is a constant demand for extensions to the language, but there are limits to every design and few significant extensions to Pascal are possible without changing the existing language. Indeed Pascal is one language where the "defects" are in many cases the result of deliberate compromises embodied in the language design objectives. It is the opinion of this author that it will prove better to complete the definition of Pascal and accept a standard language which is not significantly extended over the language defined in the Pascal Revised Report, Jensen & Wirth(1975).

This paper discusses the design of a new language intended as a development of Pascal. The language developed is not a straightforward extension of Pascal; it is about as different from Pascal as Pascal was from Algol 60. The paper is intended to be informal and is not a reference manual for the language; that will be released with the implementation of a compiler.

2. DESIGN AIMS

The language is intended to be suitable for use in a wide area of scientific and system programming. The emphasis here is on the suitability to a particular class of programming rather than the simple feasibility of use. For example, Pascal is not an attractive programming language for a large class of scientific problems simply because of the omission of the basic data type "complex".

In general the aims and objectives of Pascal apply with the following being either new or reiterated for emphasis:

* to allow more abstract algorithms and data structures to be realized directly;

* to provide the simpler, yet more powerful, control structures devised by Dijkstra (1975,1976);

* to provide an increased degree of data hiding;

* to provide a facility for parallel programming by implementing a form of communication between processes based on Hoare (1978);

* to design a language which is capable of reasonably efficient execution;

* to provide for rigorous checking of the consistency of the operations on the data, preferably during compilation;

* to provide no implicit default actions;

* to provide for the separate compilation of procedures;

* to design a language in which programmers, particularly students, can concentrate on the design of reliable algorithms and data structures;

* to keep the language "small", that is the language specification should be compact and the number of language constructs few. It would be regarded as an advantage if the language were even more compact than Pascal;

* to reduce the degree to which sequential computation intrudes into the realization of an algorithm, thus reducing the number of transient variables required.

3.   LANGUAGE ELEMENTS

Since we are discussing a development of Pascal it follows that many features of Pascal remain and it is assumed that the reader is familar with Pascal. The following is not a comprehensive definition of a complete language but rather a description of those developments which are different from Pascal. Syntax definitions, where given, are in extended BNF (Wirth 1977).

3.1 Types and Type Definitions

Class. A class type, in addition to scalar and structured types, which is similar to the class type of Simula (Dahl et al 1967), Concurrent Pascal (Brinch Hansen 1976) and Hoare(1972), is introduced. The class concept permits a collection of data structures and associated procedures, functions and selectors to realize an abstract data structure. The initialization of a class occurs implicitly at the time of entry to the block in which a class variable is declared, rather than via an explicit request as in Simula and Concurrent Pascal. The class construct permits a programmer to implement a high degree of data hiding. The implementation of a class also determines the degree of access to the data structure possible from outside the class, thus varying degrees of data security can be achieved. Within a class a procedure gives access to an action, a function access to a value and a selector access to a variable.

154

Figure 1 shows a class implementation of a list-structure. It should be noted that the realization of "list" using pointers cannot be "seen" from outside the class declaration. If a variable is declared to be of type "list"

    L: list;

then only the procedures and functions of the class can be referenced as for example L.prepend(info), L.head, etc.

```
list = class
           listptr = ↑listelement;
           listelement = record
                             content: T;
                             link: listptr
                         end;
           var
               listhead: listptr;
           procedure prepend(x: T);
           begin
               listhead := listptr(x,listhead)
           end;
           function head: T;
                     ...
           ...
           begin head := nil end;
```

Figure 1

In the example shown in Figure 2 the definition of "table" uses the type "person" as an abstract type. The actual definition could be a structured type (record) or it could be a class. The only requirement is that "person" possesses a selector named "key". The table could have been implemented in many ways other than an array (e.g. a linear list, a tree) without any difference discernible outside the class. The only requirement is that type "table" provide sufficient procedures, functions and selectors to implement the desired table functions.

```
person = ...;
table = class
           var
               A: array (...) of person;
           procedure insert(...);
           function find(k: keytype): person;
           begin
               "determine i such that A(i).key = k"
               return(A(i))
           end;
                ...
           begin ... end;
```

Figure 2

Notice that the basic structure <u>record</u> itself could be realized by a class. The following types are indistinguishable:

```
record                          class
   field1: t1;                  var
   field2: t2;                     f1: t1;
      ...                          f2: t2;
end                                 ...
                                selector field1 = f1;
                                selector field2 = f2;
                                   ...
                                begin end
```

Parameterized Types

<u>Size</u> <u>Parameters</u> Parameterized types were suggested by Wirth(1975) as a possible method of overcoming the problem, in Pascal, of passing arrays, of the same dimension but of different actual size, as arguments to the same procedure or function. The facility described here is a general form of Wirth's suggestion.

Parameterized type definition:-

> type-identifier param-list "=" type

examples

```
realvector(n: integer) = array (1..n) of real
matrix(m,n: integer) = array (1..m,1..n) of real
```

Parameterized type use:-

> var-identifier ":" type-identifier parameters

examples

```
avector: realvector(100)
amatrix: matrix(10,20)
procedure sort(value result v: realvector(n))
function product(value a: matrix(m1,n1);
                 value b: matrix(m2,n2)): matrix(m1,n2)
```

Notice that the parameters "n", "m1", n1", "m2" and "n2" declared within the procedure formal parameter section become constants (i.e., read only) whose values are the sizes associated with the actual parameters.

<u>Type</u> <u>Parameters</u> The precedent for this is Pascal itself where file-, set- and array-type declarations have the form

> identifier [parameters] "of" type

establishing a type-class.

It is proposed that the following general forms be allowed:

Definition:-

  type-identifier [formal-params] "of" formal-type-identifier "=" type

reference:-

    type-identifier [actual-params] "of" actual-type-identifier

Examples

```
table of T = class
              var
                  A: array (...) of T;
              ...
```

The Pascal type "file" can be regarded as a parameterized class:

```
file of T = class
             var
                 f: "primitive file" of T;
             procedure get;
                 ...
             procedure put;
                 ...
             ...
```

Predefined Types

Scalar Types

Integer and Boolean As for Pascal.

Character Character sets remain a problem in programming languages as we are still unable, after three decades of computing, to agree on a standard set! The only axioms which are valid for all character encodings are extremely weak:

1. the characters in the subrange '0'..'9' are ordered and contiguous;

2. characters in the subrange 'A'..'Z' (not 'a'..'z' which may not exist!) are ordered.

The intimidation of programming languages, and through them programmers, by the various whims of computer manufacturers is intolerable - character processing in Pascal is crippled severely as a consequence of accepting the above axioms. There is a strong temptation to adopt the most rational of the contending character codes for the definition of the collating sequence of characters for a particular language. If this were done then there is really only one candidate, ASCII (ISO), since none of the others could be described as rational, least of all that unbelievable mess known as EBCDIC culpably loosed on an undeserving world by IBM, and regrettably followed by some other manufacturers.

Implementation notes

1. Character data should be represented internally by at least 8 bits. On machines with 24 bit, 36 bit and 60 bit words characters should be represented by 8 bits, 9 bits and 10 bits respectively. For such machines it will not be possible to utilize any 6 bit "character" handling instructions which might exist.

2. Reading and writing of text-files may require character translation.

3. A distinction should be made between "character" and "byte" data. A byte is an integer subrange (6-bit or 8-bit) and it is expected that there will be a predefined type "byte" which will provide for the processing of special character encodings.

Against the above possible disadvantages must be weighed the advantage of program portability.

   Real and Complex To the type "real" (as for Pascal) is added the predefined class "complex" possessing a real component (.r) and an imaginary component (.i)

   Sets "Set" is a predefined parameterized type as for Pascal except that "set of char" must be implemented.

   Strings A predefined parameterized class

$$\text{"string" "of" T}$$

is introduced, where T is a scalar type-identifier.

   Pascal does not possess a true string type. An array can be used to implement the data-structure known as a string, but a string is not an array (packed or otherwise). It must be possible to reference a string as a whole or any substring of that string. In addition it should be possible to have varying length strings.

   Files and Text-files Files as for Pascal except that "file" is a predefined parameterized class. Both sequential and random access file processing procedures will be implemented.

   A text-file ("text") is a predefined parameterized class which is a structured file consisting of "pages" which in turn consist of "lines" which in turn consist of "characters". It should be possible to write any data, with the possible exception of pointers, to a text-file. In general reciprocity should exist between input and output statements, meaning that if some data has been written on a text-file by "f.write(x)" then it will be possible to recover that same data by "f.read(x)".

   Pipes

$$\text{"pipe" "of" type-identifier}$$

"Pipe" is a predefined parameterized class for communication between sequential processes. A pipe has two associated procedures "send" and "receive" by which a single item of data may be sent or received through the pipe.

Unions A predefined parameterized class "union" is introduced replacing Pascal's variant record. Pascal provided a means of representing a type-union as a variant record. The greatest weakness of this facility is that it becomes the programmer's responsibility to ensure that the tag setting correctly reflects the current status of the variant.

Example

```
R: record
          case tag: tagtype of
                  fool: (x: t1; ... );
                  idiot: (y: t2; ... );
                  ...
      end
   ...
R.tag := fool;       (1)
R.x := ...;          (2)
R.tag := idiot;      (3)
if R.y = ...         (4)
```

The reference at (4) is obviously invalid yet it may be very difficult to check since it is necessary to determine whether the field "y" has been reset since the last resetting of the tag-field. Notice that the statements at (2), (3) and (4) could be widely separated and still be analogous to the above.

The example illustrates the point that the value of the tag-field alone is not a reliable indicator of the actual variant which has been established. Thus the value of a tag-field cannot be used to determine the validity of a variant reference and this may explain why tag-field checking is omitted from many Pascal compilers.

The problem stems from the division of the action of establishing a variant into two separate actions, the setting of the tag-field (the intended variant) and the setting of the components of that variant.

There is also the disadvantage that unions are forced to be explicitly structured data and thus, for example, a union of scalar types becomes cumbersome.

Examples

```
x: union of (integer,real,char);
x := 1;  (* x.type becomes "integer" *)
if x.type = char ->
  ...
case x.type of
integer ->
real->
char->
  ...
```

Data Constructors   It is desirable to be able to initialize variables and to generate instances of a data structure within a program.
It is convenient to use the type-identifier to construct an instance of
data of that type.

Examples

```
v: integer(1);  (* v is initialized to 1 *)
x := complex(y,z)  (* x.r = y and x.i = z *)
```

In the case of scalar type-identifiers it is convenient to use them
also as type transfer functions.

Definition

```
If T1 and T2 are scalar type-identifiers
and x is an element of T1
then T2(x) is an element of T2
such that ord(T2(x)) = ord(x)
```

Examples

```
integer('a') = ord('a')
colour((ord(red)+ord(blue)) div 2)
char(i) is equivalent to Pascal's chr(i)
```

Constant Definitions

```
constant-definition = constant-identifier "=" constant-expression.
```

Constant definitions will be allowed to contain constant expressions,
that is expressions whose values can be determined at their point of
occurrence.

3.2 Procedures, Functions and Selectors

Procedures   Similar to Pascal procedures except for parameter
modes (see below).

Functions   Functions in Pascal are severely restricted in that
they may return only scalar or pointer values. This is unfortunate as
frequently it is with structured types that functions are most
required. For example, in Pascal we could define the types "point" and

"line" as follows:

```
point = record x, y: real end;
line = record p1, p2: point end
```

in order to represent points and lines in plane geometry and then we could establish an algebra of points and lines. However the algebra would be to little avail since we could not define the required functions in Pascal. If the reader thinks that the above example is too esoteric then it will be a revealing exercise to work out in detail the implementation of complex arithmetic in Pascal.

It is necessary, in order that computations on data-structures may proceed at a high level, to allow functions to return values of any type.

Figure 3 shows a complex product function which could be used if the language did not possess "complex" as a basic type.

```
type cmplxunion = union of (integer,real,complex);
function cmplxprod(value a, b: cmplxunion): complex;
begin
     do
          a.type isnt complex -> a := complex(a.0)
     []
          b.type isnt complex -> b := complex(b,0)
     od;
     return(complex(a.r*b.r-a.i*b.i, a.r*b.i+a.i*b.r))
end
```

Figure 3

Traditionally in programming languages there is a lack of uniformity in the treatment of functions which return one value and functions which return more than one value. It is recognized that functions may compute more than one value and this fact may then be used to motivate the concept of the var parameter.

It has been suggested that the semantics of procedures and functions should be describable in terms of a concurrent assignment statement (Hoare 1971, Hoare & Wirth 1973). That is,the effect of a procedure or function (as far as the var parameters and global variables are concerned) is that of a concurrent assignment of expressions to the var parameters and global variables.

Since the proposed language possesses a concurrent assignment statement it seems opportune to realize the semantics rather literally. Functions may return more than one value and may have only const or value parameters. The multiple values may be assigned to variables in a concurrent assignment statement. Figure 4 shows a simple function returning two values.

```
function minmax(const g: realvector(m)): (real,real);
var
        min,max: real;
        i: integer;
begin
        assert(m >= 1);
        min,max := g[1],g[1];
        i := 2;
        do i < m ->
                if g[i] < g[i+1] ->
                        do g[i] < min -> min := g[i]
                        [] g[i+1] > max -> max := g[i+1]
                        od
                [] g[i] >= g[i+1] ->
                        do g[i] > max -> max := g[i]
                        [] g[i+1] < min -> min := g[i+1]
                        od
                fi;
                i :+ 2
        od;
        if i = m ->
                do g[i] < min -> min := g[i]
                [] g[i] > max -> max := g[i]
                od
        [] i <> m -> skip
        fi;
        return(min,max)
end
```

Figure 4.   Function returning two values

Selectors A selector returns a variable rather than a value.
Such a facility is necessary with classes if access is to be given to
actual components of a structure rather than simply a copy of the component. For example, suppose it is required to search "mytable" of
class "table", defined in Figure 2, for an entry whose key is 'Fred'
and to increment the value in the associated field "age". The function
"find" defined in Figure 2 is of no use since it returns the value of
the record not the record itself hence

        mytable.find('Fred').age :+ 1

is not correct, in fact it is illegal. However changing "find" to a
selector rather than a function makes the above assignment both legal
and correct.

Parameters Parameters to procedures may be passed by const,
value, result or value result only.

Parameters to functions and selectors may be passed by const or
value only.

3.3 Statements

Concurrent Assignment

assignment = variable-list ":=" expression-list .

For procedural programming languages, like Pascal, variables and assignment are, for better or worse (Backus 1978), their most fundamental concepts. The state of a program is represented by the state of the variables and the assignment statement is the principal mechanism for changing the value of a variable. It is one of the objectives of a high-level programming language to reduce the number of variables required to implement an algorithm, yet languages which implement a simple assignment statement are imposing a very simple sequential mechanism for changing the state of a program: at most the value of one variable may be changed. In a situation where a change of state requires the simultaneous changing of the values of a number a variables this simple sequential mechanism may require extra variables to effect the change. As a consequence of the increase in variables the realization becomes longer and more complex than the algorithm.

Just two simple examples will be given to illustrate the above point. The first is the common case of swapping the values of two variables:

$$a, b := b, a$$
$$=> x := a; \quad a := b; \quad b := x$$

the second comes from an algorithm for reversing the order of the elements in a linear linked list:

$$r, p, p\uparrow.next := p, p\uparrow.next, r$$
$$=> x := r; \quad y := p; \quad r := p; \quad p := p\uparrow.next; \quad y\uparrow.next := x$$

The concurrent assignment appears to have been first used in CPL (Barron et al 1963) and largely ignored by programming languages since then. Its importance seems not to have been appreciated: as indicated above it is not simply (or even primarily) a notational convenience such as, for example, the multiple assignment of Algol 60.

Other Assignment Operators In addition to the normal assignment operator ":=", other forms are introduced for incrementing ":+", decrementing ":-", etc., the value of a variable. More generally:

v :? u is equivalent to v := v ? u for "?" ≠ "="

If-statement

if-statement = "if" guarded-command-list "fi" .
guarded-command-list = guarded-command {"[]" guarded-command} .
guarded-command = guard "->" statement {";" statement} .
guard = Boolean-expression .

The statement is due to Dijkstra (1975,1976). The interpretation of the statement is as follows. All the guards are evaluated and of those guarded commands whose guards are true one command is chosen arbitrarily and executed. At least one guard must be true otherwise the statement aborts.

The if-then-else-statement has attracted much comment on both its asymmetry and the complexity of the implied pre-condition for a statement nested deeply within a nested if-then-else-statement. In many cases the if-then-else-statement is another example of sequential ordering being imposed where none is required. If an ordering is required the above if-statement forces the logical complexity to be explicit since the guards will have to be mutually exclusive.

Case-statement The Pascal case-statement is retained even though it is made redundant by the if-statement, since selection on the basis of a set of constants is likely to be more efficient using a case-statement.

Do-statement

do-statement = "do" guarded-command-list "od" .

This statement is due to Dijkstra (1975,1976). The do-statement is an iterative statement which terminates when all the guards are false. While any guard is true one command whose guard is true is arbitrarily selected and executed. The comments made above on the if-then-else-statement apply similarly to the while-statement of Pascal and no clearer demonstration of the beauty of the do-statement compared with the relative ugliness of the while-statement is likely to be found than the one shown in Figure 5. The expression of Euclid's algorithm seems to have played an important role during Dijkstra's own formulation of his concept of guarded commands.

```
function gcd(a,b: posint): posint;
begin
     do a > b -> a :- b
     [] a < b -> b :- a
     od;
     return(a)
end
```

Figure 5a. Euclid's algorithm expressed with do-statement

```
function gcd(a,b: posint): posint;
begin
     while a <> b
     do begin
          while a > b do a := a-b;
          while a < b do b := b-a
        end;
     gcd := a
end
```

Figure 5b. Euclid's algorithm expressed in Pascal

Programming note It may appear at first that the statement:

if B then S

should be translated to:

    if B -> S
    [] not B -> skip
    fi

but in many cases the following translation is possible:

    do B -> S od

This second construct is stronger than the former in so far as it makes clear that the consequent of the statement implies "not B" (i.e., {B} S {not B}).

Implementation note It is important that the selection of guarded commands for both the if-statement and the do-statement is arbitrary. Requiring all guards to be evaluated and then selecting arbitrarily from those guarded commands whose guards are true will prove inefficient on a sequential machine (but not perhaps on a parallel machine). Alternatively the compiler could order the guarded commands arbitrarily (such that the order is likely to be different for different compilations) and then the guards could be evaluated sequentially with selection of the first command whose guard is true.

For-statement

```
for-statement
 = "for" variable ":=" expression "to" expression "->" statement
 | "for" variable ":=" expression "downto" expression "->" statement
 | "forall" variable "in" set-expression "->" statement .
```

The Pascal for-statement will be retained. In addition a for-statement which executes a statement for all values contained in a set, the order of selection being arbitrary, is included.

With-statement

with-statement = "with" variable-list "->" statement .

The with-statement becomes a necessity rather than a convenience, as it is in Pascal, since in general it is required in order to hold the variable returned by a selector.

3.4 Parallel Execution

par-sequence = "parbegin" proc-call {"||" proc-call} "parend"

Processes can communicate through "pipes". The implementation attempted here is different to, but based on, that suggested by Hoare(1978). In Hoare's paper processes communicate directly with a named process rather than through a named pipeline. In a network sense

Hoare's approach is to name the nodes whereas the approach here is to name the edges. There are notational advantages in the latter but a number of implementational disadvantages, one of which is the fact that the processes associated with a pipe may vary with time. In particular the termination of a process cannot be used to signal the end of a pipe. A number of constraints may be required.

Figure 6 is a realization of the procedures "disassemble", "assemble" and process "reformat" discussed in Hoare (1978).

4. SEPARATE COMPILATION

Separate compilation of procedures is a requirement for large programs and for programs which wish to use a library of procedures.

It is intended that the compiler will accept an object known as a "module" where a module consists of a definition and declaration section followed by a sequence of procedure declarations and/or a program declaration.

module = [definitions-and-declarations] {procedure} [program] .

In this way procedures at level 0 (i.e. external to the program) may be compiled separately.

4.1 External Procedures

As a consequence of separate compilation it must be possible to reference procedures which are external to the current module. In addition the facility should exist to reference and use external procedures compiled by another language compiler (in particular FORTRAN and assembler).

5. IMPLEMENTATION AND EXTENSIBILITY

No programming language is better than its implementation: the quality of the compiler and run-time support system has a profound effect on the observed quality of any programming language. This is particularly true of the language being discussed here since it is not an experimental "paper" language; one of the objectives is to produce a Pascal-like language which will be attractive to a large community of programmers. For this reason a full description of the language will not be generally available until a satisfactory implementation exists.

One of the objectives of the implementation is to produce a compiler which is portable enough to become the basis of all implementations. To achieve this the code generation will be made very "visible" and will be documented to aid transportation to various machines. The initial compiler will of course be written in Pascal and it is planned always to have a Pascal version of a compiler available for initial bootstrapping onto any machine for which a Pascal compiler exists.

One of the notable achievements of Pascal is the degree to which a family of Pascal compilers now exists, each compiler clearly based on the compiler implemented by Ammann (1970,1974). The objective here is to carry the process further and attempt to produce a "standard" compiler. This would seem to have important implications for the standardization of a language: it should be easier to revise a language if at the same time as a revised language standard is produced a revised standard compiler is also produced.

```
type charpipe = pipe of char;
procedure disassemble(result X: charpipe);
var
        cardimage: string(80) of char;
begin
        do not input.eof ->
            input.readln(cardimage);
            for i := 1 to 80 ->
                    if i <= cardimage.length ->
                        X.send(cardimage[i])
                    []  i > cardimage.length ->
                        X.send(' ')
                    fi;
                X.send(' ')
        od;
        X.close
end
```

Figure 6a.   Procedure disassemble

```
procedure assemble(value X: charpipe);
var
        c: char;
        lineimage: string(125) of char;
begin
        lineimage := '';
        do not X.end ->
            X.receive(c);
            lineimage.append(c);
            do lineimage.length = 125 ->
                output.writeln(lineimage);
                lineimage := ''
            od
        od;
        if lineimage.length = 0 -> skip
        []  lineimage.length <> 0 ->
            output.writeln(lineimage)
        fi
end
```

Figure 6b.   Procedure assemble

```
var X: charpipe;
    ...
parbegin disassemble(X) || assemble(X) parend
```

Figure 6c.   Process reformat

6. ACKNOWLEDGEMENTS

The design presented here is obviously derived from many sources. Influences are numerous and in many cases unremembered. I apologize to any whose influence has gone unacknowledged.

For stimulating discussions which preceded this design I would like to thank Ian Hayes, David Carrington, Jeffrey Tobias, Greg Rose, Carroll Morgan and Tony Gerber. I wish to thank all my colleagues at Southampton especially John Goodson, Mike Rees and Ralph Elliott for valuable discussions during my visit, even though they remain justifiably sceptical about the language described in this paper. I am grateful to David Barron for the opportunity of visiting the Computer Studies Group and the chance to commence this project. John Goodson must be thanked again for proof-reading this paper, although I am solely responsible for any remaining split infinitives.

7. REFERENCES

Ammann, U. (1970) "Pascal-6000 compiler", ETH Zurich.

Ammann, U. (1974) "The method of structured programming applied to the development of a compiler", International Computing Symp. 1973, (Günther, et al, Eds), 93-99.

Barron, D.W., Buxton, J.N., Hartley, D.F., Nixon, F., Strachey, G.S. (1963) "The main features of CPL", Computer Journal 6, 134-143.

Backus, J. (1978) "Can programming be liberated from the von Neumann style? A functional style and its algebra of programs", Comm ACM 21,8(August), 613-641.

Brinch Hansen, P. (1976) "The programming language Concurrent Pascal", I.E.E.E. Trans. Software Eng. 1,2 (June), 199-207.

Dahl,O-J., et al. (1967) "SIMULA 67, common base language", Norwegian Computing Centre, Forskningveien, Oslo.

Dijkstra, E.W.D. (1975) "Guarded commands, nondeterminacy and formal derivation of programs", Comm ACM 18,8 (August), 453-457.

Dijkstra, E.W.D. (1976) "A discipline of programming", Prentice-Hall.

Hoare, C.A.R. (1971) "Procedures and parameters; an axiomatic approach", Symposium on Semantics of Algorithmic Languages (E.Engeler, ed), Lecture Notes in Mathematics 188, Springer-Verlag.

Hoare, C.A.R. (1972) "Proof of correctness of data representations", Acta Informatica 1, 271-281.

Hoare, C.A.R. (1978) "Communicating sequential processes", Comm ACM 21,8 (August), 666-677.

Hoare, C.A.R. & Wirth, N. (1973) "An axiomatic definition of Pascal", Acta Informatica2, 335-355.

Jensen,K. & Wirth,N. (1975) "Pascal User Manual and Report", Springer-Verlag.

Wirth, N. (1971) "The programming language Pascal", Acta Informatica 1,1, 35-63.

Wirth, N. (1975) "An assessment of the programming language Pascal", SIGPLAN Notices 10,6 (June), 23-30.

Wirth, N. (1977) "What can we do about the unnecessary diversity of notations for syntactic definitions?", Comm ACM " 20,11(November), 822-823.

DOPLs : A NEW TYPE OF PROGRAMMING LANGUAGE

Graham Lee

Department of Computer Science
University of Western Australia

ABSTRACT

The importance of *operand description* in programming is
emphasised, and programming languages are classified into
Description-Oriented Programming Languages (DOPLs) and
Identifier-Oriented Programming Languages (IOPLs) according
to their *operand-description* facilities.   Several examples
are used to illustrate DOPLs, and the advantages, in terms
of the level of transparency in programs, of using DOPLs over
IOPLs.

1.   DOPLs and IOPLs

Programming languages can be classified according to their facilities
for describing which *operands* are to be used in an operation.   There are
two main classes:

* Languages which have a large variety of *operand-description*
  facilities.   These will be called *Description-Oriented
  Programming Languages* (DOPLs) [Lee, 1978].
* Languages whose only operand-description facilities are
  identifiers and names.   These will be called *Identifier-
  Oriented Programming Languages*[1] (IOPLs).

Examples of IOPLs range from very primitive languages such as a von
Neumann machine code, through the simpler high-level languages such as
Fortran, to much more sophisticated languages such as Pascal and Algol
68.

An example of a language with a large variety of operand-description
facilities is English.   In fact, one of the main differences between
English and existing programming languages lies in its use of, for
example, adjectives, participles, adverbs, nouns, pronouns and names
when describing operands.   These operand-description facilities account
for much of the expressive power of English, and it therefore seems
worthwhile to incorporate similar facilities in an algorithmic language.
The design of a DOPL can be influenced by the operand-description
facilities of English, as far as is commensurate with a formal,
unambiguous programming language.

The advantage of using a DOPL, as opposed to an IOPL, is that more
transparent, though possibly less efficient, programs can be written.
The level of operand-description facilities available in a language
greatly influences the structure of, and amount of detail in, programs.
The operand-description facilities available in a DOPL enable algorithms
to be specified without using variables, data structures, control

---

[1] This represents a change of terminology from Lee [1978]

structures with nested statements, or input statements. On the other hand, because identifiers and names can only refer to one operand at a time, all the above features are required in IOPLs mainly to support the computation of names for individual operands. IOPL programs are oriented towards specifying a detailed, controlled series of operations on *individually named operands*, whereas DOPL programs are oriented towards direct descriptions of the *whole sequence of operands* to be used in an operation. The latter is more transparent than the former. In IOPL programs, there is a conceptual gap between the explicit information given – the detailed sequence of operations on individually named operands – and the actual information required to understand the algorithm – information on the whole group of operands involved. IOPL programs cannot fill this gap, which must be bridged for each individual reading of a program. DOPL programs, on the other hand, give the latter information explicitly.

The operand-description facilities of the DOPL discussed here can be used to describe the sequence of all the operands to be used in an operation, the data for a program, the required results of an operation, to define new description facilities, and to define data structures.

Although existing languages vary in their operand-description facilities, and although there are examples of languages with operand-description facilities other than identifiers and names (see, for example, Astrahan and Chamberlain [1975], Barron [1977], Burger et al [1975], Chamberlain and Boyce [1974], Feldman and Rovner [1969], Findler [1969], Hebditch [1973], Housel and Shu [1976], Martin [1976], Potts [1970]), and although there have been suggestions for language extensions which are actually concerned with operand-description facilities (Herriot [1977], Nylin and Harvill [1976]), no existing programming language seems to have the breadth and type of operand-description facility envisaged here.

In subsequent sections, several examples are used to introduce a DOPL and to compare it to Pascal. The syntax and semantics of DOPLs are discussed in section 6. To facilitate discussion prior to this section, the following brief definitions are given. A DOPL program contains a sequence of *requests*, and is executed by using each of these requests in turn. Requests may specify operations, or define data, results or new operand-description facilities. An operational request contains *operators* and *operand descriptions*. These descriptions specify the whole sequences of operands to be used in the operation, and the request is executed by applying the operators to each of these operands in turn. In an operand description, each word is a *descriptor*, and nouns, pronouns, adjectives and identifiers are among the kinds of descriptor used. In the DOPL examples, all operators (and all operator-like terms) are in upper case, and all descriptors are in lower case. User-introduced operators and descriptors are in script.

2. THE SIEVE OF ERATOSTHENES

Consider first the following DOPL request for generating all the prime integers less than or equal to a given data integer:

PRINT each *prime* integer <= the data integer

It consists of the operator PRINT followed by an operand description which describes the sequence of operands to be used in the PRINT operation. The operand description is built from several descriptors, of which each, integer, <=, the, data, are primitive, and *prime* is user-defined.

An integer is an item in the 2-way infinite sequence of negative and positive whole numbers, and the descriptor each in the above operand description specifies all of those integers satisfying the conditions specified by the adjective *prime* and the relation
<= the data integer
Thus the operand description specifies a sequence of prime integers up to a given data integer, and the PRINT request is executed by PRINT-ing each one of these in turn.

A DOPL program for generating primes using the above request is shown in program 2.1. It consists of three requests.

```
program    prime-number generation:
DATA IS    an integer.
ADJECTIVE  prime
AS IN      prime integer
IS         integer >1
SUCH THAT  (the prime integer)
           mod
           (any integer > 1
                   and <= square root (the prime integer))
           <> 0.
PRINT      each prime integer <= the data integer
end.
```

Program 2.1   A DOPL program for generating prime numbers

The first one defines the program's data to be an integer, which can subsequently be referred to as *the data integer*. The second one defines the adjective *prime*. The line
    ADJECTIVE *prime*
specifies that a new adjectival descriptor is being defined. The line
    AS IN *prime* integer
specifies that this descriptor must be used with other descriptors which specify an integer. The line
    IS   integer > 1
says that a *prime* integer is an integer (> 1) subject to the condition following SUCH THAT, which specifies that a *prime* integer is one which is not divisible by any other integers >1.

Given the usual definition of a prime, and given that a non prime is divisible by an integer <= its square root, this program must be

correct.   It is evident from the operand descriptions used that the
printed results consist of all the primes up to the given data integer.

Consider now the Sieve of Eratosthenes.   The essential feature of
this prime-number-generation algorithm is the *removal* of multiples of
integers from a sequence initially containing all the integers between
2 and a given data integer.   First the multiples of 2 are removed,
then the multiples of 3, then the multiples of 5 (4 having been removed
because it is a multiple of 2), and so on.   At each stage, the
multiples of the next non-removed integer (which must be a prime – the
fact that it has not been removed means that it cannot be a multiple of
any integer less than it) are removed.   When all multiples have been
removed, the non-removed integers constitute the primes between 2 and
the given data integer.

This process can be specified in a DOPL by the request:

REMOVE each *multiple* <= the data integer
                of each non *remove*-ed integer
                        between 2 and the data integer

This consists of the user-introduced operator REMOVE, followed by an
operand description which is built from several descriptors, of which
each, <=, the, data, integer, of, non, between, 2, and, are primitive,
and *multiple*, *remove*-ed are not.

The operand description specifies a sequence of operands consisting of each *multiple* (<= the data integer) of each of the integers
described by the *nested operand description* (the one following of):
        each non *remove*-ed integer
                between 2 and the data integer
The request is executed by applying the REMOVE operator to each of
these operands.

Although REMOVE is a non-primitive operator, it is not necessary
to give a procedure specifying how to remove integers!   This is because
of the use of the adjective *remove*-ed, which specifies a condition
on integers which becomes true when they are used as operands of REMOVE.
Initially, no integers have been so used, and therefore the condition
        non *remove*-ed
is true of all integers to begin with.

The description:
        each integer between 2 and the integer data
specifies the sequence of integers: 2, 3, 4, ..., the data integer,
and causes each one of these to be generated in turn so that the
condition
        non *remove*-ed
can be checked.   Thus the first integer specified by the nested operand
description is 2, and the first operands specified by the entire operand
description of the request are therefore:
        each *multiple* <= the data integer
                of 2

and so the multiples of 2 are *REMOVE*-ed.   After this, the condition *remove*-ed is true of the multiples of 2.

The nested operand description now specifies the next non *remove*-ed integer, which is 3, and so

    each *multiple* <= the data integer
        of 3

is *REMOVE*-ed.   This process continues until there are no further non *remove*-ed integers.

After executing the *REMOVE* request, the prime numbers can be printed using the request:

    PRINT each non *remove*-ed integer
           between 2 and the data integer

A complete DOPL program for the Sieve process is shown in program 2.2.

program	*Sieve of Eratosthenes:*
DATA IS	an integer.
NOUN	*multiple*
AS IN	*multiple* of an integer
IS	(the integer)*(any integer >1).
REMOVE	each *multiple* <= the data integer
	of each non *remove*-ed integer
	between 2 and the data integer.
PRINT	each non *remove*-ed integer
	between 2 and the data integer
end.	

Program 2.2   A DOPL version of the Sieve of Eratosthenes

The program consists of four requests.   The first describes the data, the second defines the noun *multiple*, the third is the *REMOVE* request, and the fourth prints the primes.

The descriptor *multiple* is used as a noun (the syntax of operand descriptions is discussed in section 6) in the *REMOVE* request, and so its definition begins with NOUN.   The line
    AS IN *multiple* of an integer
specifies that *multiple* is to be used with a nested operand description which specifies one or more integers.   The line
    IS   (the integer)*(any integer >1)
defines a *multiple* to be a product of two integers.   The descriptor the in the factor
    the integer
refers back to the previous mention of an integer, which is in
    multiple of an integer.

The descriptor each specifies each item of a sequence from the first onwards.   The definition of *multiple* can be interpreted as a definition of a sequence of multiples by virtue of the factor
    any integer >1

in the expression following IS.   Thus, in the *REMOVE*-request operand description
　　each *multiple* of <an integer>
the descriptor each specifies the sequence of multiples
　　(the integer)*2
　　(the integer)*3
　　(the integer)*4
and so on.

The DOPL program can be *judged* to be correct given the definition of a prime and given that every non prime is a multiple of some integer less than it.

The DOPL program can be contrasted with the Pascal version in program 2.3.

```
program    Eratosthenes(input, output);
const     n = ?;
var  sieve : array[2 .. n] of integer;
     data, i, m : integer;
begin
read(data);
for  i := 2 to data do  sieve[i] := i;
sieve[data + 1] :=1 ;
i := 1;
repeat
       repeat i := i + 1 until  sieve[i] > 0;
       m := 2*i;
       while m <= data do
              begin
              sieve[m] := 0;
              m := m + i
              end
until i > data;
for  i := 2 to data do
       if   sieve[i] > 0 then  writeln(sieve[i])
end.
```

Program 2.3   A Pascal (IOPL) version of the Sieve of Eratosthenes

(Straight-forward representations of the sieve and of the removal operation are used in this example, in order to facilitate comparison of the two versions.   Another, more efficient and more complex IOPL version, and its proof using invariants, can be found in Hoare [1972]. This IOPL version does not necessarily represent the way in which the DOPL version would be implemented.)

This Pascal version is more difficult to understand and prove correct than the DOPL version.   Removal of multiples is done using the assignment
　　sieve[m] := 0
but because this can only reference one operand at a time, it has to be placed inside two levels of nested loop, one to vary m so that all

multiples are removed, and one to vary i so that all multiples of all primes are removed. Also, an extra loop is required to search for non-removed integers. The loops are used solely to compute the names

$sieve[m]$

of the removed multiples, and the array data structure, and the other variables, are used mainly to construct the above names.

In the IOPL version, the remove (assignment of 0 to a $sieve$ component) operation is nested inside two levels of loop, and involves several variables. Before encountering this operation, the explicit loop statements, and other nested operations, have to be read. In fact, there is no syntactic clue to the fact that the assignment to a $sieve$ component is the main operation. Rather, this has to be gathered from a complex combination of information given in several different places in the program. Once it is known that this is the main operation of the loops, the information on all the variables, which is distributed in different places in declarations, initialisations and updates, together with the explicit nested looping information, has to be gathered together and used to decide what the entire group of remove-ands and non remove-ands are. It is only this operand information which enables an understanding of the total process specified by the loops. In the DOPL version, on the other hand, the main operator REMOVE is placed first, and the sequence of all its operands is made explicit using one operand description. The detailed control information is implicit in the semantics of the descriptors used. Also, the DOPL version can define the data, and the terms $prime$ and $multiple$ (the adjective $prime$ in program 2.2 is equivalent to non $remove$-ed). For these reasons the DOPL version is more transparent than the IOPL version.

3. SORTING

Consider first the problem of sorting a sequence of data integers:

DATA IS   several integer

This could be done using the request

PRINT   smallest non print-ed data integer
UNTIL   print-ed each data integer

However, sorting in a DOPL can be specified without using a particular algorithm, by specifying what the result of sorting should be:

to   SORT a sequence of integers:
           RESULT IS $ascendingly$-$ordered$ $permutation$
                              of the parameter sequence
end

This is an example of a $procedure$. It defines the user-introduced operator SORT, by specifying what the result of an operation such as

SORT   the data sequence

should be.

The descriptor *ascendingly-ordered* can be defined as follows:

ADJECTIVE	*ascendingly-ordered*
AS IN	*ascendingly-ordered* integral sequence
IS	integral sequence
SUCH THAT	each integer of the sequence
	is - <=
	next integer of the sequence

The descriptor *permutation* (which might actually be primitive in a DOPL) can be defined as

NOUN	*permutation*
AS IN	*permutation* of sequence
IS	sequence containing each item of
	sequence
	of-which *permutation* is-being-defined
SUCH THAT FOR	any item of the *permutation*
WE HAVE	number of item = such-that-for-and
	of the *permutation*
	is - =
	number of item = such-that-for-and
	of sequence
	of-which *permutation* is-being-defined

This contains rather involved conditions in the descriptions after IS and WE HAVE. These specify that a permutation contains exactly the same items as the original sequence, but not necessarily in the same order.

The operand description after IS has the form
    sequence containing <description of items to be contained>
In the description of the items to be contained, the nested description
    sequence of-which *permutation* is-being-defined
specifies the sequence in
    AS IN *permutation* of sequence
and the
    of-which ... is-being-defined
reverses the descriptor of in
    permutation of sequence
This could be shortened using an identifier:
    AS IN *permutation* of sequence called x
after which, throughout this request, the sequence of which *permutation* is being defined can be referred to as x. It seems better not to use the identifier.

The description after WE HAVE is a Boolean expression which has the structure
    number of <description of an item of the *permutation*>
    is-equal-to
    number of <description of an item of
               the sequence of which *permutation* is being defined>
The noun such-that-for-and refers to the item described after SUCH THAT FOR. An identifier, for example y, could be used in place of this noun, if the description after SUCH THAT FOR is modified:

any item called *y*
  of the *permutation*

The use of the primitive noun such-that-for-and is to be preferred.
With this noun, it is rather more obvious which item is being referred
to than with a user-introduced identifier such as *y*, which could have
been declared anywhere in the request (or in the whole program).

An *ascendingly-ordered permutation* of a sequence can be produced
by generating sequences in lexicographic order and checking all the
conditions given in the definition, and then checking for *ascendingly-
ordered*-ness. This would be impossibly inefficient for long parameter
sequences. Even so, the *SORT* procedure is a formal specification of
sorting.

Consider now program 3.1, which is a procedure for sorting a
sequence of integers by partitioning it into three groups.

  <u>to</u> *PARTITION SORT* a sequence of integers:
    CHOOSE any parameter integer.
    RESULT IS
       result of *partition-sort*-ing
         each parameter integer < the *choose*-and,
        each parameter integer = the *choose*-and,
       result of *partition-sort*-ing
         each parameter integer > the *choose*-and
  <u>end</u>

Program 3.1 <u>A DOPL procedure for sorting by partitioning</u>

The procedure contains two requests. The first chooses one of the
integers of the parameter sequence. This is subsequently referred to as
the *choose*-and.

The RESULT IS request specifies a partition of the parameter sequence
into three groups, which contain those integers less than the chosen integer,
those equal to it, and those greater than it respectively. The commas in
the operand description of this request can be read as "followed by", and
the descriptor followed-by could be used in their place. In the description
    result of *partition-sort*-ing
      each parameter integer < the *choose*-and
the descriptor *partition-sort*-ing implies a recursive application of the
operator PARTITION SORT to the sequence of parameter integers less than the
chosen integer. There is no need to explicitly specify what the result is
for a null sequence, because the following rule can be adopted in a DOPL:

the result of performing any operation on the null sequence is the
null sequence (unless otherwise specified).

Because of the operand descriptions used, it is evident that this
procedure *recursively partitions* the parameter sequence:

<u>DEFINITION:</u>

A *recursively partitioned* sequence is either a null sequence, or a sequence comprising a left partition, followed by a middle partition consisting of several equal items, followed by a right partition, such that

(a) each item of the left partition is < the middle items,
(b) each item of the right partition is > the middle items,
(c) the left and right partitions are recursively partitioned sequences.

It is intuitively obvious that a recursively partitioned sequence is ascendingly ordered. This can be proved as follows:

<u>PROPOSITION:</u>

A recursively partitioned sequence is ascendingly ordered.

<u>PROOF</u> by reductio. Suppose not, and consider the shortest sequence which is recursively partitioned but not ascendingly ordered. This sequence must have at least two adjacent items which are out of order. These cannot both be in the same partition, otherwise a shorter, recursively partitioned but non-ascendingly ordered sequence would exist. Also, if one of these items is in the left partition, the other cannot be in the middle partition because of the stated property of the left partition. Similarly, if one of these items is in the right partition, the other cannot be in the middle. This leads to a contradiction, and so the result is proved.

*   *   *

From this proposition, program 3.1 can be *judged* to be a correct sorting procedure. A DOPL program to sort a sequence of data integers can use the request

PRINT   result of *partition-sort*-ing the data sequence

This will print the data integers in ascending order.

Another DOPL procedure for sorting by partitioning, this time into two groups called the *left-partition* and the *right-partition*, is shown in program 3.2. This procedure can be judged to be correct, given the definitions of the procedure PARTITION and the adjective *partitioned* below, by appealing to a proposition which is similar to the one above for program 3.1.

<u>to</u>   *PARTITION SORT* a sequence consisting-of 1 integer:
        RESULT IS the integer
<u>end</u>
<u>to</u>   *PARTITION SORT* a sequence consisting-of more-than 1 integer:
        PARTITION it.
        RESULT IS
              result of *partition-sort*-ing the
                    (*left-partition*, *right-partition*)
                 of the *partition*-result
<u>end</u>

Program 3.2   <u>Another DOPL partition-sorting procedure</u>

In this program, two specifications of *PARTITION SORT* are given, one
for parameter sequences which consist of only one integer, and one for
other parameter sequences.   In a DOPL, operand descriptions can be used
to specify the formal and actual parameters of a procedure.   When a
procedure is called, a case analysis on the actual parameters is performed
to match them up to an appropriate procedure specification.

The pronoun it in

        PARTITION it

is used to refer back to the previous operand description, which in this
case is the parameter sequence.   The *PARTITION* request is thus equivalent
to

        PARTITION the parameter sequence

Various kinds of pronoun can be included in a DOPL to make operand
descriptions shorter, and, if used appropriately, to make them more
transparent.

The operand description of the second RESULT IS request is *factored*,
so as to shorten it, using the pair of nouns
        (*left-partition*, *right-partition*)
It is interpreted by applying
        result of *partition-sort*-ing the
and
        of the *partition*-result
to both nouns in the pair.   The comma in the pair specifies the
concatenation of the resulting sequences.   The parentheses are used for
grouping only.

The effect of the procedure *PARTITION* can be specified as follows:

<u>to</u>   *PARTITION* a sequence consisting-of more-than 1 integer:
        RESULT IS a *partitioned permutation* of it
<u>end</u>

where the adjective *partitioned* is defined as

```
ADJECTIVE        partitioned
AS IN            partitioned integral sequence
IS               sequence comprising
                    non null sequence said-to-be the left-partition,
                    non null sequence said-to-be the right-partition
SUCH THAT        each integer of the left-partition
                 is - <=
                 each integer of the right-partition
```

There may be many *partitioned permutations* of a given sequence, and for any one of these there may be many possible *left-partitions*.   The description
   the *left- partition* of the *partition*-result
refers to whichever *left-partition* results from whichever method is used to check for *partitioned*-ness.

Although the obvious interpretation of the above procedure would involve generating permutations of the parameter sequence, there are other methods of producing a *partitioned permutation* of a sequence.   For example, the partitioning process involved in Quicksort (Hoare, 1961, 1962; Foley and Hoare 1971) an IOPL version of which is shown in program 3.3, will produce a *partitioned permutation*.

```
procedure Quicksort(var A : integerarray;
                         m, n : integer);
{To sort the components of A between the m'th and n'th}
var  r, i, j : integer;
begin if m < n then
          begin {partition A between m'th and n'th components}
          r := A[(m+n) div 2]; i := m; j := n;
          while i <= j do
               begin while A[i] < r do i := i+1;
                     while r < A [j] do j := j-1;
                     if i <= j then begin
                                    A[i] :=: A[j];
                                    i := i+1;  j := j-1
                                    end
               end;
          Quicksort (A,m,j);
          Quicksort (A,i,n)
          end
end;
```

Program 3.3   An IOPL Quicksorting procedure (from Alagic and Arbib [1978])

A specification of partitioning which is a little closer to that used in Quicksort is:

<u>to</u>   *PARTITION* a sequence consisting-of more-than 1 integer:
           CHOOSE   a parameter integer.
           RESULT IS a *partitioned permutation*
                                of the parameter sequence
           SUCH THAT each integer of the *left-partition*
                     is - <= the *choose*-and
                 and each integer of the *right-partition*
                     is - >= the *choose*-and

<u>end</u>

One of the main reasons for interest in Quicksort is that it is a very efficient sorting algorithm. Obviously, the DOPL procedures in programs 3.1 and 3.2, which are related to Quicksort in a certain sense, are far less efficient than program 3.3. However, it is less obvious that Quicksort actually sorts. In the last section of the paper, a combined DOPL/IOPL programming system is proposed. In such a system, it would be possible to express an algorithm in its gross, essential terms using a DOPL, and to transform this to an efficient IOPL version. The advantage of such a system, over an IOPL-only one, would be that, with a DOPL version which could be judged to be correct, if correctness-preserving transformations are used, the final optimised IOPL version would be known to be correct. At each stage of the transformation, proof of correctness would have a higher level, correct version to appeal to.

4.   AN INTERPRETER FOR A SIMPLE IOPL

The following is an interpreter for a simple IOPL whose programs are sequences of assignment, read, write, while, if, case and compound statements. Only simple integer variables are used, and the only operator is +.

The interpreter does not need to specify input or parsing of the source program. It is not necessary to use data structures to store the source statements or variable values.

program	*interpreter*:
NOUN	*identifier*
IS	sequence <> 'while' or 'do' or 'if' or 'then'
	or 'else' or 'case' or 'of'
	or 'begin' or 'end' or 'read'
	or 'write'
	comprising several alphabetic character .
NOUN	*value*
AS IN	*value* of integer
IS	the integer .
NOUN	*value*
AS IN	*value* of *identifier*
IS	last *value assign-ed-to* the *identifier*.
NOUN	*term*
IS	*identifier* or non-negative integer.
NOTE	the *value* of a *term* is well defined .
NOUN	*expression*
IS	several *term* separated-by '+'.
NOUN	*value*
AS IN	*value* of *expression*
IS	sum of *value* of each *term* of the *expression*.
NOUN	*relational-operator*
IS	'<' or '<=' or '>' or '>=' or '=' or '<>'.
NOUN	*Boolean-expression*
IS	*expression, relational-operator, expression.*
ADJECTIVE	*true*
AS IN	*true Boolean-expression*
IN CASE	*Boolean-expression* contains '<'
IS	*Boolean-expression*
	containing
	first *expression* having *value* <
	value of second *expression* of the
	Boolean-expression

{and similar cases for the other relational operators}.

NOUN	*assignment-statement*
IS	*identifier*, ':=', *expression*.
NOUN	*statement*
IS	*assignment-statement* or
	while-statement or
	if-statement or
	case-statement or
	compound-statement or
	read-statement or
	write-statement.
NOUN	*while-statement*
IS	'while', *Boolean-expression*, 'do', *statement*.
NOUN	*else-part*
IS	'else', *statement*.
NOUN	*if-statement*
IS	'if', *Boolean-expression*,
	'then', *statement*
	optionally followed-by *else-part*.

```
NOUN          case-specification
IS            several distinct integer separated-by ',',
              ':', statement.
NOUN          case-statement
IS            'case', expression, 'of',
              several case-specification
                      not containing integer
                          contained-in any preceding
                                  case-specification
                                  of the case-statement
                      and separated-by ';',
              'end'.
NOUN          compound-statement
IS            'begin',
              several statement separated-by ';',
              'end'.
NOUN          read-statement
IS            'read', '(', several identifier separated-by',',')'.
NOUN          write-statement
IS            'write', '(', several identifier separated-by ',',')'.
NOUN          IOPL-program
IS            compound-statement.
DATA IS       IOPL-program, several integer.
EXECUTE       the IOPL-program
to EXECUTE    a compound-statement:
   EXECUTE    each statement
end
to EXECUTE    an assignment-statement:
   ASSIGN     value of expression
   TO         identifier
end
to EXECUTE    a while-statement containing true Boolean-expression:
   EXECUTE    statement of the while-statement.
   EXECUTE    the while-statement
end
to EXECUTE    a while-statement containing non true Boolean-expression:
   DO NOTHING
end
to EXECUTE    an if-statement containing  true Boolean-expression:
   EXECUTE    statement after 'then'
end
to EXECUTE    an if-statement containing non true Boolean-expression:
   EXECUTE    statement of else-part
end
to EXECUTE    a case-statement:
   EXECUTE    statement
                  of case-specification
                      containing integer = value of expression
end
to EXECUTE    a read-statement:
   TO         each identifier
   ASSIGN     first non assign-ed data integer
end
to EXECUTE    a write-statement:
   PRINT      value of each identifier
end
end.
```

5. EULERIAN CIRCUITS IN GRAPHS

An Eulerian Circuit in a graph is a sequence of arcs such that

(a) each arc of the graph is in the Circuit exactly once,
(b) consecutive arcs in the Circuit end at and begin at the same node,
(c) the last arc in the Circuit ends at the same node at which the first one begins.

Walking around an Eulerian Circuit would involve traversing each arc once, and passing through each node one or more times. Obviously, a graph having an Eulerian Circuit (and no trivial nodes) must be connected.

Given the descriptors *node*, *graph* and *connected-to*, an *Eulerian-Circuit* of a *graph* can be defined in a DOPL (actually as a sequence of nodes, pairs of which represent the arcs) as in program 5.1. It is assumed that there is at most one arc between any two nodes, and that no node is connected to itself. Rather than use the identifiers *a* and *b* in the description after WE HAVE, the descriptions

first such-that-for-and
second such-that-for-and

could be used. Naturally, in a language with many operand-description facilities, a choice can be made in each case whether to use a defined descriptor such as an identifier, or a primitive descriptor, such as the nouns above. It seems simpler in this case to use the identifiers.

NOUN	*Eulerian-Circuit*
AS IN	*Eulerian-Circuit* of *graph*
IS	sequence of *node* of the *graph*
SUCH THAT	each *node* of the sequence is-connected-to next *node* of the sequence
AND SUCH THAT	last *node* of the sequence is-connected-to first *node* of the sequence
AND SUCH THAT FOR	any *node* called *a* of the *graph* and any *node* called *b* and connected-to *a* of the *graph*
WE HAVE	either *b* is adjacent-to *a* in the sequence
	or *b* is the last *node* of the sequence and *a* is the first *node* of the sequence
	or *b* is the first *node* of the sequence and *a* is the last *node* of the sequence
AND SUCH THAT	number of *node* connected-to any *node* of the *graph* is-equal-to 2*number of occurrences of the *node* in the sequence

Program 5.1   Definition of an Eulerian Circuit of a graph

The Eulerian Circuits of a given graph can be generated:

CHOOSE any *node* of the *graph*.
PRINT   each *Eulerian-Circuit* beginning-with the *choose*-and
              of the *graph*

Program 5.2 defines a *graph* as it might be presented for input
punched on cards:

DATA IS   *graph*   punched-on cards

The descriptors *node* and *connected-to* are also defined in program 5.2.
The descriptor said-to-be precedes a defining occurrence of a new
descriptor.   A relator is a type of descriptor which can be used in
relations.

        NOUN   *node*
        IS   several alphabetic character.
        NOUN   *connections*
        IS   several distinct *node* separated-by ','.
        NOUN   *node-information*
        IS   *node* said-to-be *connected-to*
                            each *node* of following *connections*
                            and not = any *node* of following *connections*,
                        ':', *connections*, ';'.
        NOUN   *graph*
        IS   several *node-information*   •
                            not containing *node*
                                = *node* of
                                    any preceding *node-information*
        SUCH THAT   relator *connected-to* is symmetric

        Program 5.2   Definition of a graph

From this definition, the description
        node of *graph*
means
        node of *node-information* of *graph*
and can be so interpreted by an implementation.   The semantics of
operand-description interpretation can be such as to allow the use of short
descriptions which can be automatically extended according to the defined
structure of sequences.

        The Eulerian Circuits of a data graph can be printed using the above
CHOOSE and PRINT requests.   A copy of the *graph* itself can be printed as
follows

        PRINT   the data *graph*

The question of whether or not a given connected graph has an
Eulerian Circuit can be resolved without actually generating such a
Circuit, by using the following theorem:

THEOREM (Euler)

A connected multi-graph has an Eulerian Circuit if and only if each node is connected to an even number of other nodes.

PROOF

Only if: An Eulerian Circuit, for each visit to a node, must enter and leave the node on different arcs.

If: Proceed by induction on the size of the graph.

The result is true for a graph with one arc and one node. Suppose it to be true for a connected graph with up to n arcs, and consider a graph with $n+1$ arcs. Choose any node of the graph, and any two nodes connected to the chosen one. Remove a connection from these two nodes to the chosen one, and insert a connection between the two nodes which bypasses the chosen one. This will result in a graph with either one or two components, but with one fewer arc. By the induction hypothesis, there is an Eulerian Circuit for each of these components. An Eulerian Circuit for the original graph can be made from these by replacing the inserted arc by the two removed ones, and then concatenating the two Circuits.

*   *   *

Assuming the data graph to be connected (an adjective *connected*, to be applied to graphs, can be defined in terms of the existence of *paths* between any two nodes - a path is a sequence of arcs with certain properties, and can be defined in a similar way to an Eulerian Circuit, which is a path with special properties), the following request can be used to decide whether a data graph has an Eulerian Circuit:

    IF the data *graph* does-not-contain
            node connected-to an odd number of *node*
    PRINT "This graph has an Eulerian Circuit"

This must be correct because of the above theorem.

6. DOPL SYNTAX AND SEMANTICS

A DOPL program is a sequence of requests separated by '.', and possibly followed by procedure definitions:

    NOUN   *DOPL-program*
    IS   'program', *name*, ':',
              several *request* separated-by '.'
              optionally followed-by several *procedure*, 'end', '.'.

The program is executed by using each request in turn:

    to   *EXECUTE a DOPL-program:*
    ――   *EXECUTE each request*
    end

A request is several *requestor/operand-description* pairs, where a *requestor* is an *operator*, a *preposition* or a term such as NOUN, ADJECTIVE, IS, AS IN, SUCH THAT, UNTIL:

```
NOUN       request
IS         several (requestor, operand-description)
```

An operational request is executed by applying the operators to all
the operands of all the operand descriptions.   For example, for a unary
operator:

```
to      EXECUTE    request comprising (operator, operand-description):
        APPLY      the operator
        TO         each operand of the operand-description
end
```

APPLY would be defined for each primitive and user-defined operator (in the
latter case, by executing the requests of the appropriate procedure
definition), but not for user-introduced, non user-defined operators such
as REMOVE (section 2) or ASSIGN (section 4).   The semantics of these
would be specified in terms of the associated descriptors.   For example,
the semantics of remove-ed, as in

```
remove-ed <description of an operand>
```

is

```
apply-ed REMOVE to the operand
```

and the semantics of assign-ed as in

```
assign-ed <description of an operand>
to        <description of another operand>
```

is

```
apply-ed (ASSIGN, TO)
to        (the operand, the other operand)
```

The basic structure of an operand description is

```
NOUN       operand-description
IS         several adjective-type-descriptor,
           reference, post-description
           optionally followed-by
               ('of', nested-operand-description)
```

where a reference is a description of an actual object, and may be a
noun, a pronoun or an identifier.   The adjectives either specify the
generation of all the objects specified by the reference, or possibly,
together with the post-description (an example of which is "<= the
data integer" from section 2), specify the required properties of objects.
In addition to the above structure, operand descriptions can be combined
using descriptors such as either, or, and, (,) and others.

The sequence of all the operands of an operand description used in
an operational request is the sequence comprising each referenced object
(with the properties stated in adjectives and post-descriptions) of each
object specified by the nested operand description.

7. PROPOSAL FOR A DOPL-BASED SYSTEM

A language containing a spectrum of DOPL and IOPL features would make an ideal programming system. Initially, programs could be written using the DOPL, possibly in a highly non-procedural fashion, as for example with *SORT* in section 3. Provided these were not too disproportionately inefficient (as with sorting 100 integers using a strict interpretation of *SORT*), they could be executed and used whilst a programmer and/or the implementation were refining the DOPL version to a more efficient IOPL one.

In the case of a well-defined, self-contained problem, such as sorting or the generation of primes or circuits in graphs, the DOPL version of an algorithm could be *judged* to be correct by appealing to what might be called the *factual basis of the algorithm*, this being the collection of proven properties of the objects involved in the algorithm. For example, for problems involving primes, the *factual basis* might include the definition of what is meant by a prime and propositions about the existence of factors of non primes. For problems involving circuits in graphs, the *factual basis* might include the theorem in section 5. In the case of more complex problems, such as large data-processing applications or the design of a new programming language, the DOPL version might be developed and agreed to by a committee of users and analysts, as the correct initial specification for a required system. In either case, an efficient implementation of the DOPL version could then be obtained using various automatic or manual correctness-preserving transformations.

The design of a DOPL presents a host of challenging problems. Many of these remain to be resolved. Nevertheless, the notion of *operand description*, and the incorporation of a variety of description facilities in a programming language, seem to hold the promise of a superior, general-purpose language for the future.

REFERENCES

ALAGIC, S., ARBIB, M.A., (1978): "The Design of Well-Structured and Correct Programs", Springer-Verlag, New York.

ASTRAHAN, M.M., CHAMBERLAIN, D.D., (1975): "Implementation of a Structured English Query Language", Comm. ACM, Vol. 18, No. 10, pp 580-588.

BARRON, D.W., (1977): "An Introduction to the Study of Programming Languages", CUP, Cambridge.

BURGER, J.F., LEAL, A., SHOSHANI, A., (1975) "A Semantic-Based Natural-Language Interface for Data Management Systems", Proceedings of International Conference on Systems Sciences, Hawaii, pp 218-220.

CHAMBERLAIN, D.D., BOYCE, R.F., (1974): "SEQUEL: A structured English query language", Proceedings of ACM-SIGFIDET Workshop on Data Description, Access and Control, Ann Arbor, Michigan, pp 249-264.

FELDMAN, J.A., ROVNER, P.D., (1969): "An Algol-Based Associative Language", Comm. ACM, Vol. 12, No. 8, pp 439-449.

FINDLER, N.V., (1969): "Design Features of and Programming Experience with an Associative Memory, Parallel Processing Language, AMPPL-11", Proceedings of Fourth Australian Computer Conference, Adelaide, pp 321-325.

FOLEY, M., HOARE, C.A.R., (1971): "Proof of a recursive program: Quicksort", Computer Journal, Vol. 14, No. 4, pp 391-395.

HEBDITCH, D.L., (1973) :"Terminal languages for data base access", Data Base Management, Infotech State of the Art Report 15, pp 521-541.

HERRIOT, R.G., (1977): "Towards the Ideal Programming Language", SIGPLAN Notices, Vol. 12, No. 3, pp 56-62.

HOARE, C.A.R., (1961): "Algorithm 63, Partition", "Algorithm 64, Quicksort", Comm. ACM, Vol. 4, No. 7, p 321.

HOARE, C.A.R., (1962) : "Quicksort", Computer Journal, Vol. 5, No. 1, pp 10-15.

HOARE, C.A.R., (1972): "Proof of a structured program: The Sieve of Eratosthenes", Computer Journal, Vol. 15, No. 4, pp 321-325.

HOUSEL, B.C., SHU, N.C., (1976): "A High-Level Data Manipulation Language for Hierarchical Data Structures", Proceedings of a Conference on DATA: Abstraction, Definition and Structure, SIGPLAN Notices, Vol. 8, No. 2, pp 155-168.

LEE, G., (1978): "Some design features of a Description Oriented Programming Language", Proceedings of the Eighth Australian Computer Conference, Canberra, pp 938-946.

MARTIN, J., (1976): "Principles of Data-Base Management", Prentice-Hall, Englewood Cliffs, N.J.

NYLIN, Jr., W.C., HARVILL, J.B. (1976): "Multiple Tense Computer Programming", SIGPLAN Notices, Vol. 11, No. 12, pp 74-93.

POTTS, G.W., (1970): "Natural language inquiry to an open-ended data library", Proceedings of the SJCC, Atlantic City, N.J., pp 333-342.

PROCEEDINGS OF THE SYMPOSIUM ON
LANGUAGE DESIGN AND PROGRAMMING METHODOLOGY
SYDNEY, 10-11 SEPTEMBER, 1979

A PERSONAL COMPUTER BASED ON A HIGH-LEVEL LANGUAGE

Niklaus Wirth

Institut für Informatik, ETH Zürich

Considerations of economy have in the past led to the so-called time-sharing of large computers. The premise of such systems is to project to each user the image of the entire computer being at his own exclusive disposal. This requires stringent measures of protection on programs and data of the individual participants against misbehaviour of programs and malfunctions of hardware. These measures, called overhead, are not only extensive, but also expensive.

Phenomenal advances in semiconductor technology have now increased the power of inexpensive micro-computers to the point where they can be used for tasks hitherto reserved for large scale systems. At this point, the strategy of sharing becomes of questionable value. The non-shared, personal computer is a genuine alternative and holds great promise for the future of many applications. It appears to be particularly attractive as the development tool of the software engineer; used in this function, we call it a work-station computer.

The power and usefulness of a computer does not only depend on its speed (of individual instructions) and the size of its store. It is equally much determined by the adequacy of the tools available for its use, in particular the programming language provided. It is now widely accepted that high-level languages are the only adequate tool for the development of complex systems, and these are typically the programs with which the professional software engineer is concerned. He should not have to regard his computer in terms of machine instructions and words of store, but as the mechanism implementing this high-level language.

As a consequence, a computer's design must not start with the specification of its (conventional) architecture, but rather with the definition of the programming language. In order to achieve efficiency and economy of storage, the architecture and machine code must be chosen as an optimal interface between compiler and available hardware components.

We have undertaken a research and development effort to design and build a work station computer based on a high-level language. It consists of the following main parts:

- the language Modula-2
- a 4-pass compiler generating M-code
- a file system
- a basic executive system including linker and loader
- the hardware.

In this paper, we shall concentrate on the last two points. A basic premise of this project was and is that the computer is to be programmed in only one high-level language, Modula-2, which therefore has to be a sufficiently versatile system programming language. May it suffice here to characterize Modula-2 as a product of the ancestors Pascal and Modula [1], where the major addition to Pascal is the module which, in Modula-2, also may serve as a unit of separate compilation.

The other principal factor - besides the language - to determine the structure of the hardware, is the variety of peripheral devices to be connected. Our computer utilizes (in a typical configuration) a high-resolution display as principal output device, a keyboard and a pointing device (mouse) as input devices, a disk with exchangeable cartridge as file store, and it provides a serial line interface for connection to either a communication network or (at least) a hardcopy device.

The high-resolution display with 600 lines and about 800 dots per line requires a high-band width signal for its continuous refreshing. This led to the use of a multiport memory and a display-processor that operates independently from the main processor. Since the display reads bits from the store in purely sequential order, the width of the memory data bus was chosen to be four times the width of the CPU data bus, namely 64 bits. This measure reduces the interference of the display processor with the main computing process due to cycle stealing to a few percent only.

A consequence of using a high-level language for programming is that code is separate from data. Given a multiport memory, the use of a separate port for reading instructions is obvious. As instructions are mostly read in sequential order, the large memory bus width again appears as most advantageous. The action of instruction fetching appears as a merely slight interference with the data handling activities of the main processor.

The main processor consists of a conventional arithmetic/logical unit (built with a bit-slice micro-processor) augmented by a fast stack memory and a barrel shifter. The stack was motivated by the structure of Modula-2. It is called the hardware stack or expression stack and serves to hold intermediate results during expression evaluation. It coexists but is distinct from the main and conventional "software stack" used for procedure calls and to allocate data local to these procedures.

The barrel shifter is used mainly during the interpretation of M-code instructions constructing bitmaps for the display. In contrast with most other M-code instructions which correspond to a few microinstructions only, these display instructions represent themselves as fairly complex micro-programs. It is here that a powerful computing engine is most needed.

The processor is built with Shottky TTL technology using MSI and LSI components allowing for a cycle time of 150 ns. The fast progressing VLSI technology would permit moulding of this architecture into a small number of chips.

The project has shown that significant increases in computing power can be gained not only by the use of faster chips, but also by choosing a machine architecture appropriate for high-level languages and their compilers. The same holds for the density of compiled code, i.e. economy of storage.

---

[1]   N. Wirth. Modula: A Language for Modular Multiprogramming.
       Software - Practice and Experience, 7, 3-55 (1977).

PROCEEDINGS OF THE SYMPOSIUM ON
LANGUAGE DESIGN AND PROGRAMMING METHODOLOGY
SYDNEY, 10-11 SEPTEMBER, 1979

AN EXPERIMENT IN SOFTWARE SCIENCE

Dan B. Johnston and Andrew M. Lister

Department of Computer Science
University of Queensland

ABSTRACT

This paper describes an experiment which was
undertaken for two purposes: firstly to test the
applicability of software science in the realm of
student programming, and secondly to obtain quantitative inferences about the programming language
PASCAL. The results suggest that software science
offers little in the area studied, and possible reasons
for this are discussed.

1. INTRODUCTION

Software science (Halstead, 1977; Fitzsimmons and Love, 1978;
Van der Knijff, 1978) is an embryonic experimental science which
attempts to analyse programs in terms of certain basic measures on
them. It is concerned with quantifying such program properties as
comprehensibility, likelihood of error, and effort to write, and
with establishing relationships, or "laws", which allow these
quantities to be predicted from simple measures such as counts of
operators and operands. The aim of the experiment described in this
paper was to investigate the validity of the software science laws
in the domain of student programming, and in this context to see
what, if anything, software science can tell us about the merits of
PASCAL as a programming language.

More precisely, the experiment was designed to investigate the
following areas:

(1) The correlation between the measure of "goodness" of a program
    provided by software science and the subjective assessment of
    the same program by a practised programmer (in this case a
    tutor marking the program for assessment). In particular we
    were interested to learn whether the software science measures
    could form a reliable basis for automatic grading of programs.

(2) The accuracy of certain approximations in software science.

(3) The language level of PASCAL, in the sense of "high" or "low",
    as quantified by software science.

A notable feature of the experiment was the large number of sample programs measured: about 13,000 programs written by over 500 students. Indeed the availability of this large sample was a compelling reason for performing the experiment - the opportunity seemed too good to waste! The sample is described in detail in section 3 of the paper after a brief presentation of notation in section 2. Section 4 details the measurements made and the results obtained, and section 5 discusses what conclusions can be drawn.

2. SOFTWARE SCIENCE MEASURES

The fundamental measures of software science, from which all others are derived, are (for any program)

$n1$ - number of distinct operators used
$n2$ - number of distinct operands used
$N1$ - number of operator occurrences
$N2$ - number of operand occurrences

The *vocabulary* of the program is

$$n = n1 + n2$$

and the program *length* is

$$N = N1 + N2$$

The *volume* of a program, which is the minimum number of bits required to hold it, is

$$V = N log_2 n$$

The *potential volume* V^* of an algorithm is the volume of the minimal program required to express it. Such a minimal program assumes the algorithm to be implemented as a procedure built into the language used, and therefore comprises only a single procedure call. V^* is a property of an algorithm, and is independent of the programming language used.

The ratio

$$L = V^*/V$$

is the *level* of a program, and measures the degree of compaction which would be achieved if the language used allowed the algorithm to be expressed in its minimal form.

The *effort* required to write a program is given by

$$E = V/L$$

This formulation of E is based on the number of mental discriminations required to write the program, and is therefore an indicator of the probable number of errors in the program, the time required to write it, and the effort required to understand it. The measure of "goodness" of a program which expresses a given algorithm in a given language is inversely related to E.

The final measure of software science is the *language level* of a programming language, given by the product

$$\lambda = LV^*$$

which is asserted to be constant over all well-written programs in the language. λ is the quantitative measure which corresponds to intuitive ideas of the level of a programming language.

Calculation of the quantities above for a particular program requires the measurement of $n1$, $n2$, $N1$, and $N2$ for the program, together with a knowledge of V^* for the corresponding algorithm. If $N1$ or $N2$ are not available the estimator

$$\hat{N} = n1 \; log_2 \; n1 + n2 \; log_2 \; n2$$

is claimed to be a good approximation to the length N, and if V^* is unknown then

$$L = (2 \times n2)/(n1 \times N2)$$

can be used as an approximation to the program level L (which can in turn be used to compute approximations $\hat{E}$ and $\hat{\lambda}$ for E and λ). Justification of the estimators $\hat{N}$ and $\hat{L}$ is given by Halstead (1977) on both theoretical and empirical grounds.

3. THE SAMPLE PROGRAMS

The data for the experiment consisted of 12,886 syntactically correct PASCAL programs submitted by over 500 first year students to the University of Queensland's central computer during the first semester of 1979. Syntactically incorrect programs were excluded from the sample since the measurements on these would have been somewhat arbitrary. The sample programs can be divided into two classes; *assignments*, which form part of each student's assessment, and *general programs*, which students run for interest but which are not assessed. The relevant characteristics of each class of programs are described below.

3.1 Assignments

Each student was expected to submit three assignments for assessment. The assignments may be briefly described as follows:.

Assignment 1. A program to read the subject codes and examination grades of a hypothetical student, to validate the data, and print out either the credit points obtained for each subject or an indication of a data error.

Assignment 2. A program to simulate the action of a faulty clock over a 12 hour period, printing the actual time at hourly intervals as measured by the clock.

Assignment 3. A program to read a piece of English text, print all its distinct words, and to indicate with an asterisk all the distinct words which have the same initial letter as the final word.

"Ideal" programs for each assignment, written by the lecturer in charge of the course (Lister), are given in the Appendix.

Of course not all students submitted all three assignments, and the sample size was further reduced by eliminating

(1) programs which still contained syntax errors,

(2) programs which failed to meet the stated specifications (for example by simply not working properly),

(3) programs which did more than was asked for (for example by using elaborate output layout).

The programs in categories (2) and (3), which under- or over-achieved the specifications, can be regarded as not expressing the same algorithm as the rest, and were therefore excluded on grounds of comparability. The importance of excluding these programs was not fully realised at the start of the experiment, and they were inadvertently included in the sample for the first assignment. The measurements for this assignment may therefore be slightly less reliable than those for the other two, though since the algorithm was comparatively simple we believe that the number of programs erroneously included was quite small. The final sample sizes, after all eliminations, were 423, 376, and 343 for the three assignments respectively.

A significant characteristic of the assignments was that each program expressed a known algorithm, and thus (in theory at any rate) could be associated with a known value of V^*. This implied that no approximations were necessary in calculating the various measures on the programs, particularly E and λ. It also implied that this group of programs could be used to test the validity of the estimators $\hat{E}$ and $\hat{\lambda}$. Unfortunately the determination of V^* proved to be more difficult than the available literature suggested. The problems which arose, and our solutions to them, are described in more detail in section 4.2.

Each assignment submitted to a tutor for assessment was marked on a scale 0 (very poor) to 4 (very good). This gave us the opportunity to investigate any correlation between the effort E required to write (and understand) a program and the tutor's subjective assessment of the worth of the program as indicated by the mark awarded. Of course any such correlation could be clouded by the role in the marking scheme of factors such as adequacy of comments, which are quite unrelated to program construction. For the third assignment we therefore asked the tutors to give their subjective opinion of each program's clarity on a scale 0 (lowest) to 10 (highest), and investigated whether any correlation existed between this measure and E. Eleven tutors were involved, giving a wide cross-section of experienced opinion, and each tutor assessed between 30 and 80 programs for each assignment.

3.2 General programs

During the semester the students ran a large variety of
programs which were not formally assessed. Some of these
programs were copied from lecture notes or text books, and
some were written as programming exercises. The number of
programs which were syntactically correct, and could therefore
be included in the sample was 11,744. This number includes
preliminary attempts at assignments, since we had no way of
distinguishing assignments from other programs except by what
was submitted for assessment.

The algorithms expressed by the programs in this sample
were unknown and hence the corresponding values of V^* were
also unknown. This meant the measures L, E, and λ for this
sample could not be computed and had to be replaced by the
estimates $\hat{L}$, $\hat{E}$, and $\hat{\lambda}$. However, provided that the accuracy
of the estimators was confirmed by measurements on the
assignments, the general programs were intended to provide
a useful extension of the total sample. The extent to which
this intention was fulfilled is discussed in later sections.

4. MEASUREMENTS AND RESULTS

4.1 Counting scheme

The PASCAL compiler used by students was modified to
provide the operator and operand counts $n1$, $n2$, $N1$, and $N2$.
The precise counting scheme used required some consideration
as the available literature gave few examples, none of them
for PASCAL. However, by trying to follow the philosophy
which appears to have guided earlier workers we were able to
adopt a scheme which seemed reasonable. Our resolution of
some possibly contentious problems is outlined below.

(1) Only executable text was counted, all declarative text
being ignored.

(2) Composite symbols such as *repeat...until* and *for...to...do*
were considered as single operators.

(3) Each distinct procedure call was regarded as a separate
operator, and commas between parameters were counted as
operators only for procedures (such as readln) which are
variadic.

(4) *if...then* and *if...then...else* were regarded as separate
operators, and *case...of* was regarded as a single operator
irrespective of the number of case labels used.

(5) The colon in output field width specifications was regarded
as an operator, and the field width itself as an operand.

The question of whether a different choice of counting
scheme would greatly affect our results is an open one. Work
on PL/1 programs (Elshoff, 1978) suggests that some measures,
such as V, are insensitive to changes in the counting scheme,
while others, such as $\hat{E}$ and λ, are more sensitive. Unfortunately

we did not have the resources to test Elshoff's conclusion
by trying various counting schemes in our own experiment.

4.2 Determination of V^* for assignments

The conventional derivation of V^* is to regard the
minimal form of an algorithm as a procedure call with two
operators (the procedure name and a grouping symbol) and
as many operands as there are conceptually distinct parameters.
Since each symbol is used only once,

$$V^* = (2 + n2^*) \log_2 (2 + n2^*)$$

where $n2^*$ is the number of parameters. Thus the calculation
of V^* is straightforward provided the parameters can be
readily enumerated.

Unfortunately this was not the case with the algorithms
for our three assignments. How many outputs, for example,
are there from a simulation, and how many inputs does a piece
of English text represent? The accessible literature provides
little guidance: all the examples we can find are of programs
which transform readily identifiable inputs into readily
identifiable results. Furthermore, the inputs and outputs
of these programs are unstructured atomic data items, whereas
those of our own algorithms seem to need a specification of
their structure as part of their definition. It seems
important that this structure be taken into account when
determining the minimum number of symbols in which each
algorithm can be expressed. One way of doing this is to
describe the input and output in terms of abstract structuring
operations, such as *sequence* and *pair*, as well as the atomic
data items themselves. The results of this approach are
given below.

Assignment 1

input structure : sequence of pairs (subject, grade)
input symbols   : sequence operator, pair operators, subject, grade
output structure: sequence of triplets (credit, error flag 1,
                        error flag 2)
output symbols : sequence operator, triplet operator, credit,
                        flag 1, flag 2

Since the input sequence maps one-one to the output sequence,
the sequencing operator need appear only once in a description
of the algorithm. Hence $V^* = 10 \log_2 10 = 33.22$

Assignment 2

input structure : single integer (period of simulation)
input symbols   : period
output structure: sequence of pairs (hours, minutes)
output symbols : sequence operator, pair operator, hours,
                        minutes

Since no symbol is used more than once, $V^* = 7 \log_2 7 = 19.65$

Assignment 3

input structure : sequence of characters
input symbols   : sequence operator, character
output structure: sequence of groups of characters (words)
output symbols : sequence operator, grouping operator, character

Since the two sequence operators are different,
$$V^* = 7 \log_2 7 = 19.65$$

A different approach to deriving V^* is to use the relation $V^*=LV$, and to substitute the estimator $\hat{L}$ for L. This produces an approximation $\hat{V}^*$ whose proximity to V^* is governed by the proximity of $\hat{L}$ to L. Of course it would be foolish to use a value of $\hat{L}$ derived from the sample of student programs, since one of the aims of the experiment was to test the validity of such a value. However, one program outside the sample which could be used is the "ideal" program for the assignment in question. Some justification for this is that the program contains no "impurities", and therefore should produce an estimator $\hat{L}$ which is close to the true value L (Halstead, 1977). Although it is clearly dangerous to argue from a sample of one, we feel that this derivation of an approximation to V^* serves as a useful supplement to the value of V^* obtained earlier. To put it bluntly, two derivations are better than one, particularly when neither is confidently arrived at. The values obtained by both means are shown in Table 1. V^* is the value obtained by analytic derivation, while $\hat{V}^*$ is that obtained from the ideal program. Since the discrepancies are small but significant, both values were used in subsequent calculations.

	V^*	$\hat{V}^*$	$(V^* - \hat{V}^*) / V^*$
Assignment 1	33.22	26.72	0.195
Assignment 2	19.65	22.57	-0.149
Assignment 3	19.65	17.34	0.118

Table 1

4.3 The length estimator $\hat{N}$

The operator and operand counts for each program in the sample were recorded, and from these the values of N and $\hat{N}$ were computed. The validity of $\hat{N}$ as an approximation to N was assessed by computing the mean and variance of the ratio $N/\hat{N}$ over all programs. The results were

$N/\hat{N}$:   Mean = 1.075   Variance = 0.072   Sample size = 12,886

The results suggest that $\hat{N}$ is a good estimator for N, even in the domain of student programs. This extends the area of application of the estimator beyond those already established by other workers. However, we do not regard $\hat{N}$ as a particularly important measure, since if it is possible to gather the data to compute $\hat{N}$ then it should also be possible to gather the data to compute N itself.

4.4 The level estimator $\hat{L}$

The level estimator $\hat{L}$ for each program was computed directly from the operator and operand counts. The true level L was computed for those programs (viz. the assignments) for which V^* was known - or at least for which we had a reasonable value. The validity of $\hat{L}$ as an estimator for L was then assessed by computing the mean and variance of the ratio $\hat{L}/L(=E/\hat{E})$ over all assignments. The results, using both values of V^* as derived in section 4.2, are shown in Table 2.

| Assignment number | Sample size | V | | V^* | $\hat{L}/L$ ($= E/\hat{E}$) | | |
		Mean	Std. Dev.		Mean, Variance, Std.		Dev.
1	423	491	158	33.22	1.04	0.084	0.29
				26.72	1.30	0.130	0.36
2	376	596	423	19.65	1.39	0.093	0.30
				22.57	1.21	0.071	0.27
3	343	963	575	19.65	0.93	0.045	0.21
				17.34	1.05	0.057	0.24

Table 2

Of the three means derived from the analytic computation of V^* two are reasonably close to unity, while the other (Assignment 2) is not. The average of the three means is 1.12. Of the means derived from the estimate of V^* only one (Assignment 3) is close to unity. The average of these means is 1.19. In all cases the standard deviation is about one quarter of the mean. In our view these results indicate that for the programs studied $\hat{L}$ does give a rough estimate of L, but that the estimate is too unreliable to be useful.

4.5 The language level λ

The language level λ ($= LV^*$) was computed for all assignments, using both values of V^* as derived in section 4.2. The results are shown in Table 3.

Assignment number	Sample size	V		V^*	λ		
		Mean	Std. Dev.		Mean,	Variance,	Std. Dev.
1	423	491	158	33.22 26.72	2.42 1.57	0.386 0.161	0.62 0.40
2	376	596	423	19.65 22.57	0.68 0.90	0.028 0.049	0.17 0.22
3	343	963	575	19.65 17.34	0.41 0.32	0.005 0.004	0.07 0.06

Table 3

It is apparent that whichever value of V^* is taken the value of λ declines sharply over the three assignments, and certainly does not display the constant behaviour claimed by Halstead. On reflection we do not find this surprising: indeed what is surprising is the supposition that λ ever could be constant over a range of programs written in the same language.

Since $\quad \lambda = LV^*,$
and $\quad\quad L = V^*/V,$
we have $\quad \lambda = (V^*)^2/V$

Thus for λ to be constant it is necessary for V^* to vary with the square root of V. Now V^* depends on the number of parameters of the algorithm, while V depends on the internal complexity of the algorithm. It seems most unlikely that the complexity of an algorithm is in any mathematical sense related to the number of parameters. Indeed, to take a single example, there is an infinite number of algorithms of widely varying complexity (and hence widely varying V when implemented in a particular language) which can all be expressed in the form $y := f(x)$ and which all therefore have $V^* = 4\log_2 4$.

In our view the only value of λ is as a basis for comparison of *different* programming languages. If the same algorithm is expressed in languages A and B then the ratio λ_A/λ_B can be regarded as a measure of the relative expressive power of the languages. However, this ratio is equal to V_B/V_A, so the value of λ as a measure distinct from V is negligible.

4.6 Correlation between effort measures and marks awarded

Two methods were employed for computing an effort measure for the assignments. The first was to compute the measure E from the relation $E = V^2/V^*$, using both values of V^* obtained in section 4.2. The second was to compute the estimator $\hat{E}$ from the relation $\hat{E} = V/\hat{L}$. The closeness of these measures for each of the assignments is shown in the last column of Table 2, and has been discussed in section 4.4.

Since the effort measure is claimed to be an inverse measure of the "goodness" of a program, we plotted histograms showing the distribution of both E and $\hat{E}$ against the marks awarded by tutors. Programs with a mark of 0 were omitted since their number was too small to be a valid sample. These histograms are shown in Figures 1-3. (Only the histograms for values of E computed from the analytically derived value of V^* are shown; those for E computed from the estimated value of V^* display a similar shape with a lateral transposition.)

It is clear that the histograms indicate no startling correlation between either E or $\hat{E}$ and the marks awarded. In particular, given a program with a certain value of E (or $\hat{E}$) it would be quite impossible to infer what mark the program had been given. However, there are some general overall patterns: the mean and the variance of both E and $\hat{E}$ tend to decrease as the number of marks awarded increases. The extent to which this is true is illustrated in Figures 4-6, which plot the mean and standard deviation of E and $\hat{E}$ against marks for each of the three assignments. (The kink in the graphs for Assignment 2 (Figure 5) is perhaps explained by the small number (4) of programs awarded a mark of 1.)

One further point is worth noting. The measure $\hat{E}$ we have used here is identical to the measure E_c which Gordon (1979) has suggested is a better measure of program clarity than E. If Gordon's suggestion is valid, and if the marks awarded bear any relation to program clarity (as they should), then one would expect a higher correlation between $\hat{E}$ and the mark than between E and the mark. This expectation is not borne out by the evidence of Figures 1-6. We shall return to this point in the next section, which discusses direct assessment of program clarity.

4.7 Correlation between effort measures and clarity

As mentioned in section 3.1 the tutors marking Assignment 3 were asked to give a subjective assessment of the clarity of each program. Clarity was assessed independently of the mark awarded, the aim being to isolate that quality of a program which might most closely correlate with the effort measures E and $\hat{E}$. The result is indicated in Figures 7 and 8, which show the distribution of E and $\hat{E}$ over clarity. Programs with clarity 0 and 1 were omitted, since their number (3) was too small to be a valid sample.

The observations to be made about these histograms are similar to those made in section 4.6 about the histograms over marks awarded. There is no useful correlation between either E or $\hat{E}$ and the clarity of the programs, and certainly no basis for inferring the clarity of a program from either E or $\hat{E}$.

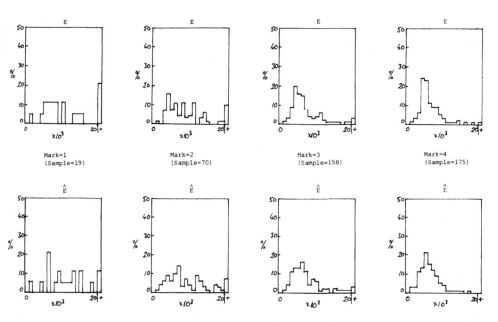

FIGURE 1 <u>DISTRIBUTION OF EFFORT MEASURES OVER MARKS AWARDED (ASSIGNMENT 1)</u>

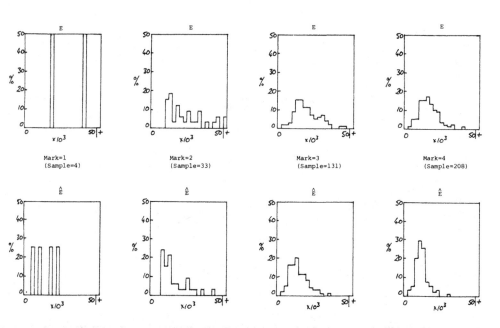

FIGURE 2 <u>DISTRIBUTION OF EFFORT MEASURES OVER MARKS AWARDED (ASSIGNMENT 2)</u>

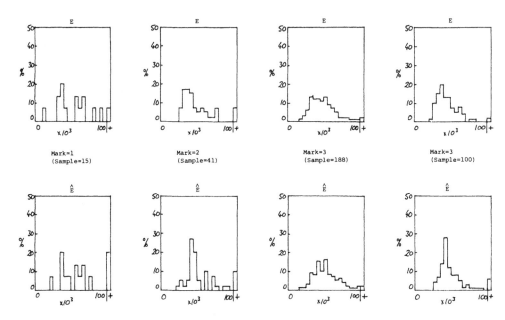

FIGURE 3 <u>DISTRIBUTION OF EFFORT MEASURES OVER MARKS AWARDED (ASSIGNMENT 3)</u>

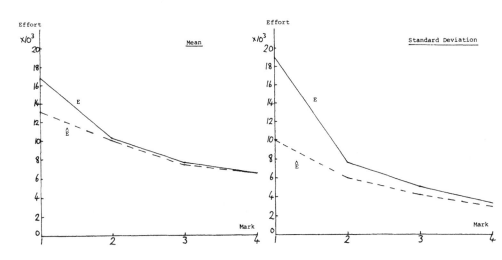

FIGURE 4 <u>MEAN AND STANDARD DEVIATION OF EFFORT MEASURES AGAINST MARK (ASSIGNME</u>

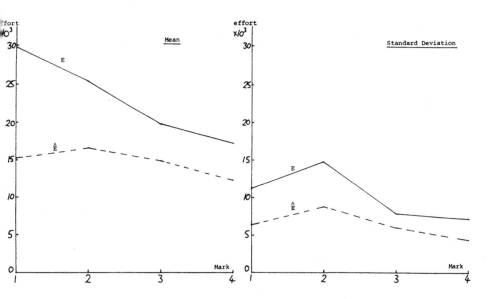

FIGURE 5 <u>MEAN AND STANDARD DEVIATION OF EFFORT MEASURES AGAINST MARK (ASSIGNMENT 2)</u>

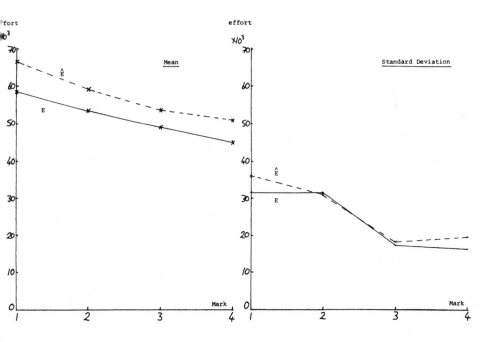

FIGURE 6 <u>MEAN AND STANDARD DEVIATION OF EFFORT MEASURES AGAINST MARK (ASSIGNMENT 3)</u>

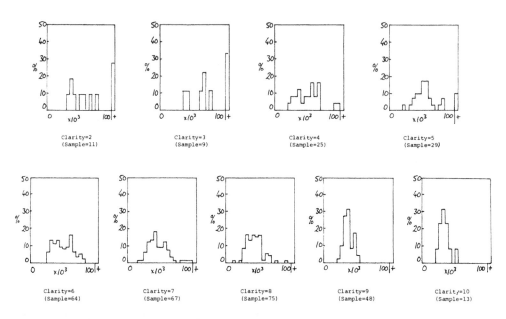

FIGURE 7 <u>DISTRIBUTION OF E OVER CLARITY (ASSIGNMENT 3)</u>

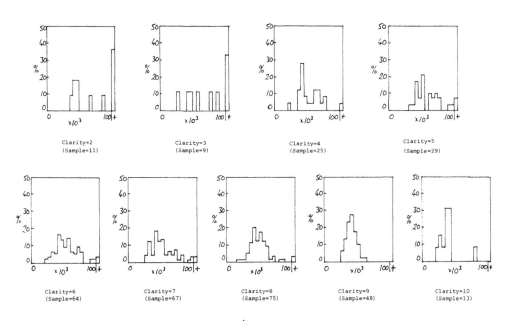

FIGURE 8 <u>DISTRIBUTION OF Ê OVER CLARITY (ASSIGNMENT 3)</u>

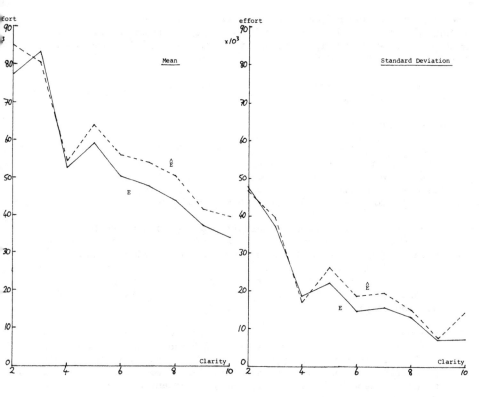

FIGURE 9 <u>MEAN AND STANDARD DEVIATION OF EFFORT MEASURES AGAINST CLARITY (ASSIGNMENT 3)</u>

However, one can detect an overall decline in the mean values of both E and $\hat{E}$ as the clarity increases, as is illustrated in Figure 9. Figure 9 also illustrates a decline in the standard deviation of both E and $\hat{E}$ as the clarity increases.

Figures 8 and 9 also indicate that Gordon's measure E_c ($=\hat{E}$) is no better indicator of clarity in this context than E.

5. SUMMARY AND DISCUSSION

The results of our experiment will probably disappoint the advocates and disciples of software science. There are a few observations which lend support to the theory, but most of our results are either negative or too weak to be useful. In terms of our original aims we can summarise them as follows:

(1)   The correlation between the effort measures and the tutors' assessment of merit and clarity was small. We can say nothing more specific than that the better programs tended to have lower effort measures, and that these measures were less widely dispersed than for the poorer programs. There are certainly no grounds for using the effort measures as the basis for automatic grading of programs.

(2)   The reliability of the length estimator $\hat{N}$ was good, at least in the mean. However, the variance of $N/\hat{N}$ indicates that there were a significant number of programs for which the estimate was not particularly accurate. In any case, for reasons indicated earlier, we do not regard $\hat{N}$ as a particularly important measure.

The level estimator $\hat{L}$ is far more important, since from it one can derive a value for E, even when V^* is unknown. Unfortunately this estimator did not prove very reliable - it showed an average discrepancy from L of nearly 40% on one assignment, and the average discrepancy over all assignments was between 10% and 20%. One reason for this may be that our values of L were themselves inaccurate, and we shall discuss this possibility in a moment.

(3)   We could find no justification whatever for using λ to quantify the language level of PASCAL. Our observations show that λ was by no means constant and for reasons discussed earlier, we would not expect it to be. In our view a meaningful measure of language level can only be relative, and can be established only by comparing the volumes of a number of algorithms programmed in different languages.

We would stress that our findings, other than that relating to language level, should not be taken as an indictment of software science as a whole. Our experiment investigated the application of the science to an area where, as far as we know, it had not been applied before. The results indicate only that in this area software science has little to offer. Some possible reasons for this are discussed below.

Firstly, it could be argued that the failure to produce many positive results is due to weaknesses in the way the experiment was conducted. Some of these weaknesses derive from the fact that our data base was transient, in the sense that the only opportunity to measure each program was on the single occasion it passed through the compiler (we did not have the resources to store the source code of all 13,000 programs). This meant that it was impossible, for example, to see how the results would have varied with different counting schemes. Similarly, there was only one opportunity to make subjective assessments of programs - at the time of marking by tutors - before they were handed back to the students and disappeared into limbo. This meant that an anomalous measurement could not be traced back to the source and the reason for the anomaly adduced: all measurements had to be taken at face value.

Another major weakness lies in the derivation of V^* (and hence L and E). As described in section 4.2 we had considerable difficulty in deciding what the value of V^* should be, and felt obliged to use two values in all calculations performed. In our defence we might mention that we performed the same calculations with other, less likely, values of V^* (covering the range $6 \log_2 6$ to $10 \log_2 10$), and although the numeric results naturally vary, the same negative conclusions apply.

A third weakness may lie in our marking scheme for assignments, which was probably too coarsely grained. A finer grain may have shown up greater differences between "good" and "bad" programs. An attempt to provide a fine grain of assessment, and at the same time to eliminate spurious factors in the marking scheme, was made by obtaining the clarity measure for Assignment 3. In the event the results from the clarity measure were no better than those from the basic marking scheme.

Perhaps the most plausible reason for our largely negative results is that student programs are often badly written, particularly in the early stages of learning. They do not always use language features to best advantage, and they often contain impurities. The presence of impurities is often quoted in the literature as being the cause of anomalies in software science measures: it seems that in the case of student programs the impurities may be sufficient to render the science almost useless. This conclusion will certainly be drawn by those who prefer to attribute our results to deficiencies in the sample rather than deficiencies in the theory.

In summary we feel that our experiment, despite its weaknesses, indicates that software science has little to offer in the area of student programming. It may also have limitations in other fields: if the science is ever to emerge as a major tool these limitations need close investigation.

ACKNOWLEDGEMENTS

We would like to thank Dr. Jean-Louis Lassez for his comments on the original plan for this experiment, and Dr. Jim Welsh for his contributions to our discussions. We are also grateful to the tutors for providing their experience and to the students who unwittingly acted as guinea pigs.

REFERENCES

Elshoff J.L. (1978) "An investigation into the effects of the
        counting method used on software science measurements",
        ACM Sigplan Notices, Vol 13, No 2.

Fitzsimmons A., Love T. (1978) "A review and evaluation of software
        science", ACM Computing Surveys, Vol 10, No 1.

Gordon R.D. (1979) "A qualitative justification for a measure of
        program clarity", IEEE Trans. on Software Engineering,
        Vol 5, No 2.

Halstead M.H. (1977) "Elements of Software Science", Elsevier
        North-Holland, N.Y.

Van der Knijff D.J.J. (1978) "Software physics and program analysis",
        Australian Computer Journal, Vol 10, No 3.

APPENDIX

```
1    PROGRAM ASS1;
2
3      VAR
4        SUBJ, GRADE, CP: INTEGER;          (*SUBJECT CODE, GRADE, CREDIT POINT VALUE*)
5        L, N: INTEGER;                     (*LOOP CONTROL, NO. OF DATA PAIRS*)
6        ERROR: BOOLEAN;                    (*TRUE IF DATA ERROR DETECTED*)
7
8      BEGIN
9        READLN(N);                         (*NO. OF DATA PAIRS*)
10       FOR L := 1 TO N DO
11         BEGIN
12           READLN(SUBJ, GRADE);           (*READ NEXT DATA PAIR...*)
13           WRITE(SUBJ, GRADE);            (*...AND PRINT IT*)
14           ERROR := FALSE;                (*NO DATA ERRORS YET*)
15           IF (GRADE < 1) OR (GRADE > 7)  (*INVALID GRADE*)
16           THEN
17             BEGIN
18               WRITE('     ERROR IN GRADE');
19               ERROR := TRUE
20             END;
21           CASE SUBJ OF
22             100, 110:
23             200, 201, 300, 301:   CP := 8;
24                                   CP := 7;
26             390, 391:             CP := 5;
27           OTHERS:
29             BEGIN
30               WRITE('     ERROR IN SUBJECT');
31               ERROR := TRUE
32             END
33           END;
34           IF (GRADE = 1) OR (GRADE = 2)
35           THEN
36             CP := 0;
37           IF NOT ERROR
38           THEN
39             WRITE(CP);
40           WRITELN
41         END
42       END.

NO ERROR(S) DETECTED
```

(*ASSIGN CREDIT POINTS FOR SUBJECT*)

(*INVALID SUBJECT*)

(*FAIL GRADES*)

(*NO DATA ERRORS DETECTED...*)

(*...SO PRINT CREDIT OBTAINED*)

```
1    PROGRAM ASS2;
2
3       VAR   AH, AM, CH, CM: INTEGER;              (*ACTUAL & CLOCK HOURS & MINS*)
4             STICKING: BOOLEAN;                    (*TRUE WHEN CLOCK IS STICKING*)
5
6
7       BEGIN
8          AH := 0;
9          AM := 0;
10         CH := 0;                                 (*CLOCK STARTS AT ZERO*)
11         CM := 0;
12         STICKING := FALSE;
13         WRITELN('      CLOCK TIME        ACTUAL TIME');
14         REPEAT                                   (*MAIN SIMULATION LOOP*)
15            AM := AM+1;                           (*ACTUAL TIME ALWAYS ADVANCES BY A MIN.*)
16            IF AM = 60                            (*ANOTHER ACTUAL HOUR DONE*)
17            THEN
18               BEGIN
19                  AM := 0;
20                  AH := AH+1
21               END;
22            IF ((CM = CH*5) OR (CM = 30)) AND NOT STICKING
23            THEN
24               STICKING := TRUE                   (*CLOCK STICKS*)
25            ELSE
26               BEGIN
27                  STICKING := FALSE;              (*NORMAL CASE*)
28                  CM := CM+1;                     (*UNSTICK CLOCK*)
29                  IF CM = 60                      (*CLOCK ADVANCES BY A MIN.*)
30                  THEN                            (*ANOTHER CLOCK HOUR DONE*)
31                     BEGIN
32                        CM := 0;
33                        CH := CH+1
34                     END
35               END;
36            IF CM = 0
37            THEN
38               WRITELN(CH, CM, AH, AM)            (*PRINT-OUT REQUIRED ON THE HOUR*)
39         UNTIL CH = 12                            (*STOP AT CLOCK'S MIDDAY*)
40      END.

NO ERROR(S) DETECTED
```

```pascal
      CONST
        CHLIM = 8;                                  (*MAX. NO. OF CHARS PER WORD*)
        WDLIM = 20;                                 (*MAX. NO. OF WORDS IN TEXT*)

      TYPE
        STRING8 = PACKED ARRAY[1..CHLIM] OF CHAR;

      VAR
        CHCNT, WDCNT, I: INTEGER;                   (*CHARACTER COUNT, WORD COUNT, AUXILIARY*)
        CH, KEY: CHAR;                              (*CURRENT CHARACTER, 1ST CHARACTER OF LAST WORD*)
        FOUND: BOOLEAN;                             (*USED IN SEARCH FOR DUPLICATES*)
        S: STRING8;                                 (*CURRENT WORD*)
        TEXT: ARRAY[1..WDLIM] OF STRING8;           (*STORAGE FOR TEXT*)

      BEGIN
        WDCNT := 0;                                 (*INITIALISE WORD COUNT*)
        WHILE NOT EOF DO                            (*INPUT & STORAGE LOOP*)
          BEGIN
            REPEAT                                  (*LOOK FOR START OF NEXT WORD IF ANY*)
              READ(CH)
            UNTIL (CH >= 'A') AND (CH <= 'Z') OR EOF;
            IF NOT EOF                              (*IF THERE WAS A WORD...*)
            THEN
              BEGIN
                CHCNT := 1;                         (*...READ IT IN*)
                REPEAT                              (*INITIALISE CHARACTER COUNT*)
                  IF CHCNT <= CHLIM                 (*DEAL WITH EACH ALPHABETIC CHAR.*)
                  THEN                              (*IF WORD NOT TOO LONG...*)
                    BEGIN                           (*...THEN...*)
                      S[CHCNT] := CH;               (*...STORE CHARACTER...*)
                      CHCNT := CHCNT+1
                    END;
                  READ(CH)                          (*...OTHERWISE IGNORE IT*)
                UNTIL (CH < 'A') OR (CH > 'Z');
                FOR I := CHCNT TO CHLIM DO          (*PAD WORD WITH SPACES*)
                  S[I] := ' ';
                FOUND := FALSE;                     (*INITIALISE TO LOOK FOR DUPLICATES*)
                I := 1;                             (*SCAN TEXT ALREADY READ*)
                WHILE (I <= WDCNT) AND NOT FOUND DO
                  BEGIN
                    FOUND := TEXT[I] = S;
                    I := I+1
                  END;
                IF NOT FOUND                        (*NOT A DUPLICATE, SO...*)
                THEN
                  BEGIN                             (*...STORE THE WORD*)
                    WDCNT := WDCNT+1;
                    TEXT[WDCNT] := S
                  END
              END                                   (*END OF DEALING WITH ONE WORD*)
          END;                                      (*END OF INPUT & STORAGE LOOP*)
        KEY := S[1];                                (*1ST. LETTER OF LAST WORD*)
        FOR I := 1 TO WDCNT DO                      (*PRINT EACH WORD, FLAGGED IF NECESSARY*)
          BEGIN
            WRITE(TEXT[I]);
            IF TEXT[I][1] = KEY
            THEN
              WRITE(' *');
            WRITELN
          END
      END.
```

NO ERROR(S) DETECTED

A CRITIQUE OF MODULA

Andrew Richardson

Department of Computer Science
University of New South Wales

ABSTRACT

MODULA and MODULA-2 are the latest major languages designed by Professor Niklaus Wirth (Wirth,1977 and Wirth,1978). They are both claimed to be high level languages suitable for the programming of dedicated computer systems, with emphasis on process control systems and device drivers. A critique of MODULA, the earlier of the two languages, is presented in this paper. The emphasis is on the "useability" of MODULA, and whether it achieves its stated goals. A compiler for MODULA has been written in BCPL by two members of the University of York, J.Holden and I.C.Wand (Cottam,1978), and this is the compiler used by the author.

1. A BRIEF DESCRIPTION OF MODULA

Areas of programming such as process control systems, device drivers and computerised equipment have long been the almost exclusive domain of Assembly code. MODULA has been designed in an attempt to reduce this domination by providing a high level language that can perform efficiently in these areas.

The language itself has a number of apparent virtues : it is a concise language (suitable for implementation on small computers); it is a "high level" language; and it is based on the now well known language PASCAL, thus being already partly familiar to many new users. It has not implemented a number of the features of PASCAL, however, as the size of the language has been been kept at a minimum to enable implementation on small machines. Whether Wirth has selected the correct features to include and omit is a matter of some contention and these differences are now examined in more detail.

1.1 PASCAL FEATURES NOT IMPLEMENTED IN MODULA

As has been said, MODULA is based closely on PASCAL. Some of the main features of PASCAL that have been omitted from MODULA are :

* Pointers/Dynamic Storage Allocation,
* Input/output facilities,
* File manipulation,
* Variant records,
* Real arithmetic,
* The "GO TO" statement,
* The "FOR" statement,
* Set types, and

* Subrange types.

By far the most annoying omission in my experience was the lack of dynamic storage allocation, and hence the absence of pointers. Pointer-based structures have the big advantage of being able to vary in size, as storage allocation takes place at run-time rather than compile-time. This property was sorely missed, one case in point being the writing of a program to scroll a GT40 display. In such a program it is necessary to represent the screen as some form of character buffer. Storage had to be allocated for the theoretical maximum number of characters that could fit on the screen, although in practice this maximum is virtually never attained. On the other hand, if some pointer facility had been available storage could have been allocated as required. It appears that the overhead involved in introducing a pointer facility would be more than compensated for by the increased efficiency of programs, especially in small computers where core space is at a premium.

The omission of set types is another decision that I would question. Although the type "bits" (which represents an array of boolean variables) can often be used in place of sets, there are still occasions when sets are very useful. For example, when a case statement is used all possible alternatives must be specified (there is no default facility in a case statement in MODULA). The easiest way to ensure this is to have a set containing all the possible alternatives and to enter the case statement only if the expression to be matched is contained in the set. The type "bits" would usually not be suitable for such a function.

Variant records and subrange types are convenient but not essential, and their omission did not cause any substantial problems.

Other omissions that could be annoying are the "GO TO" and "FOR" statements. The former can be useful when a program has a number of error conditions that require quick termination, and the latter is a very simple way of executing a loop a set number of times. The "FOR" statement is especially useful in situations where a number of arrays are being manipulated. Again, both of these instructions, although useful, are not essential and substitutes are readily available.

The three remaining omissions listed, input/output facilities, file handling capabilities and real arithmetic are logical, as MODULA is a language that would generally be used at a level where such facilities are being implemented rather than used. File manipulation facilities, for example, are not really needed when, as Wirth puts it, "the typical application of MODULA is regarded as the design of systems that implement rather than use such a file facility" (Wirth,1977). File manipulation also assumes a good deal of run-time support, which may not always be available.

With the exception of pointer-based data structures and possibly set types, the omissions have been well decided, bearing in mind that this is a language where ease of implementation and compactness are prime objectives.

The method of terminating blocks has also been changed. Commands such as "IF", "WHILE", "CASE", etc must be explicitly terminated. This is an improvement over PASCAL as it obviates the need for a compound statement and generally makes programs easier to read. For example, the PASCAL code:

```
WHILE x<y DO
    BEGIN
        a := b+c;
        inc(x)
    END;
```

becomes in MODULA

```
WHILE x<y DO
    a := b+c;
    inc(x)
END;
```

This explicit termination rule also clarifies programs containing multiply nested "IF" statements, as the "ELSE" part of each "IF" expression is clearly associated with its intended partner.

1.2 NEW FEATURES OF MODULA

1.2.1 MODULES

By far the biggest innovation introduced in MODULA has been the module (as the name suggests). Modules are self-contained units containing constants, variables, data types, procedures and processes local to the module. None of these items can be accessed outside their own module unless they are "exported" by being put in the DEFINE list of their module. Another module can then "import" these items by putting them into its own USE list.

There are three types of module: standard Modules, Interface Modules and Device Modules. Standard Modules have the property mentioned above, but no other special properties. Interface Modules have mutual exclusion properties which will be discussed in the section on signals and processes. Device Modules contain all the machine-dependent facilities and will be discussed more fully later.

Whether modules are sufficiently flexible is an interesting question. The main drawback of the present module design is that duplication of code is a possible necessity. Classes such as those in SIMULA (CDC,1975) and Concurrent Pascal (Brinch Hansen,1975) escape this problem but they are more complex and would increase the size of the compiler. Wirth appears to have made a reasonable compromise between facilities and implementation size in this area. The present modules are very clear and a definite aid to the setting out of an ordered and tidy program.

1.2.2 SIGNALS, PROCESSES AND INTERFACE MODULES

The major multi-programming feature in MODULA is the process. As far as the programmer is concerned, processes can be taken as executing in parallel with one another. Processes can be activated by more than one source, and are in general reentrant. They cannot be nested, and must therefore only occur at the outermost level of the program. Processes are controlled by three operations : "wait", "send" and "awaited". Each of these operations has an argument of type "signal", and operates only on that argument. For example,

$$send(signal1);$$

"Send" will wake up a process that was waiting for the argument signal, "wait" will put a process into the waiting state and "awaited" is a boolean variable that is true when its argument signal is being waited for somewhere in the program.

When several processes share common variables, it can be awkward to have more than one process using (and especially changing) those variables at the same time. Interface Modules have been introduced to prevent this occurring, and provide a queueing facility to ensure mutual exclusion. Several processes in an Interface Module can be waiting at once, and the process currently running does not relinquish control until it executes a "send" or a "wait" statement, at which stage the next process in the queue takes over control. There has been some criticism of this set-up (Holden and Wand, 1978), the main point of contention being that control should not be relinquished on a "send" command. There is merit in this argument from a programmer's point of view, but scheduling within an interface module would become much more complex if this suggestion were adopted, as Holden and Wand point out. No reasonable and efficient method of scheduling has been suggested that would cope with such a modified arrangement, so it appears logical to stick to the present system (which is quite acceptable).

1.2.3 DEVICE MODULES

Device Modules contain nearly all the machine-dependent areas of the language. This means that implementing MODULA on different computers will not mean rewriting the whole compiler, but chiefly only the parts of the compiler dealing with Device Modules. (The exception is the type "bits". "Bits" can be either eight or sixteen bits long, depending on the machine being used.) The separation of machine dependent areas can also be an aid to the writing of well set out programs.

The processes in a Device Module are different to standard processes, and are referred to as Device Processes. These have an ability to receive hardware interrupts through the "doio" command. This command makes the process wait for a hardware interrupt from an interrupt vector address specified in the Device Process heading. Mutual exclusion is performed in a Device Module by specifying the machine processor priority level at which the processes contained in the Device Module will run. This priority is specified in the heading of the module.

The second main feature of a Device Module is the means provided for accessing the hardware interfaces of peripherals. In a PDP-11 computer, these interfaces are represented by device registers at fixed addresses. MODULA lets the user access these registers by associating variables in a Device Module with these hardware addresses. For example, the statement

$$VAR\ dpc[172000B] : integer;$$

will assign the variable "dpc" to the memory location 172000B.

In the interests of minimising both code and the interaction between Device Processes and other areas of the program, Wirth has imposed the following restrictions:

(i) Device Processes are not reentrant (unlike other processes). This restriction has been shown to have only a slight effect on the efficiency of code generated on a PDP-11 (Holden and Wand, 1978).

(ii) Device Processes may not signal each other. This restriction is designed to minimise the switching time for Device Processes, as it means that switching between Device Processes can only occur when a hardware interrupt is received.

(iii) Device Processes may not call non-local procedures. This restriction again reduces switching time and simplifies the scheduling of processes.

The first restriction was no real problem in programming in MODULA, but the last two certainly were. These restrictions considerably reduced the clarity of large programs, with frequent "fiddles" being necessary to get around them. In one program in particular, a handler written to enable the PDP-11/45 to communicate with other computers via a party line, these restrictions were particularly awkward. Such a program relies very heavily on hardware interrupts, and thus requires large and cumbersome Device Modules, as Device Processes cannot call non-local procedures. Signalling was also a problem in this context, owing to the fact that as most of the program consisted of Device Modules most of the processes were Device Processes and thus could not signal each other. One extreme measure was a process (in a standard module) that waited for a signal from a Device Process and then relayed that signal to another Device Process - not very efficient but a step of desperation. These restrictions considerably detract from program clarity and thus must, to some extent, reduce the advantages of programming in MODULA.

There are two options open if this arrangement is to be changed. The first option would be to remove all three restrictions - restrictions (ii) and (iii) because of their serious detrimental effect on the language, and restriction (i) because it has been shown that its lifting would not involve any substantially greater overheads. I realise that this will mean a substantial increase in the complexity of the compiler but these restrictions do seriously detract from the "useability" of MODULA, and so I consider the modifications worth any but the most drastic increase in overheads.

The second option would be to standardise the modules by removing the Device and Interface Modules (as in MODULA-2). I believe that the concept of separating machine dependent areas of the language (and thus machine controlling processes) is a strong aid to the structuring of efficient programs, and therefore I would prefer the former option if it were possible.

2.   THE YORK COMPILER

The University of York Compiler (Version 1.00) was released on 20th June, 1978, and runs under the UNIX operating system. It is a four pass compiler written in BCPL and uses a sequential binary stream and in-core storage to communicate between the passes. There is no run-time storage allocation. Output is in the form of PDP-11 Assembly code.

The compiler has one major (and sometimes fatal) fault. An identifier may not be used unless it has previously been declared. In other words you can't mention an identifier in one module that has been defined in a subsequent module, even when it has duly been exported and imported. In even moderately large programs this rule is incredibly annoying. It often ruins the whole concept of modularity introduced in MODULA, and is sometimes insurmountable.

The compiler is satisfactory for compiling small, straightforward programs. It produces good quality code and does not take up large areas of core. Owing to the overlay methods employed in the compiler it is not sharable by users. Thus each user causes a new copy of the compiler to be loaded, resulting in a deterioration in system response time. This state of affairs would not be satisfactory if a number of people were using MODULA at the same time, but owing to the nature of the language and of the machines on which it will most probably be implemented, this problem should not often arise.

When one moves into larger more complex programs the compiler at its present stage of development is not satisfactory, due chiefly to the "declaration before use" rule described above. If this problem were corrected the compiler would be a satisfactory basic implementation of MODULA as presently specified.

3. IMPLEMENTATION RESTRICTIONS

MODULA has been designed with implementation on microprocessors a prime concern. The size of the language has been kept to a level that is acceptable for microprocessors, but there are a number of requirements that any computer on which MODULA is to be implemented must satisfy. The first two requirements are a direct result of MODULA's intended role as a systems programming language.

Firstly there must be a suitable form of hardware interrupts to satisfy the "doio" command. Coupled with this there must also be a facility to set processor priorities to ensure that these interrupts are processed according to the programmer's requirements. Virtually all modern micros have such facilities, and this requirement shouldn't really narrow MODULA's implementation possibilities.

Secondly there must be a way of accessing the hardware interfaces of peripherals. This is essential to provide a method of controlling any peripheral devices that may be attached to the processor. Again, most micros provide methods of access that would be acceptable to a MODULA compiler, although some do not provide as simple a system as that provided by the PDP-11 family of computers.

The third requirement is more directly connected with facilitating implementation than the previous requirements. It is mentioned by Holden and Wand (1978) and deals with the problem of implementing the reentrancy requirements of MODULA. Holden and Wand consider that some form of stack facility is essential if implementation is to be possible. They mention the INTEL 8080 as one example of a microprocessor that suffers in this area. I have had no personal experience of this problem, being involved in using rather than implementing MODULA, and

therefore cannot comment in any detail on this restriction. Suffice it
to say that a stack facility would greatly improve the chance of efficiently implementing the language.

It appears from the above requirements that MODULA could be implemented on most computers without a significant loss in effectiveness or
versatility, although some of the presently popular microprocessors
would not readily support an efficient implementation (owing to a lack
of stack facilities). It would obviously be advisable to check that a
micro satisfies the above requirements if an implementation of MODULA
is to be attempted.

4. SUGGESTED EXTENSIONS/CHANGES

4.1 POINTERS

As detailed in section 1.1 the lack of pointer-based data structures is not a practical omission. Such data structures can markedly
improve the efficiency of a program. It is therefore recommended that
run-time storage allocation be introduced so that some form of pointers
can be implemented.

4.2 SETS

I would also recommend that sets be introduced to the language,
provided that the overheads involved are not too high, as this change
is for convenience and program clarity rather than efficiency.

4.3 TYPE CHECKING

The present type checking is very rigid. This is generally an
asset but when the hardware interfaces are associated with variables
this asset becomes a nuisance and detracts from program clarity. For
example, the programmer might generally need the value of device register to be numeric, so he declares his variable as an integer type.
However, when just one bit of that integer has to be set, the rigidity
of the type checking prevents the program from setting that bit to
true, and requires the programmer to add or subtract numbers to set the
bit. This can be rather cryptic to someone else trying to follow what
the program is doing and also increases the likelihood of mistakes
being made.

I would therefore recommend the introduction of a type, more basic
than integer and bit types, in which the type checking is substantially
relaxed. Perhaps a sensible restriction would be that such a type
could only be used where device registers are involved.

4.4 DEVICE PROCESS RESTRICTIONS

As stated in section 1.2.3 I would recommend the removal of the
three restrictions on Device Processes. This would greatly improve the
flexibility of the language.

5. CONCLUSIONS

MODULA was designed to bring the advantages of high level programming into areas previously dominated by Assembly code. It was also necessary that storage requirements be kept at a minimum, so that implemation would be feasible on small computers. A compromise had to be reached between these two requirements. This compromise has generally been well decided, with the exception of the points set out in section 4. MODULA is well suited to implementation on small computers - compilers are relatively straightforward to write, the storage requirements are small, efficient code can be produced and implementation is possible on most machines.

Programs written in MODULA are far clearer and easier to write than their equivalents in Assembly code, but I would question the restrictions on device processes for the reasons stated in section 1.2.3. These restrictions are the major drawback of the language. Owing to the organisation of processes it is yet to be seen whether very large multiprocess programs could be written in MODULA. On the other hand MODULA appears very well suited to the writing of device handling programs, and it is here that MODULA makes its biggest contributions. The language is certainly a large step forward in this area.

6. BIBLIOGRAPHY

Brinch Hansen,P: "The Programming Language Concurrent Pascal", IEEE Trans. Software Eng., vol. SE-1, pp. 199-207 (1975)

Cottam,I.D.: "Functional Specification of the Modula Compiler", Report Number 13, Department of Computer Science, University of York (1978)

Holden,J. and Wand,I.C.: "Experience with the Programming Language Modula", Report Number 5, Department of Computer Science, University of York (1977)

Holden,J. and Wand,I.C.: "An Assessment of Modula", Report Number 16, Department of Computer Science, University of York (1978)

Jensen,K. and Wirth,N.: "PASCAL User Manual and Report", Springer-Verlag, New York, N.Y. (1975)

Control Data Corporation, "SIMULA Version One Reference Manual", Control Data Cyber 170 Series (1975)

Wand,I.C. and Holden,J.: "MCODE", Report Number 14, Department of Computer Science, University of York (1978)

Wand,I.C.: "Dynamic Resource Allocation and Supervision with the Programming Language Modula", Report Number 15, Department of Computer Science, University of York (1978)

Wirth,N.: "Modula: a Language for Modular Multiprogramming", Software - Practice and Experience Vol 7, 3-35 (1977)

Wirth,N.: "The Use of Modula", ibid 37-65

Wirth,N.: "Design and Implementation of Modula", ibid 67-84

Wirth,N.: "MODULA-2", Institut fur Informatik, ETH Ch-8092, Zurich (1978)

PROCEEDINGS OF THE SYMPOSIUM ON
LANGUAGE DESIGN AND PROGRAMMING METHODOLOGY
SYDNEY, 10-11 SEPTEMBER, 1979

A COMPARISON OF TWO NOTATIONS FOR PROCESS COMMUNICATION

Jim Welsh,* Andrew Lister and Eric J. Salzman

Department of Computer Science
University of Queensland

ABSTRACT

This paper compares the mechanisms for process communication, synchronisation and non-determinism in recent language
proposals by Hoare and Brinch Hansen, by both qualitative and
quantitative analyses. A significant variation in effectiveness with program class is shown.

1. INTRODUCTION

Advances in hardware technology have made networks of loosely
connected processors, each with its own local storage, an attractive
economic possibility. In doing so, they have created new problems
for programming-language designers. Parallel processing itself is
not new, and languages such as Concurrent Pascal (Brinch Hansen 1975),
Modula (Wirth 1977) and Pascal-Plus (Welsh and Bustard 1979) have
allowed the description of parallel processes for some time.
However these languages allow co-operation between processes by
means of monitors, a concept developed in the early '70s by Brinch
Hansen and Hoare (Brinch Hansen 1973, Hoare 1974). A monitor ensures
well-ordered access to shared variables by the processes which share
them, and is easily implemented when processes are executed by a
single processor, or by multiple processors with access to a common
store. The monitor concept is less natural, and its implementation
is less obvious, on processors without common store, so language
designers have sought alternative solutions.

A significant milestone has recently been passed with the
publication, by the originators of the monitor, of two new language
proposals which seek to overcome the problem. Hoare has suggested
a set of language primitives for the description of *communicating
sequential processes* (Hoare 1978), which is hereafter referred to
as CSP. Brinch Hansen has outlined a language for *distributed
processes* (Brinch Hansen 1978), hereafter referred to as DP. While
the objectives of Hoare's proposal are somewhat broader than those
of Brinch Hansen, the two proposals provide direct alternatives in
the application area chosen for DP, i.e. real-time systems implemented

---

*on leave of absence from the Queen's University of Belfast

by networks of processors with distributed storage. It is
interesting to examine their effectiveness in this area, as
demonstrated by the example programs chosen by their authors.

Both proposals adopt the process as the fundamental notion
in program construction, but differ significantly in their
mechanisms for process communication, process synchronisation, and
non-determinism within processes. Section 2 of this paper illustrates
these differences, by comparing corresponding versions of two of the
program examples given in the original papers, and makes a qualitative
assessment of the significance of these differences in program
construction. Comparative versions of the complete range of examples
used in the original papers are given as appendices to this paper and
these form the basis of a quantitative assessment presented in
Section 3. While the basis of this quantitative assessment may not
be universally accepted, an interesting correlation between the
qualitative and quantitative findings is demonstrated.

The paper is concerned only with the mechanisms for process
communication, synchronisation and non-determinism in the two
proposals. In practice they also differ on data structures, on
process structures and on process termination. Where such differences
would complicate the quantitative comparison of the communication
features, we have taken the liberty of eliminating them by adjustment
of one language or the other. The changes made are in no way a comment
on the language features involved and we apologise to their authors
for making them.

2. A QUALITATIVE COMPARISON

2.1 Communication

Both CSP and DP allow processes to communicate only by explicit
commands, but the forms chosen for these are somewhat different.

In CSP a process X outputs, or sends, information to a process
Y by executing a command of the form

$$Y \ ! \ tag(values)$$

and process Y receives, or inputs, the information by executing a
command of the form

$$X \ ? \ tag(variables)$$

Both the tags and the value and variable lists must correspond if
communication is to succeed.

In DP, communication is accomplished by one process X say,
executing a command of the form

$$call \ Y.P \ (values, \ result \ variables)$$

where process Y contains a procedure declaration of the form

 proc _P (value parameters # result parameters) ... body of P ..._

The value parameters carry information from process X to process Y,
the result parameters carry information back from Y to X.

One difference which is immediately apparent is that in CSP
each process must name the other in order to communicate while in
DP the process defining a procedure need not identify the processes
which call it. Hoare argues that this is not a significant semantic
difference, which Brinch Hansen confirms by indicating that the
implementation of a DP process must make suitable provision for the
calls on its procedures by other processes. Depending on how the
network is connected and the storage economy required, this provision
may involve identifying, or at least enumerating, the callers of each
procedure. Thus CSP makes explicit what a DP implementation must
deduce from each program.

The DP convention may not even be a significant user convenience,
for two reasons:

(1)   In some cases programming advantage is obtained from not
      having to name calling processes - the parallel array
      adder suggested as an exercise by Brinch Hansen is such
      a case - but in others a process may require other
      processes which call its procedures to pass their identity
      as parameters. Brinch Hansen's shortest-job-next scheduler
      (A4) is such a case. In the latter the programmer is
      forced to duplicate information which the implementation
      will deduce by other means, without any check on its
      equivalence. This is a first, if modest, symptom that
      the language design is at a higher level than the
      application requires, since the abstraction has removed
      information which the programmer is forced to recreate.

(2)   As Brinch Hansen points out, a complete language (based
      on his DP proposal) should provide additional notation
      to limit the access rights of individual processes to
      the procedures of other processes. This is precisely
      what CSP's process naming achieves - each process defines
      precisely the processes with which it is intended to
      communicate, and an attempt by any other process to do so
      is detectable during compilation of the program.

Clearly CSP's input and output commands are lower level
primitives than the composite procedure mechanism of DP. One
might expect therefore greater flexibility in CSP but greater
convenience (and error security) in DP. This convenience is
apparent in program examples where no real parallelism is intended,
such as Brinch Hansen's vending machine (A9). It is less obvious
in programs where parallelism is significant, because of the
additional synchronisation role which the communication mechanisms
play there.

2.2 Synchronisation

In CSP the corresponding input and output commands by which two processes communicate are executed 'simultaneously', so whichever process reaches its command first must wait until the other process reaches the corresponding command. When the communication is completed successfully both processes continue in parallel.

In DP a process which calls a procedure of another process is held up until the requested execution of the procedure is complete. This involves waiting until the called process

(a)   decides to execute the procedure on the caller's behalf, and

(b)   does so.

Throughout this period the calling process cannot engage in any other activity.

The additional waiting (b) which is inherent in a DP procedure call complicates the programmer's task in situations where the action requested by a call can and should be carried out in parallel with further activity by the caller. Such a situation is well illustrated by Hoare's set of integers example, which in its original form is as follows:

S::
content : (0..99) integer ; size : integer ; size := 0;
*[n : integer ; X ? has(n) → SEARCH ; X ! reply(i<size)
▢ n : integer ; X ? insert(n) → SEARCH;
*   [i<size → skip*
*   ▢ i=size ; size<100 →*
*   content(size) := n ; size := size+1*
]   ]
where SEARCH ≡ i:integer ; i := 0 ; *[i<size ; content(i) ≠ n → i := i+1]

The user process X sends a query *has* and then waits for a reply by means of two consecutive commands

....S ! has(x) ; S ? reply(b) ....

but to request an insertion a single command

....S ! insert(x)....

is all that is necessary. Once the process S accepts the input x the user process X continues in parallel with the insertion activity within S.

A comparable process in DP might be written as follows:

```
process S
      content : array [100] int ; size, i : int ;
      ┌──────────────────────────────────────────────────┐
      ┆ insertionrequested : boolean ; insertionvalue : int ;┆
      └──────────────────────────────────────────────────┘
      proc search (n : int)
            begin i := 1 ; do (i≤size) & (content[i]≠n) : i: i+1 end end

      proc has (n : int # answer : boolean)
            begin call S.search(n) ; answer := i ≤ size end

      proc insert (n : int)
            ┌──────────────────────────────────────────────────┐
            ┆ begin insertionrequested := true ; insertionvalue := n end ┆
            └──────────────────────────────────────────────────┘
      begin
            size := 0 ;
            ┌──────────────────────────────────┐
            ┆ insertionrequested := false ;    ┆
            ┆ cycle insertionrequested :       ┆
            └──────────────────────────────────┘
                        call S.search(insertionvalue) ;
                        if i≤size : skip |
                           (i>size)&(size<100) :
                                 size: = size+1 ; content[size]:=insertionvalue
                        end ;
            ┌──────────────────────────────────┐
            ┆          insertionrequested :=false ┆
            ┆ end                                ┆
            └──────────────────────────────────┘
end
```

Since a process calling the procedure *has* wishes to wait for
the answer to its query the determination of this answer can be
coded as the procedure body itself. However to allow the process
calling *insert* to continue while the insertion is carried out, the
procedure body is written simply to record that an insertion has
been requested. When execution of this body is completed the calling
process continues, and in parallel with this the infinite cycle in
the body of process S is resumed, to detect that an insertion has
been requested, carry out the insertion and reset the state variable
insertionrequested.

Thus to achieve the required parallelism between insertions and
the process requesting them, all of the code enclosed in boxes has to
be introduced. In no sense can this code be dismissed as the useful
redundancy of a higher level notation - it is an additional logical
framework which the program writer must conceive and the program
reader must unravel, and creates an additional area of potential
error for either. It arises because DP's abstraction of process
communication, the procedure call, includes a second phase of waiting
which this particular application, the set insertion operation, does
not require.

2.3 Non-determinism

In fact the DP process *S* is still incorrect. Because of the
non-deterministic way in which processing switches between the cycle
in the process body and the calls made on its procedures there is no

guarantee that the cycle will be resumed to carry out a requested insertion before a further call of *has* or *insert* is accepted. To guard against this possibility the *begin* at the start of each of the procedures must be replaced by

when not insertionrequested :

This all-too-easy programming error underlines a significant shortcoming of DP as a transparent programming language - the way in which non-determinism is incorporated.

Both CSP and DP recognise the need for non-determinism in programming processes which respond to unpredictably ordered external events. Both adopt Dijkstra's guarded command (Dijkstra 1976) as the means of expressing non-determinism, with trivial differences in syntax :

CSP	DP
[*guard* → *command*	*if guard : command*
☐ *guard* → *command*	┃ *guard : command*
☐	┃ ....
]	*end*
*[*guard* → *command*	*do guard : command*
☐	┃ ....
]	*end*

To enable (possibly) non-deterministic waiting CSP allows an input command $X?t( )$ to appear as a guard ; such a guard is true only when process X executes a corresponding output command, is false if process X has terminated, but otherwise implies waiting to determine the result.

Waiting in DP is expressed as *when* and *cycle* variants of the *if* and *do* commands, which imply waiting for a boolean expression guard to become true.

In CSP the guarded alternative and repetitive commands are the only source of non-determinism within a process. In DP however there is an additional non-determinism in the way in which processing switches between the process body and the external calls on its procedures. As in a conventional monitor, the points at which this switching may occur are imbedded as wait operations (i.e. *when* and *cycle* commands) within the procedures and process body itself, with no explicit structural representation of the non-determinism involved. Furthermore this non-determinism is not at the same level as that defined within the *if*, *do*, *when* and *cycle* commands themselves. Thus processing will remain within a *cycle* command in the process body as long as any of the alternatives of the cycle allow it to continue. Only when this is not so may a procedure call be started or resumed. However the process body has no priority to resume processing when a procedure call is completed or held up. As we have seen, other procedure calls may intervene and the programmer must take care of this possibility.

Both CSP and DP may be criticised for forcing the programmer
to use non-deterministic constructs to express deterministic
behaviour. However the familiar deterministic constructs *if..then..
else* and *while..do* are obvious special cases of the corresponding
guarded constructs in either language, and could easily be restored
by trivial language extension or pre-processing. This is not so
with the non-determinism between the procedures and the body of a
DP process. To impose a deterministic sequence here the programmer
must use guards composed of state variables which are reset at
appropriate points in the code. In doing so he has no syntactic
indication of the extent of the non-determinism involved, and the
presence of additional explicitly non-deterministic constructs may
complicate his task.

2.4 Scheduling

Hoare's set-of-integers example highlights the worst features
of the communication/synchronisation mechanism adopted in DP but
similar problems and logical overheads arise in example programs
used in Brinch Hansen's own paper, such as the shortest-job-next
scheduler (A4) and the sort array (A8).

Under what conditions do the disadvantages of DP's communication
mechanism not apply? Since the semantics of the DP procedure call
require that the calling process must wait, it seems ideal for
implementing processes whose job is to make other processes wait,
i.e. schedulers. From the examples given in the papers this
generalisation must be qualified in two cases :

(1) If the scheduling decision for each type of request is
    expressible as a boolean expression whose value is
    determined by the sequence of requests already serviced,
    then the scheduler may be expressed as easily in CSP - by
    prefixing the input guard representing the request with
    the boolean expression. The resource scheduler (A3) and
    the readers and writers scheduler (A5) are such cases, though
    in practice the resource scheduler can be expressed even more
    simply in CSP.

(2) If the scheduling decisions are to be taken in parallel with
    resource/user activity wherever possible, then for the reason
    already illustrated by the set of integers example the
    structure used in the DP scheduler is equivalent to that
    required in CSP and there is little difference in the volume
    of program required by either language. The shortest-job-
    next scheduler (A4) is such a case.

One example in which DP does have a significant advantage is
Brinch Hansen's alarm clock process, which is as follows :

```
process alarm
     time : int
     proc wait (interval : int)
          due : int
          begin
               due := time+interval
               when time = due : skip end
          end
proc tick ; time := time+1
time := 0
```

A comparative solution in CSP might be as follows, assuming user processes as shown:

```
[ User (i:1..n) :: ..... alarm!wait(t) ; alarm?wakeywakey()...

// alarm::
     time:integer ; time:=0;
     due:(1..n) integer ;
     i:integer ; i := 1 ; *[ i ≤ n → due(i):= -1 ; i := i+1 ];

     *[(i:1..n) interval:integer ; user(i)?wait(interval)→
                         due(i) := time+interval
      □(i:1..n) due(i)=time →
                         user(i)!wakeywakey() ; due(i) := -1
      □ realtimeclock?tick() →
                         time := time+1
]        ]
```

Both solutions assume that the tick step is sufficiently long for the alarm clock to service all necessary users between ticks.

This problem is particularly suited to DP for the following reasons:

(1)   The DP procedure *wait* encapsulates the waiting requirement of each user process clearly and concisely, without reference to the other processes involved.

(2)   The procedure *tick* produces the only changes necessary in the alarm clock environment, so no explicit cycle is required as the process body.

(3)   The separate copies of the local variable *due*, which are created for the processes calling *wait*, provide an implicit data structure over exactly those processes with calls outstanding - in CSP an explicit array over all user processes is declared.

(4)   In determining which processes may continue, the implementation of the DP alarm clock logic inspects only the *due* variables of those actually waiting; in the CSP version all elements of the *due* array are inspected and must therefore be initialised and reset to default value for non-waiting processes.

All four of these factors make the DP program easier to
construct, easier to understand, and less prone to error than
the CSP version. Advantages (3) and (4) are significant in that
they are not illustrated elsewhere in the set of program examples
considered. Note also that they are dependent on the procedural
encapsulation of communication.

As far as efficiency is concerned points (3) and (4) deserve
further consideration. The explicit array *due* in the CSP version
is not a storage overhead since the DP implementation must set aside
at least as much storage for the activation records as the user
processes may require by all waiting concurrently. The reduction
in computation (4) which the DP program achieves is an exploitation
of the underlying set of suspended procedure executions which the
DP implementation must maintain. A comparable efficiency could be
achieved in CSP by explicitly creating a similar set of waiting
users, but at additional programming effort. This efficiency could
affect the feasibility of such a clock process in a real-time
environment.

2.5 Classes of distributed process

In brief the alarm clock example epitomises the advantages
of DP over CSP while the set of integers example epitomises its
disadvantages. However factor (2) on the alarm clock above gives
a significant clue to the conditions under which DP is effective.

The example DP processes considered in the evaluation may be
sub-divided into three classes:

Class 1:   A DP process which consists of a set of procedures,
           and a body which terminates before any procedures
           calls are allowed, is a monitor in the conventional
           sense, but with explicit wait and implicit signal
           operations as provided by guarded regions.

Class 2:   A DP process which contains no procedures and
           consists solely of a body is a process in the
           conventional sense whose only communication is
           by synchronised procedure calls to other (monitor-
           like) processes.

Class 3:   By bringing together the process and monitor as a
           single "distributed process" concept DP creates a
           third class of process in which the sequential
           execution of the process body is non-deterministically
           interleaved with execution of calls on its monitor-
           like procedures.

It is the class 3 process which realises the full potential
of each processor in a distributed network - for asynchronous
parallel activity interleaved with synchronised communication
sequences. However the retention of the monitor procedure as
the only means of communication in DP enforces a textual and
logical split between the synchronised communication sequence
and its asynchronous consequence within the process, interposing
a subtle non-determinism which the programmer often has to override
by additional code.

In contrast a CSP process adopts monitor-like behaviour by
executing a non-deterministic loop with an appropriate input guard
for each monitor call. In some cases the waiting required of the
'caller' is expressible as a boolean precondition to the input guard;
in others it may be expressed as the boolean guard of a second
'signalling' command in the same non-deterministic loop. The extent
to which synchronisation persists once an input 'call' is accepted
is freely determined by the position of the corresponding output
response, if any, and the asynchronous consequence follows immediately
and deterministically in the process text. Any additional activity
by a class 3 process in parallel with its users can be added to the
same non-deterministic loop without any additional structure.

Thus while DP seems to graft the monitor and process concepts
together to allow a clumsy expression of class 3 'processes', CSP
enables the characteristics of each class to be synthesised from a
single concept, the guarded loop, by the inclusion of separate input
and output commands, and input guards.

3. A QUANTITATIVE COMPARISON

The qualitative comparison given in section 2 is illustrated
using two programs only, but is based on experience of translating
the complete set of example programs given in each proposal into
the notation advocated in the other. The appendices A1-16 show
the results of that effort.

Such a collection of small but significant programs in two
languages invites some quantitative comparison. A quantitative
method for measuring program characteristics by examination of their
source text has been developed by Halstead under the general title
Software Science (Halstead 1977). Despite the simplistic and sometimes startling hypotheses on which it is based some significant
success has been claimed for the approach (Fitzsimmons and Love 1978).
Halstead's measures are obtained by counting

$$\text{the number of distinct operators} \quad n_1,$$
$$\text{the number of operator occurrences} \quad N_1,$$
$$\text{the number of distinct operands} \quad n_2,$$
$$\text{and the number of operand occurrences} \quad N_2,$$

in each program. From these the program 'volume' V is given by

$$V = (N_1 + N_2) \; log_2(n_1 + n_2)$$

Thereafter Halstead postulates that.

(1) The level of abstraction in a program is given by

$$L = V^*/V$$

where V^* is the minimal volume possible for the algorithm.

(2) An appropriate measure of language level is

$$\lambda = LV^* = (V^*)^2/V$$

(3) The effort involved in writing a program is measured by

$$E = V/L = V^2/V^*$$

Thus, in comparing versions of the same algorithm in two programming languages, the ratio of the measured volumes V_1/V_2 is an inverse measure of the relative language levels (and the square of this ratio is a measure of the relative effort involved in the program's construction).

To compare the effect of the different mechanisms for communication, synchronisation and non-determinism in CSP and DP by use of Halstead's measures it is essential that other differences in the two languages do not interfere. To this end the programs given in the appendices differ from the originals in the following ways:

(1) The CSP proposal makes no suggestions on the range of data types and data structures that a complete language should provide, while the DP proposal includes arrays, sets and bounded sequences, with appropriate operations for each, together with a *for* statement enabling the processing of arrays and sets, component by component. For comparison purposes the CSP examples have been rewritten assuming an exactly equivalent set of features.

(2) The DP proposal makes the use of semicolon delimiters optional. To make counting easier all semicolons which denote explicit sequencing in a DP process have been made explicit in the process text.

(3) In his discussion Hoare suggests an abbreviated notation for declaring input variables, writing *X?T(n:integer)* rather than *n:integer ; X?T(n)*. This abbreviation has been used throughout the CSP examples as it corresponds more closely to an input parameter declaration in DP.

The precise strategy to be used in counting operators and operands in the CSP and DP programs also required careful consideration. The accessible papers on software science give limited examples, in languages very different from CSP and DP. However from these the following general strategies are apparent:

(1) Only executable program text is counted, all declarative text being ignored.

(2) Composite combinations of symbols such as *if then* or *while do* are considered to be single operators.

(3) Where control operations refer to other points in a program text, e.g. *goto* or *call*, each combination of operation and distinct label or name is considered a distinct operator.

For DP and CSP these strategies were interpreted as follows:

(1) In DP all declarations and procedure headings were ignored. In CSP all declarations were ignored, including those within input commands such as $X?T(n:integer)$; however in a subsequent input to an existing variable such as $X?T(n)$ the variable n was counted as an operand occurrence.

(2) In DP the combinations

$$
\begin{array}{lll}
\underline{if} & : & \underline{end} \\
\underline{do} & : & \underline{end} \\
\underline{when} & : & \underline{end} \\
\underline{cycle} & : & \underline{end}
\end{array}
$$

were considered to be four distinct operators, with imbedded occurrences of

$$ | \quad : $$

denoting a further auxiliary operator. Likewise the combination

$$ \underline{for}\ x\ \underline{in} \quad : \quad \underline{end} $$

was considered a single operator (and declaration of x). Similar arguments give the following combinations as operators in CSP :

$$
\begin{array}{lll}
[& \rightarrow &] \\
*[& \rightarrow &] \\
\square & \rightarrow & \\
*[x\ \underline{in} & \rightarrow &]
\end{array}
$$

(3)   In DP each distinct combination of the form

$$\underline{call}\ P.t(\ \ )$$

was considered a distinct operator.   In CSP each of
the forms

$$P!t(\ \ )$$
$$P?t(\ \ )$$

was considered a distinct operator.

One problem area was the treatment of bound variables in
CSP's guarded arrays, such as:

$$(i : 1..n)\quad P(i)?t(.....)\quad \rightarrow\quad .....i.....i.....$$

How should the introduction and use of i be counted?   After some
consideration the following procedure was adopted:

(1)   The initial $(i : 1..n)$ was considered to be declarative
and was therefore ignored.

(2)   Each subsequent occurrence of i on either side of the $\rightarrow$
was counted as an operand occurrence.

(3)   The parentheses() enclosing i in $...P(i)?....$ were not
counted as a subscripting operation,   since the process
array name P cannot occur without them - a similar
attitude was taken on all purely syntactic parentheses,
commas, etc. throughout the two languages.

The details of the precise counting method to be used for any
language are clearly open to dispute.   Experiments by Elshoff (1978)
suggest that, while some software science measures are sensitive to
minor variations in counting strategy, the volume measure V is not.
What matters in comparing CSP and DP is that the two counting
strategies used should be consistent and should reflect the
significant programming differences imposed by the two notations.
It is on this assumption of fairness that interpretation of the
results depends.

Application of the chosen counting strategy to the programs
given as Appendices A1-A16 produced the results shown in Table 1.

Program example	DP					CSP					λDP/λCSP
	n_1	N_1	n_2	N_2	V	n_1	N_1	n_2	N_2	V	
A1. Message buffer	8	10	3	7	58.8	13	17	3	8	100	1.70
A2. Character stream	14	27	9	24	231	14	26	8	22	214	0.93
A3. Resource scheduler	4	6	3	8	39.3	3	3	1	2	10.0	0.25
A4. S-J-N scheduler	20	49	10	43	451	20	48	10	44	451	1.00
A5. Readers and writers	8	15	3	20	121	15	20	4	14	144	1.19
A6. Alarm clock	7	10	5	10	71.7	11	21	9	20	177	2.47
A7. Dining philosophers	14	16	6	13	125	16	20	5	13	145	1.16
A8. Sorting array	16	47	10	50	456	17	43	6	42	385	0.84
A9. Vending machine	13	37	10	36	330	16	33	8	30	289	0.88
A10. Copier	4	10	6	12	73.1	3	3	1	1	8.00	0.11
A11. Squasher	9	37	10	42	336	8	17	3	13	104	0.31
A12. Disassembler	5	7	4	5	38.0	5	6	3	3	27.0	0.71
A13. Division 1	8	13	6	12	95.2	8	15	6	14	110	1.16
A13. Division 2	10	30	13	32	280						0.39
A14. Set of integers	18	47	14	40	435	16	34	9	28	288	0.66
A15. Integer semaphore	5	7	3	10	51.0	9	12	5	12	91.4	1.79
A16. Eratosthenes' sieve	16	31	8	29	275	14	22	5	20	178	0.65

Table 1 : Program examples with software science data and resultant λ ratio

Programs A1 to A9 are those used by Brinch Hansen to illustrate the features of DP; programs A10 to A16 are used by Hoare to illustrate the features of CSP. The following additional programs in Hoare's paper were discarded for the reasons given:

(1) The ASSEMBLE process is too dependent on process termination in CSP to be represented fairly in DP.

(2) The recursive FACTORIAL array of processes is unrealistic.

(3) The bounded buffer is equivalent to Brinch Hansen's message buffer (A1).

(4) The matrix multiplication array is too dependent on features not provided in DP.

In translating a CSP process which accepts input from another process P and later returns an output response, one must decide in DP whether the process P is to wait for the response, or is to be allowed to continue in parallel and request the response later - in CSP this is determined solely by the "calling sequence" used in P. Since this distinction is crucial to the qualitative assessment, Hoare's division process (A13) was translated into two DP forms which demonstrate the difference involved. Division 1 provides a single

procedure which forces the user process P to wait; Division 2
provides one procedure which inputs the dividend and divisor,
and another which collects the remainder and quotient when they
are available.

The following comments may be made on the results shown in
Table 1:

(1)　The resource scheduler (A3) and the copier process (A10),
which is a one-character buffer, are represented so
nearly optimally in CSP that they may be discounted as
pathological cases.

(2)　For several of the examples, such as the readers and
writers scheduler (A5), the dining philosophers
(A7) and the integer semaphore (A15), the actions coded
in DP and CSP are identical. The advantage shown for DP
by the λ ratio is due entirely to the fact that in DP the
initial execution of the process body followed by the
repeated execution of calls on its procedure is implicit
in the process syntax, while in CSP it must be expressed
explicitly by coding of the form

> *...initialisation...;*
> **[inputguard → ......*
> *[] inputguard → ......*
> *...................*
> *]*

This inherent advantage of DP applies throughout the
coding of all class 1 processes.

(3)　The λ-ratios show an extreme advantage for DP in the
alarm clock process, and a significant advantage for
CSP in the set of integers process, in accordance with
the preceding qualitative assessment. Given that software
science is a statistical science, and that the counting
strategy used may be open to criticism, the precise value
of the λ ratio for each example is not highly significant,
but the variation of λ ratios with process class is.
Discarding the pathological cases, and re-ordering the
examples in descending λ-ratio order gives the results
shown in Table 2.

Program	$\lambda DP/\lambda CSP$	Class
Alarm clock	2.47	1
Integer semaphore	1.79	1
Message buffer	1.70	1
Readers and writers	1.19	1
Dining philosophers	1.16	1
Division 1	1.16	1
Shortest job next scheduler	1.00	3
Character stream	0.93	2
Vending machine	0.88	1
Sort array	0.84	3
Disassembler	0.71	2
Set of integers	0.66	3
Sieve	0.65	3
Division 2	0.39	3
Squasher	0.31	3

Table 2 Program examples in descending λ ratio order
showing correlation with process class

Table 2 clearly shows that of program examples for which DP
is either better or comparable to CSP by λ measurement all but
one are of class 1 or 2, i.e. either conventional monitors or
conventional processes. All but one of the examples in which CSP
has a significant advantage are of class 3. Thus these quantitative
results show a close agreement with the qualitative assessment in
section 2.

4. CONCLUSION

The faults found with DP in comparison to CSP are typical of
those to which any higher level notation is liable, namely that
the higher level abstraction removes from the user either access
to information, or a freedom, which his application requires. From
the examples considered, the constraints of a procedural communication
mechanism make class 3 processes more difficult to construct in DP
than in the lower level CSP. This is borne out by both the qualitative and quantitative analyses of the examples chosen. It seems
therefore that CSP has struck a better level of language features for
such programs, and creates less unwanted non-determinism than DP.

Is this the whole story? The example programs were presumably
chosen by their authors to illustrate each language feature, rather
than to provide a representative sample of the potential program set
of each language. We in turn have used them simply because they were
there. In the end the success of a language is determined by the
actual application programs which have to be written in it, not by
the toy programs beloved by language designers and academics. Of
the examples considered, one showed advantages of DP which were not
illustrated elsewhere, and which are dependent on its procedural

encapsulation of communication. If the real world's application programs of class 3 exploit these advantages more than the examples used in the papers then the relative effectiveness of the two languages may be different from that found here.

ACKNOWLEDGEMENTS

The contents of this paper are the result of a series of group discussions with our colleagues Paul Bailes, Bob Buckley, Rick Stevenson and Greg Smith. Their contribution to the final outcome is gratefully acknowledged.

REFERENCES

Brinch Hansen P.[1973]   "Operating System Principles", Prentice-Hall, Englewood Cliffs, N.J.

Brinch Hansen P.[1975]   "The programming language Concurrent Pascal", IEEE Transactions on Software Engineering, Vol 1, No 2.

Brinch Hansen P.[1978]   "Distributed processes", Comm.ACM, Vol 21, No 11.

Dijkstra E.W.[1976]   "A Discipline of Programming", Prentice-Hall, Englewood Cliffs, N.J.

Elshoff J.L.[1978]   "An investigation into the effects of the counting method used on software science measurements", ACM Sigplan Notices, Vol 13, No 2.

Fitzsimmons A., Love T.[1978]   "A review and evaluation of software science", ACM Computing Surveys, Vol 10, No 1.

Halstead M.[1977]   "Elements of Software Science", Elsevier North-Holland Inc., N.Y.

Hoare C.A.R.[1974]   "Monitors: an operating system structuring concept", Comm.ACM, Vol 17, No 10.

Hoare C.A.R.[1978]   "Communicating sequential processes", Comm.ACM, Vol 21, No 8.

Welsh J., Bustard D.W.[1979]   "Pascal-plus - another language for modular multiprogramming", Australian Computer Science Communications, Vol. 1, No. 1.

Wirth N.[1977]   "Modula : A programming language for modular multiprogramming", Software - Practice and Experience,Vol 7, No 1.

APPENDICES

A1 : Message buffer

Brinch Hansen's example of a bounded buffer is as follows:

```
process buffer
    s : seq[n]char
    proc send(c:char)  when not s.full : s.put(c) end
    proc rec(#v:char)  when not s.empty : s.get(v) end
    s := []
```

A comparable CSP solution is as follows:

```
buffer ::
    s : seq(n)char ;
    s := () ;
    *[ ¬ s.full ; X?send(c:char) → s.put(c)
    □ ¬ s.empty ; Y?rec() → v:char ; s.get(v) ; Y!rec(v)
    ]
```

Comments: (i) The CSP solution requires an explicit loop
            *[....□....] to express the non-deterministic
            sequencing of send and receive operations ;
            in CSP this is implicitly expressed. A similar
            difference is observable in all class 1 (monitor)
            programs.

           (ii) The CSP solution requires a two-step calling
            sequence in the receiver process Y
                buffer!rec() ; buffer?rec(x)
            to simulate a call to a procedure with a result
            parameter.

A2 : An input character stream

Brinch Hansen programs a process which reads card images and
sends a corresponding stream of characters to a buffer, as follows:

```
process stream
    b : array[80]char ; n,i : int
    do true :
    call cardreader.input(b) ;
    if b=blankline : skip |
       b≠blankline :
           i := 1 ; n := 80 ;
           do b[n]=space : n := n-1 end ;
           do i≤n : call buffer.send(b[i]) ; i :=i+1 end
    end ;
    call : buffer.send(newline)
    end
```

A comparable CSP process is as follows:

```
stream ::
*[ cardreader?input(b:(1..80)char) →
     [ b=blankline → skip
     □ b≠blankline →
           n,i : integer ;
           i := 1 ; n := 80 ;
           *[ b(n)=space → n := n-1] ;
           *[ i≤n → buffer!send(b(i)) ; i := i+1]
     ] ;
     buffer!send(newline)
]
```

Comment: The CSP version replaces <u>do true : input call ; ....</u>
              by *[inputguard → .....
          which in CSP also takes care of the termination of
          the inputting (cardreader) process, but otherwise
          the solutions are equivalent in all but syntax.

A3 : A resource scheduler

Brinch Hansen gives the following DP coding of a monitor which
schedules the use of a single resource:

```
process resource
      free : bool
      proc request  when free : free := false end
      proc release  if not free : free := true end
      free := true
```

Assuming user processes user (1..n), a suitable CSP scheduler
is as follows:

```
resource ::
*[ (i:1..n) user(i)?request() → user(i)?release() ]
```

Comments: (i)   The CSP solution allows only a non-deterministic
                  choice between competing user requests. In DP
                  the non-determinism also includes the release
                  operations, and the state variable free has to
                  be introduced.

           (ii)   The DP scheduler stops if a release operation
                  is attempted when the resource is already free;
                  the CSP version ignores such operations.

           (iii) The CSP requirement for naming user processes
                  means that the scheduler accepts a release
                  operation only from the user who last acquired
                  it; to achieve the same control in DP requires
                  a user identity parameter in each procedure.

A4 : shortest-job-next scheduler

Brinch Hansen gives the following (class 3) process as a shortest-job-next scheduler, in which the next job is decided in parallel with the current job's use of the resource whenever possible:

```
process sjn
      queue : set[n]int ; rank : array[n]int
      user,next,min : int

      proc request(who,time:int)
            begin queue.include(who) ; rank[who] := time ;
                  next := nil ; when user=who : next := nil end
            end

      proc release  user := nil

      begin queue := [] ; user := nil ; next := nil ;
            cycle
                  not queue.empty & (next=nil) :
                        min := maxint ;
                        for i in queue :
                              if rank[i]≥min : skip |
                                 rank[i]<min : next := i ; min := rank[i]
                              end
                        end |

                  (user=nil) & (next≠nil) :
                        user := next ; queue.exclude(user)
                  end
            end
      end
```

Assuming user processes users(1..n) an equivalent CSP process is as follows:

```
sjn ::
      queue : set(n)integer ; rank : (1..n)integer ;
      user,next : integer ;
      queue := () ; user := nil ; next := nil ;

      *[ (i:1..n) users(i)?request(time:integer) →
                  queue.include(i) ; rank(i) := time ; next := nil
      [] (i:1..n) users(i)?release() → user := nil

      [] next=nil ; ¬ queue.empty →
                  min : integer ; min := maxint ;
                  *[ i in queue →
                        [ rank(i)≥min → skip
                        [] rank(i)<min → next := i ; min := rank(i)
                  ]        ]
      [] user=nil ; next≠nil →
                  users(next)!ok() ; user := next ;
                  queue.exclude(user) ; next := nil
      ]
```

Comments: (i) Each solution involves four non-deterministically interleaved code fragments, whose interleaving is controlled by the same variables. In CSP the four fragments form a single non-deterministic command.

(ii) In CSP reactivation of a user is separated from the code which accepted the request; however this separation allows this reactivation to precede, rather than follow, the corresponding housekeeping within the scheduler, and precludes the interleaving of any further request processing, so a higher degree of parallelism is possible.

A5 : A readers and writers scheduler

Brinch Hansen shows the following solution to the readers and writers problem:

```
process resource
    s : int
    proc startread  when s≥1 : s := s+1 end
    proc endread     if   s>1 : s := s-1 end
    proc startwrite when s=1 : s := 0   end
    proc endwrite    if   s=0 : s := 1   end
    s := 1
```

The following CSP process solves the same problem:

```
resource ::
    readers : set(n)int ; readers := () ;
  *[ (i:1..n) ¬ (i in readers) ; user(i)?startread()  →
                                              readers.include(i)
   ▯ (i:1..n)    i in readers ; user(i)?endread()     →
                                              readers.exclude(i)
   ▯ (i:1..n)    readers.empty ; user(i)?startwrite() →
                                              user(i)?endwrite()
   ]
```

Comments: (i) As in the resource scheduler the deterministic sequence for *startwrite* and *endwrite* operations is expressed directly in CSP; however non-deterministic selection between *startreads*, *endreads* and *startwrites* is required.

(ii) By replacing the state variable s by the set *readers* the CSP version validates user identity at little extra cost; to do the same in DP requires an identity parameter in each procedure, a set of readers, and a boolean flag for writing.

(iii) Because the waiting condition is expressible as a boolean expression prefixing an input guard the CSP solution encapsulates the waiting process as neatly as in DP.

A6 : An alarm clock

Brinch Hansen suggests the following process to enable other user processes to wait for a specified interval of time, where the actual progress of time is signalled by a regular tick operation:

```
process alarm
      time : int
      proc wait(interval:int)
            due : int
            begin due := time+interval ;
                  when time=due : skip end
            end
      proc tick   time := time+1
      time := 0
```

The same effect is provided by the following CSP process:

```
alarm ::
      time : integer ; due : (1..n)integer ;
      time := 0 ; *[ d in due → d := -1 ] ;
   *[ (i:1..n) user(i)?wait(interval:integer) →
                                    due(i) := time+interval
   ▢ (i:1..n) due(i) = time →
                              user(i)!wakeywakey() ; due(i) := -1
   ▢ realclock?tick() → time := time+1
   ]
```

Comments: see text.

A7 : The dining philosophers problem

Brinch Hansen gives the following solution to the dining philosophers problem:

```
process Philosopher[5]
      do true : ..... call table.join(this)....
                        call table.leave (this).....end
process table
      eating : set[5]int
      proc join(i:int)
            when ([i⊕1,i⊖1] & eating)=[] : eating.include(i) end
      proc leave(i:int)
            eating.exclude(i)
      eating := [ ]
```

An exactly equivalent solution is possible in CSP:

Philosopher (i:1..5) ::
  *[true → ....table!join().......table!leave()....]

table ::
    eating : set(5)integer ; eating := () ;
  *[(i:1..5) ((i⊕1,i⊖1) & eating)=() ;
              Philosopher(i)?join() → eating.include(i)
    ▯ (i:1..5) Philosopher(i)?leave() → eating.exclude(i)

    ]

Comment: The table process is another example of a scheduler
          in which the waiting condition is expressible as a
          boolean expression prefixing an input guard.

A8 : Sorting array

Brinch Hansen's version of this example is confusing in that it
uses a sequence of length ≤ 2 to hold the items within each element
process at any moment, but also accesses and rearranges them by
subscript as if the sequence is an array. The following version uses
two variables and a load count instead of the sequence, and gives a
smaller software science volume than Brinch Hansen's original:

process Sort[n]
      x, temp, load, rest : int

    proc put(c:int) when load=0 : x := c ; load := 1 |
                          load=1 : temp := c ; load := 2 end

    proc get(#c:int) when load=1 : c:= x ; load := 0 end

    begin
          load := 0 ; rest := 0 ;
          cycle
              load=2 :
                  if x≤temp : call Sort[succ].put(temp) |
                      x>temp : call Sort[succ].put(x) ; x:=temp
                  end;
                  rest := rest+1 ; load := 1 |

              (load=0) & (rest≠0) :
                  call Sort[succ].get(x) ;
                  rest := rest-1 ; load := 1
          end
      end

An equivalent CSP array is as follows:

Sort(i:1..n) ::

*[Sort(i-1)?put(x:integer) →

        count : integer ; count := 1 ;
        *[count>0 ; Sort(i-1)?put(temp:integer) →
                [x≤temp → Sort(i+1)!put(temp)
                ▯ x>temp → Sort(i+1)!put(x) ; x:=temp
                ] ;
                count := count+1
        ▯ count>0 ; Sort(i-1)?get() →
                Sort(i-1)!got(x) ; count := count-1
                [count=0 → skip
                ▯ count>0 → Sort(i+1)!get() ;
                        Sort(i+1)?got(x)
]   *]*   *]*

Comments: (i) In the CSP version the first *put* operation which
                    loads a previous empty process element is
                    distinguished from those which follow; the count
                    variable ensures that the process reverts to this
                    initial empty state when the last value has been
                    extracted.

           (ii) In the CSP version the balancing actions required
                    of each process after it services a *get* or *put*
                    request are coded to follow the servicing code
                    deterministically. In the DP version the load
                    variable controls the non-deterministic inter-
                    leaving of the four code fragments required.

A9 : A vending machine

    Brinch Hansen gives the following process defining the behaviour
of a single vending machine:

process vending machine
    items,paid,cash : int
    proc insert(coin:int) paid := paid+coin
    proc push(#change,goods:int)
        if (items>0) & (paid≥price) :
            change := paid-price ; cash := cash+price ;
            goods := 1 ; items :=items-1 ; paid := 0 |
        (items=0 or (paid<price) :
            change := paid ; goods := 0 ; paid := 0
        end
    begin items := 50 ; paid := 0 ; cash := 0 end

A similar process in CSP is as follows:

Vending machine ::
   items,paid,cash : integer ;
   items :=50 ; paid :=0 ; cash := 0 ;
  [user?insert(coin: integer) → paid := paid+coin
  □ *user?push() →*
      [*items>0 ; paid≥price →*
          user!deliver(paid-price,1) ;
          cash := cash+price ; items := items-1
      □ *(items=0) ∨ (paid<price) →*
          user!deliver(paid,0)
      ] *;*
      paid := 0
  ]

Comment: The CSP solution is slightly neater because the return of the results of a *push* operation can be coded as direct output commands, rather than as assignments to formal parameters.

A10 : A single character buffer

Hoare gives the following CSP process which acts as a single character buffer between processes *west* and *east*:

    *x :: *[west?put(c:char) → east!get(c)]*

An equivalent buffer might be programmed in DP as follows:

    <u>process</u> *x*
       c : char ; cready : bool ;
       <u>proc</u> *put(u:char)* <u>when</u> <u>not</u> *cready :*
                     c := u ; cready := true <u>end</u>
       <u>proc</u> *get(#v:char)* <u>when</u> *cready :*
                     v := c ; cready := false <u>end</u>
       cready := false

Comments: (i) As with the resource scheduler (A3) the deterministic sequence of *put* and *get* operations is expressed explicitly in CSP. In DP it must be superimposed on an inherently non-deterministic sequence by means of the state variable *cready*.

        (ii) A slightly shorter if obtuse solution can be expressed in DP by declaring *c* as a bounded sequence of maximum length 1, thus
                        c : <u>seq[1]</u>char
        (cf. A1) but comment (i) still applies.

All : A squasher

Hoare also gives the following example, which is again a single character buffer, but which replaces each pair of consecutive asterisks by an upward arrow:

$x ::$ *[*west?put(c:char)* →
     [*c≠asterisk* → *east!get(c)*
     ☐ *c=asterisk* →
       west?put(c) ;
       [*c≠asterisk* → *east!get(asterisk)* ; *east!get(c)*
       ☐ *c=asterisk* → *east!get(upwardarrow)*
    ]   ]   ]

A DP solution to the same problem is as follows:

process x
    c : *char* ; *state* : *int*
    proc put(u:char) *when* *state=cempty* :
                              $c := u$; *state* := *cfull* *end*
    proc get(#v:char)
       when *state=cready* : $v := c$; *state* := *cempty* |
           state=asteriskfirst : $v :=$ *asterisk* ;
                         state := *cready*
      end
    begin
      state := *cempty* ;
      cycle *state=cfull* :
        if *c≠asterisk* : *state* := *cready* |
        c=asterisk :
        state := *cempty* ;
        when *state=cfull* :
         if *c≠asterisk* : *state* := *asteriskfirst* |
          c=asterisk : $c :=$ *upwardarrow* ;
                  state := *cready*
        end
       end
     end
   end
 end

Comments: (i) In the CSP solution the state of the buffer at any moment is represented by its point of execution, with distinct input and output commands for each state. In DP all input and output must pass through the procedures *put* and *get* with the process body keeping track of the state in which any particular call of *put* or *get* occurs.

(ii) A DP solution using a two character buffer to solve the same problem may be simpler, but the above is typical of the coding required of any 'intelligent' buffer which vets the data received before transmitting it.

A12 : A card image disassembler

Hoare gives the following process to read card images and output them character by character to a process x inserting an extra space at the end of each card. It is similar to, but simpler than, Brinch Hansen's character stream (A2). Using the for construct imported from DP it is trivially programmed in CSP as follows:

```
east ::
    *[ cardfile?read(cardimage:(1..80)char) →
                *[ c in cardimage → x!put(c) ] ;
                x!put(space)
    ]
```

The DP solution is as follows:

```
process east
        cardimage : array[80]char
        do true :
            call cardfile.read(cardimage) ;
            for c in cardimage : call x.put(c) end ;
            call x.put(space)
        end
```

A13 : A division routine

Hoare gives the following process as a means of providing an integer division facility for a user process X :

```
Division ::
    *[ X?div(x,y:integer) →
            quot,rem : integer ;
            quot := 0 ; rem := x ;
            *[ rem≥y → rem := rem-y ; quot := quot+1 ] ;
            X!ans(quot,rem)
    ]
```

This can be implemented in DP in two ways according to whether the user process X is to be forced to wait for the answer. If it is, then a process providing a single procedure suffices:

```
process Division 1
        proc div(x,y:integer#quot,rem:integer)
        begin
            quot := 0 ; rem := x ;
            do rem≥y : rem := rem-y ; quot := quot+1 end
        end
        skip
```

However if the user process is to be allowed to continue while the answer is being computed, a process with two procedures and an interleaved process body is required:

```
process Division 2
        Y,R,Q : int ; state : int
        proc div(x,y:integer)
            when state=idle : R := x ; Y := y ;
                                    state := active end
        proc ans(#quot,rem:integer)
            when state=done : quot := Q ; rem := R ;
                                    state := idle end
        begin
            state := idle ;
            cycle state=active :
                Q := 0 ;
                do R≥Y : R := R-Y ; Q := Q+1 end ;
                state := done
            end
    end
```

Comment: The two processes illustrate clearly the differences between class 1 and class 3 processes in DP, and the programming overheads which it imposes on the latter.

A14 : A set of integers

Hoare gives the following process as a representation for a set of integers, in which insertions are carried out in parallel with continued execution of the requesting process x. For ease of comparison an imbedded procedure-like formulation has been adopted for the search subroutine.

```
S :: content : (0..99)integer ; size,i : integer ;

    search(n:integer) ≡
        ( i := 0 ; *[ i<size ; content(i)≠n → i := i+1 ] )

    size := 0 ;
    *[ x?has(n:integer) → search(n) ; x!reply(i<size)

    [] x?insert(n:integer) → search(n) ;
                        [ i<size → skip
                        [] i=size ; size<100 →
                            content(size) :=n ; size := size+1
    ]                   ]
```

A DP process allowing the same parallelism is as follows:

```
process S
    content : array[100]int ; size,i : int ;
    insertionrequested : boolean ; insertionvalue : int ;
    proc search(n:int)
        begin i := 1 ;
            do (i≤size)&(content[i]≠n) : i:=i+1 end end

    proc has(n:int#answer:boolean)
        when not insertionrequested :
            call S.search(n) ; answer := i≤size end
    proc insert(n:int)
        when not insertionrequested :
            insertionrequested := true ;
            insertionvalue := n end

    begin
        size := 0 ;
        insertionrequested := false ;
        cycle insertionrequested :
            call S.search(insertionvalue) ;
            if i≤size : skip |
                (i>size)&(size<100) :
                    size := size+1 ;
                    content[size] := insertionvalue
            end ;
            insertionrequested := false
        end
end
```

Comments: see text.

A15 : An integer semaphore

Hoare implements an integer semaphore as follows:

```
S :: val : integer ; val := 0 ;
    *[ (i:1..100) X(i)?V() → val := val+1
     □ (i:1..100) val>0 ; X(i)?P() → val := val-1
    ]
```

The DP solution is very similar:

```
process S
    val : int
    proc V  val := val+1
    proc P  when val>0 : val := val-1 end
    val := 0
```

Comment: This is a third example of a scheduler in which the
         waiting condition is trivially expressed as a boolean
         prefix to an input guard.

A16 : A prime number sieve

Hoare gives the following process array as the core of a sieve to find prime numbers, in which the processes deal concurrently with the different trial numbers percolating through the sieve. For comparison purposes the boundary processes are omitted as these involve different techniques for their definition in CSP and DP.

```
Sieve(i:1..100) ::
    p,mp : integer ;
    Sieve(i-1)?test(p) ;
    print!prime(p) ;
    mp := p ;
    *[Sieve(i-1)?test(m:integer) →
            *[ m>mp → mp := mp+p ] ;
            [ m=mp → skip
            [] m<mp → Sieve(i+1)!test(m)
    ]          ]
```

A DP process array with the same effect is as follows:

```
process Sieve(100)
    p,mp,m :int ; testing : bool
    proc test(t:int) when not testing : m := t ;
                                        testing := true end
    begin
        testing := false ;
        when testing :
            p := m ;
            call print.prime(p) ;
            mp := p ;
            testing := false ;
            cycle testing :
                    do m>mp : mp := mp+p end ;
                    if m=mp : skip |
                        m<mp : call Sieve[succ].test(m)
                    end ;
                    testing := false
            end
        end
    end
```

Comment: Again the significant difference is that in the DP process all input must pass through the procedure *test*, and that the interleaving of this and the process body must be controlled by the state variable testing.

AUTHORS' AFFILIATIONS

Brian Cohen   Department of Computer Science, University of New South Wales,
                           P.O. Box 1, Kensington, N.S.W., 2033, Australia.

Ria Follett   Department of Computer Science, University of New South Wales,
                           P.O. Box 1, Kensington, N.S.W., 2033, Australia.

Norman Y. Foo   Basser Department of Computer Science, University of Sydney,
                           Sydney, N.S.W., 2006, Australia.

Don Herbison-Evans   Basser Department of Computer Science, University of Sydney,
                           Sydney, N.S.W., 2006, Australia.

Jan B. Hext   Basser Department of Computer Science, University of Sydney,
                           Sydney, N.S.W., 2006, Australia.

Dan B. Johnston   Department of Computer Science, University of Queensland,
                           St. Lucia, Queensland, 4067, Australia.

Graham Lee   Department of Computer Science, University of Western Australia,
                           Nedlands, Western Australia, 6009, Australia.

Andrew M. Lister   Department of Computer Science, University of Queensland,
                           St. Lucia, Queensland, 4067, Australia.

Prabhaker Mateti   Department of Computer Science, University of Melbourne,
                           Parkville, Victoria, 3052, Australia.

Geoffrey J. Nolan   Basser Department of Computer Science, University of Sydney,
                           Sydney, N.S.W., 2006, Australia.

Paul Pritchard   Department of Computer Science, University of Queensland,
                           St. Lucia, Queensland, 4067, Australia.

Andrew Richardson   University of New South Wales,
                           P.O. Box 1, Kensington, N.S.W., 2033, Australia.

Dennis M. Ritchie   Bell Laboratories,
                           Murray Hill, New Jersey, 07974, USA.

Ken Robinson   Department of Computer Science, University of New South Wales,
                           P.O. Box 1, Kensington, N.S.W., 2033, Australia.

Jeffrey Rohl   Department of Computer Science, University of Western Australia,
                           Nedlands, Western Australia, 6009, Australia.

Eric J. Salzman   Department of Computer Science, University of Queensland,
                           St. Lucia, Queensland, 4067, Australia.

Claude Sammut   Department of Computer Science, University of New South Wales,
                           P.O. Box 1, Kensington, N.S.W., 2033, Australia.

Jim Welsh   Department of Computer Science, University of Queensland,
                           St. Lucia, Queensland, 4067, Australia.

Niklaus Wirth   Institut für Informatik, ETH-Zentrum,
                           CH-8092, Zürich, Switzerland.

49: Interactive Systems. Proceedings 1976. Edited by A. Blaser
C. Hackl. VI, 380 pages. 1976.

50: A. C. Hartmann, A Concurrent Pascal Compiler for Mini-
nputers. VI, 119 pages. 1977.

51: B. S. Garbow, Matrix Eigensystem Routines – Eispack
de Extension. VIII, 343 pages. 1977.

52: Automata, Languages and Programming. Fourth Colloquium,
versity of Turku, July 1977. Edited by A. Salomaa and M. Steinby.
69 pages. 1977.

53: Mathematical Foundations of Computer Science. Proceed-
s 1977. Edited by J. Gruska. XII, 608 pages. 1977.

54: Design and Implementation of Programming Languages.
ceedings 1976. Edited by J. H. Williams and D. A. Fisher. X,
pages. 1977.

55: A. Gerbier, Mes premières constructions de programmes.
256 pages. 1977.

56: Fundamentals of Computation Theory. Proceedings 1977.
ed by M. Karpiński. XII, 542 pages. 1977.

57: Portability of Numerical Software. Proceedings 1976. Edited
V. Cowell. VIII, 539 pages. 1977.

58: M. J. O'Donnell, Computing in Systems Described by Equa-
s. XIV, 111 pages. 1977.

59: E. Hill, Jr., A Comparative Study of Very Large Data Bases.
40 pages. 1978.

60: Operating Systems, An Advanced Course. Edited by R. Bayer,
M. Graham, and G. Seegmüller. X, 593 pages. 1978.

61: The Vienna Development Method: The Meta-Language.
ted by D. Bjørner and C. B. Jones. XVIII, 382 pages. 1978.

62: Automata, Languages and Programming. Proceedings 1978.
ed by G. Ausiello and C. Böhm. VIII, 508 pages. 1978.

63: Natural Language Communication with Computers. Edited
eonard Bolc. VI, 292 pages. 1978.

64: Mathematical Foundations of Computer Science. Proceed-
s 1978. Edited by J. Winkowski. X, 551 pages. 1978.

65: Information Systems Methodology, Proceedings, 1978.
ed by G. Bracchi and P. C. Lockemann. XII, 696 pages. 1978.

66: N. D. Jones and S. S. Muchnick, TEMPO: A Unified Treat-
t of Binding Time and Parameter Passing Concepts in Pro-
mming Languages. IX, 118 pages. 1978.

67: Theoretical Computer Science, 4th GI Conference, Aachen,
ch 1979. Edited by K. Weihrauch. VII, 324 pages. 1979.

68: D. Harel, First-Order Dynamic Logic. X, 133 pages. 1979.

69: Program Construction. International Summer School. Edited
L. Bauer and M. Broy. VII, 651 pages. 1979.

70: Semantics of Concurrent Computation. Proceedings 1979.
d by G. Kahn. VI, 368 pages. 1979.

71: Automata, Languages and Programming. Proceedings 1979.
d by H. A. Maurer. IX, 684 pages. 1979.

72: Symbolic and Algebraic Computation. Proceedings 1979.
ed by E. W. Ng. XV, 557 pages. 1979.

73: Graph-Grammars and Their Application to Computer
nce and Biology. Proceedings 1978. Edited by V. Claus, H. Ehrig
G. Rozenberg. VII, 477 pages. 1979.

74: Mathematical Foundations of Computer Science. Proceed-
1979. Edited by J. Bečvář. IX, 580 pages. 1979.

75: Mathematical Studies of Information Processing. Pro-
dings 1978. Edited by E. K. Blum, M. Paul and S. Takasu. VIII,
pages. 1979.

76: Codes for Boundary-Value Problems in Ordinary Differential
tions. Proceedings 1978. Edited by B. Childs et al. VIII, 388
s. 1979.

77: G. V. Bochmann, Architecture of Distributed Computer
ems. VIII, 238 pages. 1979.

Vol. 78: M. Gordon, R. Milner and C. Wadsworth, Edinburgh LCF.
VIII, 159 pages. 1979.

Vol. 79: Language Design and Programming Methodology. Proceedings, 1979. Edited by J. Tobias. IX, 255 pages. 1980.

This series reports new developments in computer science research and teaching – quickly, informally and at a high level. The type of material considered for publication includes:

1. Preliminary drafts of original papers and monographs

2. Lectures on a new field or presentations of a new angle in a classical field

3. Seminar work-outs

4. Reports of meetings, provided they are

   a) of exceptional interest and

   b) devoted to a single topic

Texts which are out of print but still in demand may also be considered if they fall within these categories.

The timeliness of a manuscript is more important than its form, which may be unfinished or tentative. Thus, in some instances, proofs may be merely outlined and results presented which have been or will later be published elsewhere. If possible, a subject index should be included. Publication of Lecture Notes is intended as a service to the international computer science community, in that a commercial publisher, Springer-Verlag, can offer a wide distribution of documents which would otherwise have a restricted readership. Once published and copyrighted, they can be documented in the scientific literature.

Manuscripts

Manuscripts should be no less than 100 and preferably no more than 500 pages in length.
They are reproduced by a photographic process and therefore must be typed with extreme care. Symbols not on the typewriter should be inserted by hand in indelible black ink. Corrections to the typescript should be made by pasting in the new text or painting out errors with white correction fluid. Authors receive 75 free copies and are free to use the material in other publications. The typescript is reduced slightly in size during reproduction; best results will not be obtained unless the text on any one page is kept within the overall limit of 18 x 26.5 cm (7 x 10½ inches). On request, the publisher will supply special paper with the typing area outlined.
Manuscripts should be sent to Prof. G. Goos, Institut für Informatik, Universität Karlsruhe, Zirkel 2, 7500 Karlsruhe/Germany, Prof. J. Hartmanis, Cornell University, Dept. of Computer-Science, Ithaca, NY/USA 14850 or directly to Springer-Verlag Heidelberg.

Springer-Verlag, Heidelberger Platz 3, D-1000 Berlin 33
Springer-Verlag, Neuenheimer Landstraße 28–30, D-6900 Heidelberg 1
Springer-Verlag, 175 Fifth Avenue, New York, NY 10010/USA

ISBN 3-540-09745-7
ISBN 0-387-09745-7